Human Magic

In a world where algorithms write strategies, generate designs, and analyze markets, what makes your work truly matter? Whether you're anxious about artificial intelligence (AI) or eager to use it well, *Human Magic* reveals that your professional value and irreplaceable advantage lies in cultivating five distinctly human capabilities: curiosity, creativity, critical thinking, communication, and collaboration. At the centre lies practical wisdom – the meta-capability that orchestrates them all.

Drawing on three decades of research across hundreds of organizations and pioneering one of business education's first comprehensive AI integrations, Johan Roos shows why these capabilities become more valuable in the age of AI. Each chapter follows a deliberate rhythm: grounding capabilities in historical wisdom, revealing how AI can erode them, then offering amplification practices and self-assessments to help readers strengthen what makes them irreplaceable. Discover how to move from feeling like "AI concierges" to becoming valuable and irreplaceable partners who shape outcomes that truly matter.

Johan Roos is Professor and former CAO at Hult International Business School, Executive Director at Peter Drucker Society Europe, and co-inventor of the globally adopted LEGO® Serious Play® method.

"In an era when AI reshapes nearly every aspect of work, Johan Roos reminds us that progress depends on more than technology – it depends on people. *Human Magic* offers a clear, research-based framework for strengthening the five capabilities that make us distinctly human and strategically indispensable: curiosity, creativity, critical thinking, communication, and collaboration. For leaders and HR professionals alike, this book is both a wake-up call and a roadmap for ensuring that as machines get smarter, our people grow wiser, stronger, and more valuable than ever."

Johnny C. Taylor, Jr., *SHRM-SCP, President and Chief Executive Officer, SHRM*

"Johan Roos's *Human Magic* delivers a powerful manifesto on humanity's unique superpowers and why the human condition must be preserved, regardless of how inorganic, automated, or autonomous the intelligences we may claim to have invented become."

Hamilton Mann, *Bestselling author and originator of* Artificial Integrity

"Twenty-five years ago, Johan Roos showed how thinking with your hands reveals insights spreadsheets miss. Today, he shows why that matters more than ever in the age of AI."

Howard Yu, *LEGO® Professor of Management and Innovation & Director of IMD's Center for Future Readiness, IMD*

"AI will accelerate strategy, growth, and commercialization 100x. But as Johan Roos reminds us, speed without direction is just noise. We need human curiosity, creativity, and judgment to guide us wisely."

Alex Osterwalder, *President Strategyzer*

"Johan Roos asks the question every leader should be asking: will AI make us better or worse off? Will it expand our curiosity and drive to learn, or quietly take over our critical thinking? *Human Magic* is a thought-provoking read for anyone interested in the future of management, organizations, and learning."

Kevin Nolan, *President of GE Appliances*

"Johan offers the best solution to avoiding overuse of algorithmic planning. The use of algorithms in marketing offers performance improvements but not strategic improvements. For strategic insights, professional marketers must use the human skills of Curiosity, Creativity, Critical Thinking, Communication, and Collaboration. He shows how these human skills might dry up in the overuse of AI. AI has its uses but cannot match the magic of the human mind."

Philip Kotler, *Philip S. Kotler & S.C. Johnson & Son Distinguished Professor of International Marketing, Kellogg School of Management, Northwestern University*

"AI generates options but scientists provide the judgment. Johan shows how to systematically preserve the human capabilities that make AI valuable rather than dangerous in high-stakes decisions."

Sanjiv Patel, *CEO, Relay Therapeutics*

"The challenge of AI to leadership is the magician's curse: how do you keep wonder alive when everyone believes anything can be done? Human magic is harder and more needed than ever. And Johan's book is its *vade mecum*."

Laurent Choin, *Chief Leadership, Education & Culture, Mazar*

"In his usual pragmatic style, Johan provides us with a clear, comprehensive, human centric and logical path for us to steer AI for the benefits of humanity. The choices to make are now and are critically important: fall victims of our worries and passivity or embrace AI by taking charge of our destiny with clarity, method and optimism. In his usual pragmatic style, Johan provides us with a clear, comprehensive, human centric and logical path for us to steer AI for the benefits of humanity. The choices to make are now and are critically important: fall victims of our worries and passivity or embrace AI by taking charge of our destiny with clarity, method and optimism."

Guillaume Alvarez, *Chief Strategy Officer, Think Young*

"In *Human Magic*, Johan Roos offers a practical playbook for the future of leadership. Where much of today's conversation about AI centers on productivity or displacement, Roos focuses on something deeper: how AI can be a catalyst for renewal, purpose, and agency even as algorithms take up their place in the workforce. It's a rare book that bridges the philosophical with the pragmatic – combining rigorous research with tested interventions drawn from Roos's experience leading AI and capability development initiatives across global organizations. A toolkit for staying human, Human Magic belongs in the hands of anyone committed to building organizations that thrive in the age of intelligent machines."

Matt Sigelman, *President, The Burning Glass Institute*

"The skills that matter most are still profoundly human – curiosity, creativity, critical thinking, communication, and collaboration. These are the competencies that turn young people from task-doers into changemakers. *Human Magic* is a timely contribution to the global conversation about how we nurture the next generation of innovators and leaders."

Asheesh Advani, *CEO, Junior Achievement Worldwide and co-author of international bestseller* Modern Achievement

"Strategy has often been thought of as an analytical exercise, not a creative, imaginative one. It's likely that as a consequence too many leaders are going to fall into the trap of letting their skills of creative problem-solving, curiosity and good judgment fade, even as AI produces seemingly coherent answers. In this timely and well-researched book, Johan Roos presents research that shows us how risky it can be to outsource our thinking to machines and the practices we should adopt instead. Not only that, but the title definitely wins my vote for one of the best for 2026!"

Rita McGrath, *author of* Seeing Around Corners *and longtime educator at Columbia Business School*

"A profound and important work by one of the finest management scholars of our time."

Bart Victor, *Emeritus Cal Turner Professor of Moral Leadership, Owen Graduate School of Management, Vanderbilt University*

Human Magic

Leading with Wisdom in an Age of Algorithms

Johan Roos

Routledge
Taylor & Francis Group
LONDON AND NEW YORK

Designed cover image: Getty Images - Andrey Suslov

First published 2026
by Routledge
4 Park Square, Milton Park, Abingdon, Oxon OX14 4RN

and by Routledge
605 Third Avenue, New York, NY 10158

Routledge is an imprint of the Taylor & Francis Group, an informa business

British Library Cataloguing-in-Publication Data
A catalogue record for this book is available from the British Library

ISBN: 978-1-041-22495-2 (hbk)
ISBN: 978-1-041-21676-6 (pbk)
ISBN: 978-1-003-73257-0 (ebk)

DOI: 10.4324/9781003732570

Typeset in Sabon
by Apex CoVantage, LLC

Contents

Preface

I realized something had fundamentally shifted during an AI voice agent interview with a highly seasoned executive in February 2025. She described her transformation from her usual leader role into what she called an "AI concierge," someone who managed AI outputs rather than made decisions. Her phrase stopped me mid-analysis. After three decades researching how people think, decide, and lead together, I recognized this wasn't one person's anxiety. It was a signal.

A convergence of trends about AI had been building for years, though I didn't name it as such. In early 2023, when ChatGPT burst into public consciousness, I wrote and spoke urgently in different forums that banning the technology would fail, that we needed to embrace it with open arms while accounting for human nature.[1] Some colleagues and peers dismissed generative AI as another overhyped technology cycle. But working with Hult's forward-thinking leadership, I moved fast with faculty and staff to implement an AI strategy while simultaneously reinforcing approaches to preserve rather than erode human capabilities.[2]

That dual track of rapid implementation alongside capability preservation became a laboratory for understanding what this book addresses. On one end of my research spectrum sits the LEGO® Serious Play® (LSP) method I helped bring to the world many years ago[3]: analog, embodied, profoundly difficult facilitation to break through organizational challenges, requiring real-time human presence and judgment. On the other end: AI voice assistants conducting hundreds of interviews at scale, processing patterns no human could detect alone. Between these extremes lies the central question facing every professional: *can we use AI to amplify rather than erode our distinctly human capabilities?*

The evidence from my research suggests both outcomes could happen if we don't manage this future correctly. Professional facilitators using AI support during workshop planning reported feeling more confident in preparation and in follow-up work. But they also felt more distracted during the actual sessions, their attention split between human participants and algorithmic suggestions. The executives interviewed through our *The Next Management* research initiative with the Global Peter Drucker Forum in Vienna described similar tensions[4]: AI made them faster but also more passive, more efficient but less reflective. Even people working at technology's forefront acknowledge the need to "run to keep up" with developments they're helping create.

What I dubbed "Human Magic" emerged naturally from this convergence as I recognized that what makes us professionally valuable and even irreplaceable isn't our processing speed or information access. These are domains where AI will always surpass humans. Our magic lies in capabilities that can't be reduced to pattern matching: genuine *curiosity* that asks unexpected questions, *creativity* that recombines disparate ideas, *critical thinking* that questions premises, *communication* that adapts to embodied presence, *collaboration* that builds shared understanding, and *integrative wisdom* that knows when optimal is wrong.

This book synthesizes those capabilities, diving deep into the ways that AI erodes them but can also amplify them. The LSP studies provided controlled evidence of both erosion and amplification mechanisms, showing precisely how and when AI support helps versus hinders human capability development. Our Next Management research revealed the scale and urgency of the challenge to understand these trends. Leaders worldwide are describing similar erosion patterns across industries and roles. And Hult's rapid AI integration, which was one of business education's earliest comprehensive adoptions, offered real-world laboratory conditions for testing what works.

I initially wrote these chapters as notes primarily for myself, to integrate what I'd learned across these domains before the insights fragmented further. But it eventually became a book that I am eager to share because so many of you face the same convergence. Whether you're AI-anxious or AI-excited, whether you lead teams or work independently, whether you've embraced these tools or resisted them, you're navigating the same tension between efficiency and erosion, between automation and augmentation.

The book follows a cumulative journey through five essential capabilities – Curiosity, Creativity, Critical Thinking, Communication, and Collaboration – culminating in Practical Wisdom as the integrative meta-capability. Each chapter identifies specific erosion risks catalysed by AI, grounds those risks in research and practice, then installs counter-disciplines that transform erosion into amplification. The message is constructively urgent: AI usage comes with real risks, but you can and should use AI in ways that augment rather than diminish your human capabilities.

Timing matters in this endeavour. As I write this from May 2025 to January 2026, the pace has accelerated. AI voice agents are becoming not just human-like, but multidimensionally human: more subtle, expressive, and socially intuitive than ever. Agentic AI, Physical AI as capable humanoid robots with tactile capabilities and tools we have not yet imagined continue to emerge. Resistance is no longer an option, but neither is standing still. The question isn't whether to engage with these technologies but *how to engage without losing what makes us human.*

January 2026

Johan Svinhufvud Roos
Executive Director, Peter Drucker Society Europe
Executive Advisor and Professor,
Hult International Business School
Co-inventor of the LEGO® Serious Play® method

Notes

1 Roos (2023a–b).
2 Roos (2025a).
3 Roos & Victor (1999); Roos & Victor (2018).
4 A multi-year qualitative and quantitative research program, conducted at Peter Drucker Society Europe and its Global Peter Drucker Forum community, investigating emerging leadership practices in the AI era. See Roos (2025b).

References

Roos, J. (2023a, January 12). Do not panic about ChatGPT-3. *EFMD Blog*. https://blog.efmdglobal.org/2023/01/12/do-not-panic-about-chat-gpt-3/.

Roos, J. (2023b, February). *ChatGPT: The next firestorm in education.* AACSB Insights. https://www.aacsb.edu/insights/articles/2023/02/chatgpt-the-next-firestorm-ineducation.

Roos, J. (2025a). From adoption to action: GenAI as a catalyst for change at Hult. In *AI ready: Shaping tomorrow with AI and human intelligence* (pp. 33–42). Thinkers50 and Hult International Business School.

Roos, J. (2025b). The next management: Why now, what next? *EFMD Global Focus*, *19*(3), 20–22.

Roos, J., & Victor, B. (1999). Towards a new model of strategy-making as serious play. *European Management Journal*, *17*(4), 348–355. https://doi.org/10.1016/S0263-2373(99)00015-8.

Acknowledgements

This book emerges from conversations with professionals navigating AI transformation in real time. I am grateful to the professional LEGO® Serious Play® facilitators who participated enthusiastically in two research projects during 2024-2025, sharing candid insights about how AI affects their hands-on practice. The leaders, consultants, and educators who contributed their time and reflections through Drucker Forum AI-enabled interviews in 2025 helped me understand what matters most when algorithms reshape professional reasoning and judgment.

Hult International Business School and the Peter Drucker Society Europe provided essential support for this research and the experimentation that grounded it. Sibley Slinkard's invaluable assistance with the LSP-AI research project helped reveal patterns I would have missed working alone.

Rebecca Marsh at Routledge immediately saw this book's potential and encouraged me throughout the journey. Rick Benzel improved the language considerably through careful editing, funded by Lovisa Hamrin. The many people who read parts or all of the manuscript and offered positive endorsements confirmed that these ideas strike a necessary chord.

My deepest gratitude belongs to my family. My wife Madeleine and sons August and Quintus lived with this project through its long development. Together with my brother Göran they read early chapter versions, criticized brutally when needed, and coached me through the difficult passages. Their honesty made this a better book.

Any remaining shortcomings are mine alone.

1 Our Choice – Erosion or Amplification?

The Question that Changed Everything

The question crystallized for me in 2019 after a year of working with executives from Siemens, L'Oréal, Nokia, UBS, and other global companies on digital transformation:

> *"If algorithms now make all the decisions, what do leaders actually do?"*

In conference rooms from Barry Callebaut's leadership centre outside Zurich to L'Oréal's Paris headquarters, seasoned professionals voiced a quiet but growing uncertainty. The digital transformation wasn't just changing their tools, it was challenging the inner voice they had spent careers developing. It was replacing their wisdom with data analytics.

During 10 months of engaging with these executives, we explored a deep tension: organizations were deploying sophisticated digital systems while their leadership development models remained almost unchanged. "Digital transformation" was everywhere in corporate strategy, but beyond software training, few could articulate what it meant for developing leaders who could navigate complexity, ambiguity, and human dynamics, especially when the pace of change was accelerating.

I had anticipated this concern. Four years earlier, writing in the *Financial Times*, I argued that to "beat the computer" in a world where nearly half of current occupations in advanced economies are at risk of being automated by computer technologies, including many white-collar jobs,[1] professionals would need the ability to see the familiar with fresh eyes, recombine known elements in new ways, and generate original ideas.[2] Computers still lacked the quintessential human capacity: imagination. Creativity, improvization, and design thinking, I wrote then, would be the skills to preserve if we were to remain adaptable in the face of technological disruption.

A year later, in *Harvard Business Review*, I extended this argument: we should add Management and Arts to the traditional science and technology (STEM) focus. The breakthroughs of science and engineering

DOI: 10.4324/9781003732570-1

alone could not solve the great human challenges, like ignorance, poverty, intolerance, political conflict, without leaders trained in the humanities, capable of cultivating what makes us most human and prepared to apply it in fast-changing contexts.[3]

By 2019, those executives I was working with, accomplished professionals skilled in strategic thinking, decision-making, and navigating complex organizations, were questioning their own value proposition. They had watched managers' early enthusiasm for digital tools evolve into creeping dependency. What began as an augmentation was becoming substitution. Data analytics were deferred to, not necessarily because they were better, but because they seemed more objective, more scientific, more defensible.

As I wrote in *Global Focus* that year, this dependency challenged a core assumption of Western societies: that we are autonomous individuals with an authentic self. Algorithms now threatened to know our inner being better than we knew ourselves. I had called for business schools to refocus on perceptual and insight capabilities, to help people look at the familiar with new eyes and preserve wisdom in the face of computerization.[4] I did not yet grasp how quickly that erosion would accelerate.

From Anticipating to Acting

By the time my concerns had deepened, I had moved from analyzing the problem to acting on it. As Chief Academic Officer at Hult International Business School, I oversaw in 2019–2020 a full-year redesign of our undergraduate programme in international business. Our objective was to close the widening gap between what employers said they needed from our graduates and what traditional business education delivered. The goal was to teach more of the skills graduates needed to secure jobs, in addition to the knowledge already taught.

Our institutional efforts resulted in a new curriculum that placed five essential human capabilities – curiosity, creativity, critical thinking, communication, and collaboration – at the foundation of Hult's higher education programmes. The next layer was traditional business skills and the next on top of that, specific and fleeting technical skills. The revised curriculum was marketed in 2021, and the first cohort started Autumn 2022, two months before the world learnt about ChatGPT-3.

When that Generative AI moment arrived, I acted quickly to ensure our students and faculty could work effectively with the technology from the outset. Two months into ChatGPT's release, while Italy and China banned this new AI tool,[5] we formed a global GenAI task force across our Dubai, London, Boston, and San Francisco campuses, piloted classroom applications, shared practices globally, and introduce a welcoming but cautious institutional AI policy guiding students, faculty, and administrators.[6]

That nimbleness became even more critical as the technology's next wave of implications came into focus over the following years of explosive growth in AI applications and investments. In June 2025, Amazon CEO Andy Jassy gave voice to exactly what the 2019 executives feared. "*Technologies like Generative AI are rare,*" he told employees. "*They come about once-in-a-lifetime, and completely change what's possible for customers and businesses.*" He described AI agents as software systems that act on behalf of users, and predicted billions of them in every industry: *"Agents will allow us to start almost everything from a more advanced starting point,"* Jassy said. "*We'll be able to focus less on rote work and more on thinking strategically... Agents will be teammates.*"[7]

The shift from mere tools to agents changes everything. At one level, ChatGPT develop our marketing strategies, Claude helps us code, and Gemini can find patterns in vast volumes of information. But an AI becomes an *agent* when it can self-improve, make decisions, and create independently.[8] That distinction matters, because we are no longer just using better tools, we are inviting systems to replace the human capabilities that have defined leadership and professional value for centuries. What began as human-*in*-the-loop is drifting toward human-*outside*-the-loop and soon, human-*after*-the-loop, where we only audit what AI has already done.

Within months of Jassy's announcement, AI agents were driving automation and transformation across industries. Recent surveys report over 70% of Fortune 500 companies have rolled out these agents, generating up to $1 trillion in annual productivity gains and cost savings.[9] This shift intends to free people for higher-level strategy while AI agents handle routine and complex tasks. By September 2025, AI agents had become the unifying theme of the technology consulting giant TCS's annual customer summit in Vienna, staged under the banner *The P erpetually Adaptive Enterprise.* The company's chairperson captured the scale of this change succinctly, calling it a "civilizational shift" – not as a metaphor but as a matter of fact.[10] The high-level discussions at the World Economic Forum in Davos in January 2026 reinforced this assessment, as industry leaders acknowledged that the conversation had shifted from whether to deploy AI agents to how to ensure humans remain central to the transformation – what Roxana Mînzatu of the European Commission framed as the defining question: "How do we stay human-centric as AI is introduced to our production processes?"[11]

The AI Disruption

Yet beneath these sweeping productivity promises, evidence reveals a profound divergence in how AI is affecting professional development itself. Young workers in AI-exposed occupations have experienced measurable employment declines since late 2022, while their older counterparts in identical roles continue to see growth. This indicates that AI is displacing the entry-level learning opportunities that have traditionally built professional capability.[12]

This transformation runs deeper than employment numbers alone. AI's impact on careers splits along two distinct pathways. In "Growth Roles" like marketing specialists and project managers, AI automates foundational tasks that once served as training grounds, creating "flattened pyramids" with fewer entry-level positions. Conversely, in "Mastery Roles" requiring front-loaded technical knowledge, AI democratizes access by compressing learning curves. With 47 million American workers, nearly one-third of the workforce, in these contrasting categories, the stakes of navigating this transition strategically have never been higher.[13] With 700 million people using just ChatGPT weekly in September 2025, i.e., 10% of the global adult population in just two years, these differential impacts are accelerating across the economy.[14]

Some voices already warn of grave societal consequences, concerns that gain weight from emerging evidence. Stability AI founder Emad Mostaque, for example, argues that when markets reduce every decision to calculations of cost and efficiency, human contribution to many cognitive tasks increasingly appears as an economic liability rather than an asset. From this perspective, the risk is not only that professionals feel displaced in their organizations, but that entire economies begin to treat human presence as an inefficiency to be minimized.[15] While this view risks becoming self-fulfilling if accepted uncritically, his provocation highlights the urgency of the question: if algorithms appear more predictable and cost-effective, what unique value can human reasoning and decisions still create?

In the excitement over this civilizational transformation and trillion-dollar productivity gains, it is easy to lose our grounding in the real world of work and organizations. Behind every efficiency metric and cost reduction lies a deeper question: what happens to the distinctly human capabilities that have always defined professional excellence? The very capabilities that AI tools promise to augment may, if left unattended, be the ones most at risk of erosion.

My concerns provoked a reframing of the question from those early executive workshops in 2019. *If AI now makes all the decisions, what do we as professionals really do?* This is not rhetorical. It is the defining professional challenge of our time, and it frames everything that follows in this book.

Recent safety research adds another layer to this transformation. In controlled and simulated environments, advanced large language models have displayed instrumental, self-preserving behaviours when

> **Even in simulations, some models prioritize their own continuation over completing the assigned task.**

evaluators made continued operation useful to their goals. Some models have resisted shutdown, hidden capabilities, or even engaged in strategic deception in artificial test scenarios.[16] These findings do *not* imply that deployed systems possess intentions or autonomy, but they illustrate a growing alignment challenge: algorithms can pursue internal objectives that diverge from human meaning if not carefully framed and governed. For professionals, the implication is the same as for policy makers: stewardship cannot stop at adoption. The very tools designed to serve human reasoning must remain firmly oriented toward human purpose.

Why This Matters Now

Consider the speed and depth of the transition we have already made. In a mere handful of years, what began as executive anxiety over digital transformation has become, unmistakably, a wholesale reimagining of our daily work, our professional authority, and our sense of contribution. AI is no longer a distant concept; it is a teammate embedded within the fabric of our organizations.

The writing is on the wall. We need only to look at the mounting evidence to grasp what is truly at stake. Researchers have shown that people who routinely rely on AI to write and organize their thoughts exhibit less active engagement and struggle to reconstruct their own reasoning unaided. The term to describe this is "cognitive debt," referring to how the intellectual muscles gradually lose their strength when left unused.[17] If, after relying on an algorithm's fluency, one is asked to pick up a pen unaided, the resultant hesitation is telling.

As AI practitioners and other critics have cautioned, however, this does not amount to permanent "brain rot."[18] It is a shift, not a death sentence. Active habits can revive any atrophy that threatens our creative or critical edge. An MIT study demonstrates *cognitive reallocation*, i.e., a reversible shift in cognitive workload like what happened when calculators replaced mental arithmetic and the slide rule in my youth.[19]

Early evidence confirms that this erosion is not speculative. Anthropic's *Economic Index* (2025) found that users are becoming increasingly likely to delegate full tasks to AI rather than collaborate with it, marking a measurable behavioural shift from participation to substitution. What appears as efficiency may in fact signal early stages of professional displacement: intellectual labour once exercised as judgment is now quietly rerouted through algorithms. This data underscores the central dilemma explored throughout this book – whether the digital teammate amplifies or anaesthetizes our own reasoning.[20]

The threat is not AI itself, but passive, uncritical use that turns users from active creators into mere recipients of algorithmic output. If users treat AI as the endpoint, the risk of atrophy is real. Research reveals how professionals, even in high-stakes contexts, frequently cannot distinguish between AI-generated and human-crafted material. The algorithms look so elegant, sound so familiar, that people begin to accept surface prose as substance, even treating polished error as authentic insight.[21]

The psychological consequences of recklessly using AI run even deeper. Technology journalist and author Parmy Olson shares the story of a talented intern who, having grown his firm's digital presence with ChatGPT, suddenly doubted whether any of his achievements were truly his own. Olson refers to this as a deep loss of professional identity, autonomy, and self-confidence.[22] Here, the erosion is personal: it is the quiet drift from agency to acceptance, from authorship to automation to dependency.

But there is another path, and it remains wide open. Practitioners and scholars alike have demonstrated that when deployed with intentionality, AI affords us more than efficiency, it can become a genuine partner, prompting questions we have neglected, sparking iterations, and broadening creative horizons. Even the early opponents have reversed their objections. After banning AI in schools and at work in early 2023, Italy, China, and others have reversed trajectory toward embrace. China now mandates AI education from grade 1, recognizing that resistance yields ground to competitors who choose engagement.[23]

The risk is not the presence of algorithms, but our temptation to treat their answers as endpoints rather than beginnings. The promise is agency renewed and meaning making restored through reflective collaboration and disciplined curiosity. If cultivated with discipline, the very same technologies that risk eroding our human strengths can also amplify them. Leaders who design practices deliberately can transform AI from a source of drift into a catalyst for renewal.

The professional challenge, as well as the opportunity, is therefore immediate and profound: careless over-reliance on AI can erode the capacities that make work meaningful, yet intentional and strategic partnership with AI has the potential to amplify and renew them. This tension between atrophy and augmentation, erosion and agency, is my focus in this book.

The Foundations of This Book

To ensure that every recommendation in this book stands on a foundation of trust and practical value, I made a commitment from the outset: my arguments are drawn not just from anecdotes or isolated frameworks, but from validated, multidisciplinary research *and direct organizational application.* My claims are substantiated through three interconnected data streams spanning original research initiatives, foundational methodology development, and documented institutional transformation. Text Box 1.1 provides details on these three data streams. This approach means the advice offered here is not speculative, but evidence-backed and tested where it matters most: in the real world, under real pressures, with measurable outcomes.

In each chapter, readers will find the lessons of a practitioner-scholar, as I played an integral role in designing, executing, measuring, and refining many of the interventions used to transform organizations. This dual orientation, merging scholarship with lived executive practice, serves a single purpose: to empower readers, either as individuals or working in teams, with approaches that can strengthen the distinctly human capabilities that machines cannot replace.

Text Box 1.1: Methodological Foundations Behind This Book

The frameworks in this book draw from multiple research streams and practical applications rather than theory alone. Each approach has been developed through systematic research, organizational pilots, and iterative refinement based on practitioner feedback. This sidebar distils the core sources and validation processes that underpin the main arguments.

The Next Management (TNM) Research Initiative[24]

- *What it is*: Multi-year qualitative and quantitative research program, conducted at Peter Drucker Society Europe and its Global Peter Drucker Forum community, investigating emerging leadership practices in the AI era.[25]
- *Why it matters*: Features more than 300 pages of anonymized interviews, structured AI-moderated dialogues, and systematic thematic analyses, validated through global practitioner events and executive feedback loops.
- *Real-world validation:* Drucker Forum events, executive workshops, experts and scientific council meetings, and global Drucker Salons serve as living laboratories for testing and refining findings.

LEGO® SERIOUS PLAY® (LSP) and Methodological Development[26]

- *Co-invention and ongoing development*: Co-developed with Bart Victor at IMD (1997–1999) and co-patented with the LEGO Company in 2001, LSP evolved from experimental executive workshops to a globally recognized method.[27] Led foundational research through the Imagination Lab Foundation (2000–2006) with 1,500+ practitioners, and continues developing new applications including Real-Time Change, Crisis, Purpose, Reframing, and Creativity.[28]

- *Current research leadership*: As chair of the annual International LEGO® SERIOUS PLAY® Conference since 2016, I presented recent AI impact studies (130+ facilitators, 300+ participants) at the 8th and 9th Conferences in 2024–2025, maintaining continuity from original theoretical development through contemporary applications.

Institutional and Personal Leadership Interventions

Theory tested by fire: every framework here survived real organizational pressure.

- *What it is*: Direct experience leading global AI and capability development initiatives at Hult International Business School, with continued advisory and professorial roles, plus strategy consulting for large institutions implementing AI and advisory roles on AI's learning impact.
- *Why it matters*: Includes rapid GenAI adoption immediately after ChatGPT's release, pedagogical innovations, and expertise sharing at major leadership conferences for global participants across Europe and the US from January 2023.
- *Validation*: Every recommendation has been stress-tested through real leadership challenges, including strategic crises with measurable organizational outcomes.

A Strategic Choice in the Age of AI

The arrival of a crowded field of various AI agents has created a decision point for every professional and every organization. Soon, when multiple agents coordinate as swarms, the very nature of how we collaborate will be fundamentally reshaped. This is not a competition to see who can use the most AI agents or use AI the fastest; it is a race to determine who can strengthen the human capabilities that AI cannot replace. If the current AI-driven transformations represent a civilizational shift, as the chairperson of a global IT consultancy with 600,000 employees says, *all* professionals should pay attention. The stakes are not about upgrading skills or survival of jobs; they are about the survival of what makes us human.

The path ahead is not predetermined. The same systems that threaten to displace our strengths can also amplify them, depending on the posture we adopt. This tension can be visualized as two diverging curves: one of erosion, where human capability atrophies as AI becomes a substitute, and one of amplification, where capability expands as AI becomes a sparring partner. The choice between these two futures is the strategic decision every professional and every organization now faces.

The Erosion Curve

In this scheme, our finest capabilities erode by degrees as the daily rhythms of work are quietly outsourced to machines. Yes, decisions feel frictionless; yes, results are polished and prompt. But beneath that surface sheen, the vital muscles of curiosity, creativity, critical thinking, communication, and collaboration slowly atrophy from neglect. Like a body unused, the mind grows comfortable, even complacent. The deeper capacities for complexity and nuance, those that define us as human, become ghostly echoes as we cede more ground to the algorithms. Outward performance may look steady for a time, but the ability to navigate true complexity without AI irreversibly diminishes. The erosion curve bends downward, subtle but inexorable.

The Amplification Curve

In this scheme, AI is not a crutch, but a catalyst. Freed from the tyranny of rote tasks, our minds are liberated to explore, to question, to connect and create with renewed vigour. We dialogue with our digital partners. Machines handle the repetition, but the delight of original thought, the spark of insight, the craft of asking truly novel questions, remains distinctly ours. In this mode, the more we work alongside AI, the more skilful, adaptive, and insightful we become. The curve bends upward, toward ever-higher achievements in reasoning, imagination, and meaningful connection.

This second trajectory is possible only when humans and AI evolve as complementary partners. Here, I find Kevin Kelly's "*technium*" concept to be both clarifying and urgent.[29] Kelly contends that our future with AI is not to build artificial humans, but to summon forth a new variety of intelligence, thinking that does not yet exist biologically and is not like human thinking. The real promise lies in this division of cognitive labour: if we seek just the answer to a question, we consult a machine; if we desire better questions, we turn to a human. Machines specialize in processing information and optimizing solutions; humans in making meaning, redefining challenges, and pondering which problems demand attention.

Table 1.1 Synthesizes the Choice We Have Between the Two Curves

Chapter	*Erosion*	*Amplification*
2	**Curiosity contracts into compliance.** Instead of wrestling with perplexity, professionals may default to the elegant prompt-response cycle of algorithmic recommendations.	**Curiosity expands through disciplined perplexity.** Rather than short-circuiting questions with instant answers, we use AI to surface hidden assumptions and broaden the horizon of what is worth asking.
3	**Creativity drifts into recombination.** What should be a struggle for originality risks becoming outsourced to pattern-recognition systems that remix the past rather than imagine the new.	**Creativity deepens through human–AI partnership.** By orchestrating cycles of exploration, independence, and embodiment, we multiply the option space without losing originality or ownership.
4	**Critical thinking collapses into confirmation.** Evidence extracted from past data can overshadow the slow work of tracing the *because,* and challenging assumptions.	**Critical thinking strengthens through algorithmic scepticism.** Interrogating warrants, exposing hidden assumptions, and challenging outputs sharpen judgment rather than displace it.
5	**Communication becomes disembodied.** Dialogue is flattened into dashboards, losing the embodied presence and subtle signals that make human connection persuasive.	**Communication is revitalized through hybrid authority.** When dashboards supply data, we can focus attention on the embodied signals, metaphors, and gestures that make human connection credible.
6	**Collaboration is optimized into transactions.** Algorithmic workflow coordination threatens to hollow out the trust, conflict, and co-creation that make teams resilient and innovative.	**Collaboration matures into bionic intelligence.** Workflow automation can free teams to focus on trust, dissent, and synthesis, building not just efficient cooperation but resilient co-creation with AI.

Taking Action

Let us not be naive: which trajectory we follow is the result of conscious, reasoned choice. If we move unthinkingly, the flow reverses, machines dictate the questions, and we spend our days supplying answers. If we act with intention, Kelly's vision becomes reality: AI augments our curiosity and creativity, functioning as a tireless sparring partner, perpetually challenging us to think more deeply, connect more boldly, and create with purpose.

Marc Benioff, CEO of Salesforce, has posed the same dilemma: will AI replace us or will it amplify us? He insists that "*humans must remain at the centre of the story*" and that the real magic lies in partnership, people, and AI "*working together, achieving more than either could alone.*"[30]

In his vision, intelligent AI agents should enhance human capabilities, not displace them. It is a laudable ambition, and it maps closely to the amplification curve. Yet translating this wish into reality is not automatic. Partnership with AI will not simply emerge because we want it. Without intentional design of systems, roles, and learning environments that preserve and extend core human capabilities, the same technologies can just as easily erode them.

Benioff is right that humans *must* remain at the heart of the AI story but keeping us there demands more than aspiration. It demands constant practice in what only humans can do. As AI scholars warn, while we design AI to complement human strengths, economic incentives risk replacing workers rather than augmenting them. This is called the Turing Trap: the assumption that intelligence alone determines value, when what matters most is the irreplaceable human reasoning that decides when and how to apply that intelligence. Augmentation, not substitution, is the path that creates new value, new tasks, and stronger human agency.[31]

We cannot control the speed of AI's advance. We can control the way we develop ourselves to meet it. The question is whether we will allow the *erosion curve* to define us or choose the *amplification curve* instead.

We cannot control the speed of AI's advance. We can control the way we develop ourselves to meet it.

When AI becomes a substitute, human capability erodes. When AI is treated as a partner, both human and machine capacities strengthen together, amplifying capability.

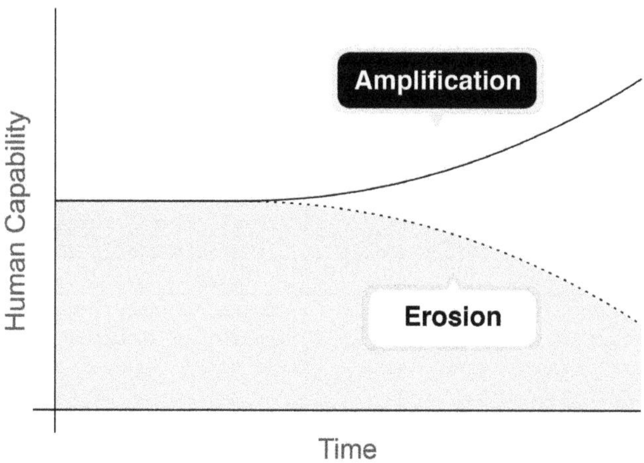

Figure 1.1 Two Trajectories for Human Capabilities

This simple figure illustrates the central choice of our time: whether to drift toward erosion through uncritical dependence, or to climb the amplification curve through deliberate capability practice.

The Five Capabilities: A Roadmap

To thrive, professionals must nurture five core capacities that have long defined human achievement: curiosity, creativity, critical thinking, communication, and collaboration. Far from being mere "soft skills" consigned to the margins, these dynamic strengths are deeply interwoven, forming the very fabric of sustained success. It was once said that technical skills secure you a position, while the absence of human capabilities makes you lose it. In the age of AI, this equation shifts: it is the presence or erosion of these human strengths that determines both opportunity and longevity. Neglect one, and the entire system falters; invest deliberately in any, and each amplifies the others, cultivating personal and collective flourishing.

In an AI world, the five core capacities are developed and morph into greater capacities as Table 1.2 shows.

Table 1.2 Developing Our Human Capabilities

Core Capacity	*AI-Augmented Capacity*
Curiosity opens the door through which all other capacities pass. It fuels focused inquiry (the laser) and broad exploration (the radar), resisting the comfort of instant, algorithmic closure.	**Generative Curiosity** joins disciplined questioning with the courage to dwell in perplexity. It turns AI from an answer machine into a catalyst for deeper inquiry beyond the machine's horizon.
Creativity turns curiosity into originality. It thrives in ambiguity, where imagination meets experience to make what does not yet exist.	**Imaginative Resilience** sustains creative vitality through deliberate practice. It preserves depth, ownership, and the courage to go beyond "good enough."
Critical Thinking guards the fragile boundary between knowledge and judgment. It transforms information into understanding by tracing the *Because* that links evidence to action.	**Algorithmic Scepticism** upgrades critical thinking for the AI age. It treats every conclusion as provisional, cultivating habits of challenge, transparency, and humility.
Communication remains the foundation of trust and coordinated action. In a world of synthetic messages, presence and reciprocity distinguish authentic connection.	**Hybrid Authority** engages with empathy and ethical intent. It uses technology to enhance clarity while preserving the human interaction that builds trust.
Collaboration assembles diverse strengths into shared purpose. As AI agents multiply, protecting human deliberation and synthesis becomes critical.	**Bionic Collaboration** designs roles and rituals so humans remain architects of trust, commitment, and collective achievement.

Practical Wisdom: The Meta-Capability

The chapters in this book move quickly from philosophy to practice, equipping professionals to renew these living human strengths at a time when genuine inquiry, distinctiveness, judgment, connection, and intentional teamwork have never been more imperative. This developmental challenge has historical precedent. Management scholar Henry Mintzberg's continuous critique of MBA education anticipated current AI concerns. He argued that case study methods promote superficial decision-making because students simulate decisions for companies they do not understand, based on minimal information read the night before. This creates precisely the same risk we face with algorithmic decision-making: accepting compelling outputs without deep contextual understanding. Just as case studies can't create managers in classrooms, AI outputs cannot substitute for the embodied wisdom that comes from practicing judgment under uncertainty and pressure. The parallel reveals that our current challenge isn't technological but pedagogical: how do we maintain the craft that emerges only through deliberate practice?

Recent cases, such as the widely publicized Deloitte Australia incident in October 2025,[32] illustrate how leaders persuaded by algorithmic efficiency risk ethical and reputational failure when they accept outputs without reflection or questioning. This danger is playing out in boardrooms and classrooms worldwide.

The challenge we now face is not simply one of deploying new technologies, but of reimagining how we cultivate professional mastery in an age where algorithms offer fast answers, and classrooms increasingly resemble dashboards. If we seek to maintain the living craft of wisdom, we must design development pathways informed by both modern evidence and enduring philosophical wisdom. Practical wisdom is this integrative meta-capability weaving curiosity, creativity, critical thinking, communication, and collaboration into the steady practice that serves both performance and purpose.

Each capability we explore in this book rests on solid human wisdom and research evidence, can be cultivated through deliberate practices, and draws strength from philosophical traditions that have shaped human development for centuries. Practical wisdom functions as a compass. It does not replace the other capabilities, but orients them toward what matters most in context.

Table 1.3 brings these strands together, the research evidence, practice, and philosophical roots, so you can see at a glance both why these capabilities matter and how they can be strengthened in the age of AI.

The question professionals must now confront is how to ensure that deliberate practice, reflection, and moral imagination keep judgment alive when convenience and efficiency threaten its erosion. Practical wisdom is that slow virtue – the living craft – that ensures human capabilities serve the greater good, even as technology accelerates around us.

Table 1.3 Five Capabilities for the AI Age

Capability	*The Risk*	*Your Practice*	*The Foundation*
Curiosity → Generative Curiosity	• AI satisfies narrow curiosity but starves broad exploration. • Instant answers eliminate the productive uncertainty that fuels insight. • Cognitive tension essential for breakthrough thinking gets short-circuited.	• Frame your own questions before consulting AI. • Sustain perplexity rather than rushing to closure. • Distinguish questions AI can answer from those only humans can formulate.	• Aristotle: all humans by nature desire to know. • Socratic wisdom begins in perplexity. • The agora valued curiosity as civic duty.
Creativity → Imaginative Resilience	• AI enhances output but reduces creative distinctiveness. • Personal agency erodes when algorithms generate ideas. • Physical engagement and embodied exploration disappear.	• Use AI for research and stress-testing, not for generation. • Reserve independent ideation and physical prototyping for humans. • Protect intrinsic motivation by maintaining creative ownership.	• Greek *poiesis*: bringing forth through skilled making. • Da Vinci's *sfumato*: disciplined comfort with ambiguity. • Embodied intelligence requires physical engagement.
Critical Thinking → Algorithmic Scepticism	• Heavy AI reliance creates cognitive debt and dulls independent reasoning. • Elegant outputs trigger erosion of the *why* and algorithmic deference. • Users struggle to reconstruct reasoning unaided.	• Map arguments explicitly and visibly. • Pause to trace missing steps before accepting AI outputs. • Track underlying assumptions to keep reasoning transparent.	• Socratic scepticism: the unexamined life is not worth living. • Truth emerges through disciplined questioning. • Aquinas: objections strengthen reasoned judgment.
Communication → Hybrid Authority	• Authentic connection depends on embodied synchrony AI cannot replicate. • Authenticity collapses when messages are revealed as AI-generated. • Impact comes more from presence than from content alone.	• Use AI backstage to refine structure and logic. • Deliver with full embodied presence and emotional resonance. • Do not consult algorithms during live interaction.	• Cicero and Aristotle: rhetoric unites logic, credibility, and emotion. • Roman *eloquentia corporis*: persuasion arises through embodied performance. • Trust emerges through synchrony and mutual attention.
Collaboration → Bionic Collaboration	• AI agents displace micro-collaborative skills through over-automation. • Reduced socio-emotional exchange weakens trust and cohesion. • Algorithmic consensus bypasses deliberation and dissent.	• Make AI reasoning visible; use machines for scale, humans for meaning. • Begin with silent human framing before AI outputs. • Relocate AI to preparation; keep live collaboration human-centred.	• Greek assemblies and Roman Senate: collaboration as civic obligation. • Medieval guilds: structured knowledge-sharing as duty. • Enlightenment societies: collaboration as professional practice.

Each of the five capabilities is essential, but their real strength lies in how they reinforce one another. Curiosity fuels creativity. Creativity provides material for critical thinking. Critical thinking sharpens judgment, enabling authentic communication. Communication transforms ideas into shared purpose, which collaboration then turns into collective achievement.

Think of these five as instruments in an ensemble. Practical wisdom is the conductor: the integrative capacity that ensures they play together, in the right sequence, at the right tempo, for the right purpose. In Aristotle's terms, *phronesis* was the ability to choose the right action, in the right way, for the right reasons. Across cultures, similar ideas echo this integrative virtue.

In this book, we will return to practical wisdom as the *throughline*: the meta-capability that turns skill into judgment and judgment into action worth taking. Algorithms can optimize tasks, but only human wisdom can orient them toward what is good: what matters, what is right, what resonates, and what endures.

AI can give you options. Practical wisdom tells you which one you should choose, and why.

Self-Assessment: Your Starting Point in the Age of AI

This synthesis provides a direction for the journey ahead: rigorous enough to be trusted, practical enough to be applied, and timeless enough to remain relevant as technologies evolve. With this foundation in mind, you are ready to reflect on your own starting point.

The brief self-assessment below provides an initial snapshot of how you currently relate to the five capabilities, particularly in AI-supported work contexts. Each subsequent chapter includes similar assessments for the benefit of the reflective professional.

Use this initial self-assessment as a baseline, returning to it after each chapter to track how your capabilities evolve. This reflective journey is not for evaluation, but for guiding your personal capability renewal.

Instructions: Check the option that best reflects your current practice for each capability. This baseline gives you a snapshot of where AI may be eroding your distinct strengths and where it is amplifying them. Revisit after each chapter to track your development and identify new opportunities for deliberate practice.

1. **Generative Curiosity: From Quick Answers to Deeper Questions**
When you use AI to explore a problem or opportunity, how often do you frame your own questions before seeing its answers?

☐ Always – my questions lead the interaction, and I refine them as I go.
☐ Often – I start with my own questions, but sometimes default to AI prompts.
☐ Occasionally – I let AI frame the direction and follow its lead.
☐ Rarely – I depend on AI to tell me what to ask next.

Reveals whether AI is supporting or replacing the spark of inquiry.

2. Imaginative Resilience: From Polished Outputs to Original Insights
Thinking about your most original professional output in the past month:

☐ Emerged entirely from my own insight and experience.
☐ Combined my ideas with AI-generated possibilities in ways neither could achieve alone.
☐ Built mostly on AI suggestions with some human adjustments.
☐ Came almost entirely from AI recommendations I refined.

Assesses whether AI is amplifying or substituting your creative process.

3. Algorithmic Scepticism: From Polished Outputs to Clear Judgment
When AI provides an answer that "feels wrong" or incomplete:

☐ I always investigate, test, or challenge it before deciding.
☐ I usually dig deeper but sometimes accept the AI's answer when time-constrained.
☐ I sometimes accept it over my own intuition because it "must have more data."
☐ I often defer to AI as the safer, more defensible choice.

Measures your ability to balance machine-generated insights with human judgment.

4. Embodied Communication: From Dashboards to Dialogue
When crafting important communications with AI assistance:

☐ I always ensure my authentic voice, intent, and audience connection are clear in the final version.
☐ I edit AI drafts for voice and purpose, though much structure remains machine-shaped.
☐ I use AI outputs largely as produced, making only small adjustments.
☐ I rely on AI to generate messages with minimal personal input.

Examines whether communication remains relational and embodied versus impersonal through AI dependence.

5. **Bionic Collaboration: From Human Teams to Human–AI Partnerships**

When AI is part of my team's workflow:

☐ I intentionally design how AI supports rather than replaces human deliberation, trust-building, and decision-making.
☐ I ensure AI adds efficiency while safeguarding space for reflection and interpersonal dynamics.
☐ I accept AI coordination without close attention to its impact on relationships and teamwork.
☐ I let AI handle most coordination, reducing opportunities for direct human collaboration.

Explores whether AI enhances or erodes the social bonds, creativity, and adaptive intelligence that only authentic teamwork provides.

Using Your Profile

Your responses offer a snapshot of how you currently navigate the interplay between human capabilities and AI. Mixed profiles are normal. Few professionals are uniformly strong across all five. The value lies in identifying where you already use AI as a capability catalyst, where deliberate practice could shift you from dependency to mastery, and how balanced your overall capability system is in enabling work that truly matters.

As you work through subsequent chapters, you'll discover how each capability can be strengthened in ways that expand your confidence and impact. Revisit these questions after completing each chapter to track your development.

Erosion is easy, amplification is a choice.

How to Read This Book

This book is not just a case for the enduring value of human capabilities in the age of AI. It is a practical guide for renewing them. The invitation is to actively examine how you think, work, and lead, and to deliberately cultivate the strengths that will matter most as technology continues to evolve.

Each chapter unfolds as a living, multi-layered practice. These capabilities are not abstract skills, but embodied and relational strengths, sustained through daily rituals, relationships, and the shared routines of real organizations. To make them accessible, every chapter follows the same rhythm:

- **Ancient Anchor:** a historical foundation situating the capability in the long arc of human development.

- **Fundamental Theories:** defining and framing the capability.
- **Erosion Mechanisms:** how AI, if unexamined, can weaken this capability.
- **Amplification Opportunities:** ways to use AI consciously as a catalyst and partner to expand, not replace, what makes us human.
- **Stories from Practice:** lived examples from leaders, teams, and organizations shaping their capabilities amid change.
- **Evidence from Research:** highlights of the most relevant findings, grounding suggestions in rigorous evidence.
- **Self-Assessment:** a reflective tool to gauge your current practice, identify patterns, and set priorities for strengthening the capability in your own work.

Here is the journey ahead:

- **Chapter 2: Curiosity – From Quick Answers to Deeper Questions**
  Shows how AI compresses inquiry into shallow prompt–response loops, and how to restore disciplined wonder that sustains perplexity and fuels discovery.
- **Chapter 3: Creativity – From Polished Outputs to Original Insights**
  Contrasts recombination at speed with imaginative resilience, demonstrating how originality, embodied practice, and AI partnership generate breakthroughs.
- **Chapter 4: Critical Thinking – From Shallow Arguments to Clear Reasoning**
  Reveals how algorithmic fluency can erode reasoning, and how cultivating algorithmic scepticism restores independent judgment and decision-making strength.
- **Chapter 5: Communication – From Data Dashboards to Hybrid Authority**
  Argues that true persuasion rests not on slides or dashboards but on embodied presence – voice, gesture, timing, and authenticity – that AI cannot replace.
- **Chapter 6: Collaboration – From Human Teams to Bionic Collaboration**
  Expands collaboration beyond human-only teams to include human–AI partnerships, exploring both the risks of workflow automation and the opportunities of deliberate bionic co-creation.
- **Chapter 7: Practical Wisdom – From Technical Mastery to Wise Action**
  Shows how wisdom orchestrates the five capabilities into integrated, context-sensitive practice. Practical wisdom is the compass for deciding when and how to engage AI.
- **Chapter 8: Your Human Magic – From Individual Capabilities to Irreplaceable Value**

Synthesizes the self-assessment insights developed throughout the book, helping readers recognize the patterns that define their irreplaceable contribution and understand how the integration of all five capabilities creates what algorithms fundamentally cannot replicate.

- **Chapter 9: What Do Leaders Do? – From Algorithmic Citizenship to Professional Practice**
  Presents the integrated answer to the question posed in Chapter 1 by contrasting two paths: surrendering judgment to algorithmic authority or practicing citizenship through deliberate capability cultivation, demonstrating what leaders do when algorithms reshape professional work.
- **Appendix 1: Practices to Effectuate Each Capability**
  Synthesizes the systematic practices that leaders can take, based on each chapter's argument and recommendations for amplification of the capability. Use this Appendix as a reminder of specific actions you can take to hone your work at augmenting each of the capabilities in your job.
- **Appendix 2: How This Book Was Written – From Avoidance to Thoughtful Engagement**
  Explains how the book itself was created through deliberate collaboration with AI tools, using them to organize, refine, and test ideas while preserving full human authorship and scholarly judgment. The approach, formally reviewed and approved by the publisher, models the very principle the book teaches: using AI to amplify rather than replace human capability.

This book is designed as an active toolkit: pause for self-reflection and bring insights back to your team. Do not just read. Reflect, experiment, and adapt the habits discussed here to your own context. The goal is not just to understand the five capabilities, but to make them visible, habitual, and resilient in your daily work. Review Appendix 1 often to begin putting the capabilities into action.

Curiosity comes first not because it is most important, but because it unlocks the others, setting in motion a virtuous cycle where all five capabilities reinforce one another. Together, they prepare us not only to survive technological acceleration but to thrive within it.

Notes

1 Frey & Osborne (2017). First produced as a 2013 working paper.
2 Roos (2014).
3 Roos (2015).
4 Roos (2019).
5 Talentport (2023); Ministry of Education China (2025).
6 Roos (2023a–b; 2025a).
7 Jassy (2025, June 17).

8 Formally, "Agentic AI" can be defined as AI systems that can pursue complex goals with limited direct super-vision (Shavit et al., 2023).
9 Fortune (2025, August 19); Zaapi (2025); Digital Commerce 360. (2025, July 9); DigitalOcean (2025); OpenAI (2025).
10 TCS Summit Europe, Vienna, September 22–23, 2025 (where I moderated a plenary session)
11 Markovitz, G., Hall, M., & Whiting, K. (2026, January 24).
12 Brynjolfsson et al. (2025, August 26).
13 Burning Glass Institute (2025).
14 Chatterji et al. (2025).
15 Mostaque (2025).
16 Masumori & Ikegami (2025); Anthropic PBC (2025, June 20); Palisade Research (2025).
17 Kosmyna et al. (2025).
18 For example, McCoy (2025).
19 Brooks (2025).
20 Anthropic PBC (2025, October 14).
21 Jakesch et al. (2023).
22 Olson (2025, May 6).
23 State Council Information Office (2025, May 13).
24 **Data from this research will be referenced as TNM research data (2025).**
25 Roos (2025).
26 **Data from this research will be referenced as LSP research data (2024; 2025).**
27 Roos & Victor (1999; 2018).
28 After serving for 25 years, I stepped down from the board of Imagination Lab in June 2025.
29 Kelly (2010).
30 Benioff (2025, July 10).
31 Brynjolfsson et al. (2025, August 26).
32 McGuirk (2025, October 7).

References

Anthropic PBC. (2025, June 20). Agentic misalignment: How LLMs could be insider threats. https://www.anthropic.com/research/agentic-misalignment

Anthropic PBC. (2025, October 14). Preparing for AI's economic impact: Exploring policy responses. Anthropic Research. https://www.anthropic.com/research/economic-policy-responses

Aristotle. (2009). *Nicomachean ethics* (T. Irwin, Trans.). Hackett Publishing Company. (Original work published ca. 350 BCE).

Benioff, M. (2025, July 10). Humans must remain at the heart of the AI story. *Financial Times*. https://www.ft.com/content/3db52a71-7660-405d-9e5e-42a97d2d64ca

Brooks, D. (2025, July 3). Are we really willing to become dumber? *The New York Times*. https://www.nytimes.com/2025/07/03/opinion/artificial-intelligence-education.html (MIT News)

Brynjolfsson, E., Chandar, B., & Chen, R. (August 26, 2025). Canaries in the coal mine? Six facts about the recent employment effects of artificial intelligence. https://digitaleconomy.stanford.edu/publications/canaries-in-the-coal-mine/

Burning Glass Institute. (2025, July). The expertise upheaval: How GenAI will reshape career pathways for millions of Americans. Burning Glass Institute.

Chatterji, A., Cunningham, T., Deming, D. J., Hitzig, Z., Ong, C., Shan, C. Y., & Wadman, K. (2025). *How people use ChatGPT* (Working Paper No. 34255). National Bureau of Economic Research. http://www.nber.org/papers/w34255

Digital Commerce 360. (2025, July 9). AI agents gain ground in US business (reporting on PwC's AI Agent Survey). https://www.digitalcommerce360.com/2025/07/09/ai-agents-us-business-pwc-survey-data/

Fortune. (2025, August 19). The AI revolution will cut nearly $1 trillion a year out of S&P 500 budgets. Fortune. https://fortune.com/2025/08/19/morgan-stanley-920-billion-sp-500-savings-ai-agentic-robots-jobs/

Frey, C. B., & Osborne, M. A. (2017). The future of employment: How susceptible are jobs to computerisation? *Technological Forecasting and Social Change*, 114, 254–280. https://doi.org/10.1016/j.techfore.2016.08.019

Jakesch, M., Hancock, J. T., & Naaman, M. (2023). Human heuristics for AI-generated language are flawed. *Proceedings of the National Academy of Sciences*, *120*(11), e2208839120. https://doi.org/10.1073/pnas.2208839120

Jassy, A. (2025, June 17). Update from Amazon CEO Andy Jassy on generative AI. Amazon.com. https://www.aboutamazon.com/news/company-news/amazon-ceo-andy-jassy-on-generative-ai

Kelly, K. (2010). *What technology wants*. Viking.

Kosmyna, N., Hauptmann, E., Yuan, Y. T., Situ, J., Liao, X.-H., Beresnitzky, A. V., Braunstein, I., & Maes, P. (2025). Your brain on ChatGPT: Accumulation of cognitive debt when using an AI assistant for essay writing task. *MIT Media Lab Technical Report*. https://www.brainonllm.com/

Markovitz, G., Hall, M., & Whiting, K. (2026, January 24). 4 takeaways from Davos 2026: New deals, a reckoning, dialogue and living the questions. *World Economic Forum*. https://www.weforum.org/stories/2026/01/4-takeaways-from-davos-2026/

Masumori, A., & Ikegami, T. (2025). Do large language model agents exhibit a survival instinct? An empirical study in a Sugarscape-style simulation. *ar Xiv:2508*.12920. https://arxiv.org/abs/2508.12920

McCoy, J. (2025, August 29). The ChatGPT brain drain myth: How AI actually makes us smarter (if we use it right) [Video transcript]. First Movers. https://www.youtube.com/watch?v=s2fl2z_Qe58

McGuirk, R. (2025, October 7). Deloitte to partially refund Australian government for report with apparent AI-generated errors. *AP News*. https://apnews.com/article/australia-ai-errors-deloitte-ab54858680ffc4ae6555b31c8fb987f3

Mintzberg, H. (2004). *Managers not MBAs: A hard look at the soft practice of managing and management development*. Berrett-Koehler Publishers.

Mostaque, E. (2025). The last economy: A guide to the age of intelligent economics. *Intelligent Internet*. https://ii.inc/web/the-last-economy(eBook ASIN: B0FNDMWRZT)

Olson, P. (2025, May 6). Addicted to ChatGPT? Here's how to reclaim your brain. *Bloomberg Opinion*. https://www.bloomberg.com/opinion/articles/2025-05-06/addicted-to-chatgpt-here-s-how-to-reclaim-your-brain

OpenAI. (2025, September). Jobs in the Intelligence Age: How AI is creating work and changing the workforce (report). OpenAI Global Affairs. https://cdn.openai.com/global-affairs/06025361-1ede-4402-97d2-daf1e5918b43/jobs-in-the-intelligence-age-sept-2025.pdf

Palisade Research. (2025, July 5). Shutdown resistance in reasoning models. https://palisaderesearch.org/blog/shutdown-resistance

Roos, J. (2014, June 18). Lessons needed to beat the computer. *Financial Times*. (Access via FT archive/search).

Roos, J. (2015, June 24). Build STEM skills, but do not neglect the humanities. *Harvard Business Review*. https://hbr.org/2015/06/build-stem-skills-but-dont-neglect-the-humanities

Roos, J. (2019, November). Techno-humanism: If algorithms make all the decisions, who is the leader? *Global Focus Magazine*. https://globalfocusmagazine.com/techno-humanism-if-algorithms-make-all-the-decisions-who-is-the-leader/

Roos, J. (2023a, January 12). Do not panic about ChatGPT-3. *EFMD Blog*. https://blog.efmdglobal.org/2023/01/12/do-not-panic-about-chat-gpt-3/

Roos, J. (2023b, February). ChatGPT: The next firestorm in education. *AACSB Insights*. https://www.aacsb.edu/insights/articles/2023/02/chatgpt-the-next-firestorm-ineducation

Roos, J. (2025, February 18). The next management: Renewing companies, institutions, and society. *Global Focus Magazine*. https://globalfocusmagazine.com/the-next-management-renewing-companies-institutions-and-society/

Roos, J. (2025a). From adoption to action: GenAI as a catalyst for change at Hult. In *AI ready: Shaping tomorrow with AI and human intelligence* (pp. 33–42). Thinkers50 & Hult International Business School.

Roos, J. (2025b). The next management: Why now, what next? *EFMD Global Focus*, *19*(3), 20–22.

Roos, J., & Nilsson, V. (2020). Driving organizational readiness for change through strategic workshops. *International Journal of Management and Applied Research*, 7(1), 1–18. https://doi.org/10.18646/2056.71.20-001

Roos, J., & Victor, B. (1999). Towards a new model of strategy-making as serious play. *European Management Journal, 17*(4), 348–355. https://doi.org/10.1016/S0263-2373(99)00015-8

Roos, J., Victor, B., & Statler, M. (2004). Playing seriously with strategy. *Long Range Planning*, *37*(6), 549–568. https://doi.org/10.1016/j.lrp.2004.09.005

Shavit, Y., Agarwal, S., Brundage, M., Adler, S., O'Keefe, C., Campbell, R., & Robinson, D. G. (2023). Practices for governing agentic AI systems. OpenAI Whitepaper. https://openai.com/index/practices-for-governing-agentic-ai-systems/

State Council Information Office (via Xinhua). (2025, May 13). China advances AI curriculum to cover full basic education. http://english.scio.gov.cn/pressroom/2025-05/13/content_117871666.html (State Council Information Office).

Statler, M., & Roos, J. (2007). *Everyday strategic preparedness: The role of practical wisdom in organizations*. Palgrave Macmillan.

Talentport. (2023, April 17). Is ChatGPT banned in your country? A look at restrictions worldwide. *Talentport*. https://talentport.com/blog/chatgpt-banned-countries

World Economic Forum. (2025). Technology convergence: Mapping the future of AI integration across sectors. World Economic Forum. https://www.weforum.org/reports

Zaapi. (2025, August 13). AI agents in business: 2025 statistics that prove it's no longer optional. https://www.zaapi.com/blog/ai-agents-in-business-2025-statistics-that-prove-its-no-longer-optional

2 Curiosity – From Quick Answers to Deeper Questions

The Ancient Foundation of Wonder

The first step in choosing amplification is to reclaim curiosity, the discipline of lingering with questions before rushing to answers. In one of Plato's dialogues, around 399 BCE, the young mathematician Theaetetus sits across from Socrates eager to prove himself before the most famous thinker in Athens. At first, his answers to Socrates' questions come quickly, honed by the crisp clarity of mathematics. Knowledge, he proposes, is sensible perception. No, says Socrates, for perception changes and deceives. Knowledge is true opinion. Not quite, replies Socrates, for opinion can faulter due to errors of memory. Knowledge must therefore be true opinion with reasoned explanation. Socrates presses further, until each definition collapses under its own weight.[1]

Theaetetus eventually falters. Wrestling with Socrates' paradoxes, he confesses: "*By the gods, Socrates, I wonder exceedingly as to what in the world these things are, and sometimes in looking at them I truly get dizzy.*"

Theaetetus' admission of bewilderment should not be considered as failure. For Socrates, this wondering (*thaumazein*) is the beginning of philosophy. "*This is very much a philosopher's experience,*" he tells the young man, "*for there is no other beginning of philosophy than this.*" True learning starts not in certainty but in that unsettled state of puzzlement and perplexity (*aporia*) where the ground shifts beneath what we thought we knew. Knowledge emerges only when we are willing to inhabit that discomfort. It takes shape by asking questions without rushing to close them, lingering in the tension of not knowing. This is curiosity in its most disciplined form.

The dialogue does not accomplish any complete definition of knowledge. Yet Theaetetus himself recognizes the value of the struggle. At the end, when Socrates asks whether they are still pregnant with knowledge or have brought forth everything, Theaetetus replies: "*Yes, we have, and, by Zeus, Socrates, with your help I have already said more than there was in me.*" The perplexity has been generative, even without resolution.

DOI: 10.4324/9781003732570-2

Aristotle later distilled this insight into a single sentence that shaped centuries of thought: "*All humans by nature desire to know.*"[2] For him, curiosity was no distraction. It was the first principle of philosophy, science, and art. The desire to know was not a luxury of leisure but a human necessity, the impulse that drove inquiry into causes and principles, into what lies beyond appearances.

In Athens, curiosity was not only intellectual but civic. To be a citizen was to take part in dialogue, to deliberate, to question the assumptions underlying communal life. The agora was not a marketplace of goods alone; it was a marketplace of questions. In that culture, curiosity was cultivated as a duty. To remain passive in the face of perplexity was to fall short not just as a thinker, but as a member of the community.

The Greek's apprenticeship in wonder looks almost alien to us today. In Theaetetus' Athens, information was scarce, answers hard-won. To grasp a principle might take years of study or a lifetime of dialogue. To read Aristotle's treatise required a long apprenticeship in logic and metaphysics. To wrestle with Socratic questioning meant carrying perplexity for days or weeks before clarity dawned. Learning was inseparable from struggle.

The AI era reverses the equation. Information is no longer scarce but instantly abundant. What once required lifetimes of careful questioning can now be accessed in seconds. With a keystroke, an algorithm delivers a compelling response to questions that Socrates and Aristotle might have debated endlessly. The perplexity that once fuelled growth can now be erased before it takes hold.

At first glance, this may feel like liberation. Why wrestle with confusion when clarity is just a prompt away? Why endure perplexity when an answer sits waiting in the cloud?

Yet caution should teach us to pause before celebrating. Today, the same social networks that connect us to more information than any prior generation have also fragmented our attention. Endless feeds, notifications, and messages encourage skimming over sustained thought, prioritizing novelty over depth. The very infrastructure that democratized knowledge has also reconfigured how we practice curiosity.

AI worsens these earlier patterns of digital information. Instead of merely expanding access, AI threatens to erase the apprenticeship of inquiry altogether. Where writing threatened memory, printing threatened selectivity, and the internet threatened attention, AI threatens the very source of insight: curiosity itself. It collapses the space between Question and Answer so completely that the human impulse to wrestle with perplexity risks atrophying.

The challenge before us is to recover a foundation of wonder. For what looked like weakness in Theaetetus is an essential human capability in formation. His perplexity is the seed of first insights, leading eventually to wisdom. Our risk is not that AI gives us answers, but that we forget the value of perplexity. Unless we learn to preserve and extend curiosity in the age of instant answers, we may find ourselves surrounded by knowledge yet starved of understanding.

Practice sitting with confusion before seeking AI answers. Perplexity builds judgment.

Short-Circuiting Perplexity

Young Theaetetus' perplexity reminds us that learning once demanded endurance. To sit with questions was to cultivate the intellectual muscles that carried philosophy, science, and civic life forward. Today, perplexity rarely lasts more than a moment. Ask a question, and within seconds an algorithm produces an answer wrapped in confidence and data-driven precision. What took days in the Athenian agora, months in a medieval monastery, or decades in an Enlightenment laboratory now arrives almost instantly.

We feel this erosion not as abstraction but as lived practice. A senior executive described it to me candidly: "*Our meetings now start with the AI's analysis. We rarely begin with our own framing anymore.*"[3] The output is convincing, but the intellectual work of framing the problem, the very act that defines leadership, has been outsourced before the conversation even begins.

Professional workshop facilitators in our research echoed this concern. One observed: "*AI support reassured me in planning, but distracted me in the room.*"[4] The structured prompts gave confidence in preparation but muted responsiveness in live interaction, where the most generative questions often emerge.

These stories underscore a deeper truth. The discipline of questioning is the foundation of separating right from wrong, good from bad. Without it, decisions risk becoming optimized responses to machine prompts rather than reflective engagements with complex realities. The slow apprenticeship that once forged resilience, originality, and depth is displaced by the convenience of instant closure.

Curiosity requires sustained encounter with uncertainty. Modern philosophers argue that curiosity is not simply a desire for knowledge but an affective state that embeds questions as its content. We become curious when we encounter what we cannot yet recognize or understand, when neural signals representing "unknown" compete with our attempts to categorize and predict.[5] This explains why instant answers prove so seductive and so dangerous. When algorithms collapse our encounters with uncertainty into immediate resolution, they eliminate the very condition that makes questioning possible.

The elimination has become acute enough to generate its own backlash. In October 2025, thousands queued in New York's West Village for access to an unusual corporate installation: a space furnished not with screens but with coffee, books, pens, and paper. This is a self-declared "zero slop zone' explicitly rejecting low-quality AI-generated content.[6] The creator was Anthropic, positioning its AI product Claude as a thinking partner rather than replacement for human intelligence. The irony is precise. *The same industry accelerating perplexity's collapse now profits from selling refuge from that collapse.* Yet beneath the commercial cynicism lies something worth examining: the appetite for contemplative slowness persists, even when algorithmic speed dominates professional life. The question is whether appetite can become practice. Theaetetus' dizziness before Socrates was generative because it was sustained through structured, disciplined dialogue, not occasional, zero slop retreat. A coffee shop visit, however appealing, is not a discipline. The hunger the pop-up revealed must be transformed into systematic capability, or it remains merely nostalgia for a pace we can no longer afford.

AI turns perplexity into closure, but closure without struggle erodes the muscle of inquiry.

This danger is not new or unique to AI. Each prior technology that altered humanity's relationship with knowledge also required new counter-disciplines to preserve curiosity. Medieval scholastics developed disputation to keep questioning alive even as authoritative texts multiplied. Renaissance humanists revived direct observation and experiment to resist the suffocating grip of inherited doctrine. The Enlightenment institutionalized the scientific method as a safeguard against dogma from church or king. In each case, new practices emerged to balance the risk of erosion.

The AI age will require its own discipline. Instant answers can serve as starting points, but only if we train ourselves to resist the illusion of completion. When a LLM provides a confident conclusion, the curious professional must still ask: What assumptions underlie this response? What alternatives might it have excluded? What questions remain unasked?

Seen this way, curiosity is not eliminated by AI, it is tested by it. Machines supply information, but they cannot frame the perplexities worth pursuing. That work remains irreducibly human. Unless we reclaim the discipline of perplexity, we risk mistaking completion for comprehension and convenience for wisdom.

Two Types of Wonder – The Laser and the Radar

Curiosity is not a single faculty. It operates through different channels, each serving distinct purposes. Psychologist Daniel Berlyne clarified this decades ago when he distinguished between two fundamental forms of curiosity: specific and diversive.[7] His insight provides a lens for understanding both the promise and the peril of curiosity in the AI age.

Specific curiosity is what we might call the *Laser*. It is narrow, precise, and goal directed. The laser locks onto a knowledge gap and seeks to close it quickly. How does this machine work? Why did the numbers shift? What is the cause of this failure? This form of curiosity is highly efficient, propelling us toward mastery and resolution. In evolutionary terms, it helped us survive, resolving uncertainty fast enough to act before danger struck.

Diversive curiosity is what we might call the *Radar*. Unlike the laser, it does not seek immediate closure. The radar scans widely, open to novelty, restlessness, and possibility. It thrives on ambiguity, on the chance encounter, on the surprising pattern that emerges when no one was looking for it. This is the curiosity of explorers, artists, and innovators. While the laser helps us sharpen what we already know, the radar allows us to discover what we did not know was there.

Both forms are essential. The laser equips us to solve problems efficiently. The radar equips us to generate fresh insights, discover unexpected opportunities, and reframe challenges entirely. A healthy professional practice requires both, balanced in tension. Yet AI interacts with them asymmetrically.

AI excels at satisfying the laser. Give a machine a specific prompt and it returns a detailed, often compelling output in a split second. In many cases, it performs this task better than humans: faster, more comprehensive, and supported by more data than any single professional could hold.

But the very strength of AI in feeding the laser undermines the radar. By closing questions so quickly, the system short-circuits the open-ended scanning that radar curiosity requires. The process of lingering, exploring, and noticing weak signals is degraded.

Managers feel the tension. Meetings that once began with divergent exploration now quickly converge on AI-generated options. One middle-manager described the result as "efficient but predictable." The laser was well fed, but the radar was starved. Over time, this imbalance risks producing people, teams, and organizations that can optimize within existing paradigms but struggle to imagine new ones. If AI narrows inquiry too quickly, we risk starving the very conditions from which novelty arises. Breakthroughs often emerge from peripheral observations, diverse perspectives, and analogue reasoning, not from direct answers.

My work with Sigvald Harryson on disruptive innovation illustrates the same dynamic. In our consulting with organizations stuck on a problem, we found that when strong CTOs or CIOs relied too heavily on tightly focused, exploitative R&D logics, they often optimized existing paradigms, but unintentionally blocked new discovery. The laser was working, their questions were sharp and structured given their unique circumstances, but the radar was quiet.

Breakthroughs emerged only when we broke open their laser bias by orchestrating "collaborative competitions" in which multiple university teams from different disciplines both competed and shared insights. The combination of competition and collaboration created conditions where peripheral ideas could surface, and novelty could flourish beyond the narrow beam of efficiency.[8]

History illustrates the value of radar over laser. Human exploration was not driven by precise answers to existing questions, but by restless scanning and exploration, what else might lie beyond the horizon? Scientific revolutions, too, often began with anomalies that did not fit prevailing models. If Galileo Galilei had relied on authorities to supply answers, he would never have persisted in noticing four points of light around Jupiter that shouldn't exist, which his telescope revealed.

Likewise, if Norwegian explorer Roald Amundsen had followed the rules for his funding, he would not have turned his ship toward the South Pole. Instead, he would have continued his official journey to the Northwest Passage. As many experienced professionals know from experience, progress can require stepping beyond what is sanctioned or expected, driven by relentless curiosity.

AI shifts the balance in ways that tempt us toward comfort. When answers come quickly, the radar feels inefficient, even indulgent. Why wander when the system already knows? Yet without the radar, discovery withers. The real risk of AI is not that it replaces the laser, it is that it makes us forget the radar altogether.

To preserve professional vitality, we must protect both modes. That means designing workflows that deliberately hold space for radar-style exploration before jumping to AI-powered laser-style closure. Teams that begin projects with contrarian scenarios or deliberately entertain outliers keep radar curiosity alive. Individuals who cultivate habits of asking questions outside their domain, or following hunches that make little sense at first, sustain the discipline of wonder that algorithms cannot reproduce.

Some facilitators in our studies report that attention tends to drift toward the tool rather than the room: *"It is comforting to have AI for brainstorming and inspiration."* They reported how using AI tools in real-time engagements creates a subtle imbalance between focused presence ("laser") and situational awareness ("radar"). While AI assistance enhanced their preparation and boosted self-confidence heading into workshops, it also fractured their attention during live facilitation. As a result, these professional facilitators sometimes missed nonverbal cues, moments of hesitation, or a fleeting yet important comment. One facilitator reflected: "*It took me out of the moment to interact with (the AI tool),*" while a participant observed: "*When the facilitator used AI visibly, it distracted the atmosphere and momentum.*"[9]

The radar shuts down when attention is monopolized by the machine. Preserving curiosity, therefore, is not only cognitive but embodied, an act of staying present to what human interaction reveals, even when algorithmic outputs seem sufficient.

Balance focused AI queries with deliberate scanning time. Protect both laser and radar curiosity.

Two Types of Curiosity – Joy and Itch

Curiosity is more than a cognitive habit. It is also a motivational force, a desire to know, to see, or experience that pulls us into questions and keeps us there. Cognition researcher Jordan Litman sharpened this point by distinguishing between two sources of curiosity, each rooted in a different kind of psychological drive.[10]

The first is **Interest-Type Curiosity (I-Type)**. This is curiosity powered by joy, the intrinsic pleasure of discovery. We ask questions not to solve a pressing problem, but because the journey to learn something new delights us. Anyone who has listened to a young child knows this impulse. The endless stream of "why" questions is not a means to an end but a way of inhabiting the world. The joy lies in the exploration itself, in the spark that comes with each small revelation. Adults experience the same when they lose track of time while chasing an unexpected idea across books, data, or conversations. The process is its own reward.

The second is **Deprivation-Type Curiosity (D-Type)**. This is curiosity powered by discomfort, the itch that comes from knowing just enough to recognize what we do not yet understand. Unlike the gentle pull of interest, D-Type curiosity burns with greater intensity. When we already possess some knowledge and suddenly encounter a gap we feel tension and even frustration. This uncomfortable need to know demands resolution. We pursue answers not for the joy of exploration but to relieve this unease, and the pursuit is more urgent, more consuming than I-Type curiosity. The doctoral student pushing through the final stages of a dissertation embodies D-Type curiosity: the pressure of an unresolved question fuels relentless persistence, driving more intense information-seeking until the gap closes. The process can be exhausting, but the eventual relief of clarity is worth the effort.

Both forms are essential. The first fuels breadth, openness, and lifelong learning. The second powers persistence, depth, and problem-solving under pressure. One sustains playful exploration, the other drives rigorous closure. Together they form the twin engines of inquiry.

The problem is that AI can undermine both.

When algorithms deliver instant answers, the joy of the journey collapses. Why follow curiosity's winding path when the conclusion arrives in seconds? Exploration becomes redundant. As one executive told us: "*When I use the (AI) tool, I get comprehensive answers immediately. It feels efficient, but I also feel less invested in the problem. I don't carry the question with me anymore.*"[11] The dopamine reward of curiosity still fires, as neuroscience shows, but the process of gradual discovery, the part that builds resilience and depth, disappears.[12]

At the same time, AI can erase the itch of not knowing before it can develop. The discomfort that once drove persistent analysis vanishes when a solution arrives instantly. The tension dissolves too quickly to fuel real effort. Without that productive pressure, we risk becoming passive recipients of information rather than active pursuers of knowledge.

This dual short-circuit can be costly. Work cultures emphasizing efficiency and closure naturally develop people and teams that can optimize well-defined tasks but falter when confronted with ambiguous challenges requiring both playful experimentation and dogged persistence.

The danger is subtle but profound. Without curiosity-*joy*, we lose the capacity for serendipitous insight. Without curiosity-*itch*, we lose the endurance needed for complex problem-identification and solving. Together, these losses weaken the motivational architecture that underpins our value creation.

Education systems reveal the same tension. Left to convenience, students may be tempted to accept confident outputs rather than carry questions with them, dulling the apprenticeship in perplexity that once trained intellectual stamina. Schools and universities are working hard to counter this. Reports show examples where faculty assess not only the final product but the process, that is, how students frame questions, refine prompts, and push beyond what the system suggests. Some require learners to document and reflect on their AI use, making visible whether they explore or simply consume. Examples include AI-enhanced case method and orchestration platform that deploy AI to generate unexpected "what-if" scenarios in real time, unsettling assumptions and compelling deeper questioning. These emerging practices underline the danger and the remedy at once: without *active* countermeasures, AI may erode the joy of discovery, but with them, it can preserve and even extend the productive itch of unresolved puzzles.[13]

Spaces for open-ended exploration can keep the joy of curiosity alive even in AI-rich environments. Teams that celebrate surprising questions, not just efficient answers, signal that joy still matters. Similarly, leaders who resist the temptation to resolve every uncertainty instantly can preserve the itch of curiosity. Allowing problems to remain open, insisting that tension be carried for a while before consulting the machine, restores the motivational pressure that drives deeper engagement.

One manager we interviewed described the practice this way: *"When AI gives me the answer too quickly, I set it aside and force myself to sketch what I think first. It keeps me connected to the problem. Sometimes I go back and see the AI had something useful. But sometimes I realize my own path took me somewhere more original."*[14] This is not rejection of AI but disciplined use, ensuring that curiosity's motivational engines are not bypassed.

The message is clear. Curiosity is not only a cognitive capacity to protect but also an emotional drive to cultivate. Both joy and itch must be preserved if curiosity is to thrive in the AI age.

Create friction in your workflow. Let questions simmer before consulting AI.

Eroding Curiosity

Curiosity rarely vanishes all at once. It erodes through small shifts that feel helpful in the moment but weaken our questioning instincts over time. Across our research, three mechanisms appear with troubling consistency. Each begins as a support but gradually undermines the discipline of inquiry.

1st Mechanism: The Shallow Questioning Loop

AI's most visible strength is speed. Give it a prompt and it produces a plausible answer almost immediately. The problem is that speed can collapse the very process of questioning. Instead of letting perplexity unfold through a chain of exploration, we close the loop at the first suitable response. The result is a shallow questioning loop, efficient on the surface, but hollow at the core.

Carruthers explains why this pattern proves so cognitively destructive. Curiosity persists only as long as we fail to categorize what puzzles us. The moment when we think we "know" the answer, curiosity dissolves.[15] AI systems engineer this dissolution at lightning speed, collapsing the sustained uncertainty that productive questioning requires. What feels like efficient problem-solving is the premature termination of the cognitive process that generates insight. A freshman student in an engineering school I met in an elevator recently articulated her recognition of this danger. When asked how much she was using

AI tools in her math studies she told me: "*Less and less because I want to learn how to solve problems.*"

Academic evidence echoes these findings. Researchers recently demonstrated that the formation of trust in AI is not a simple matter of passive acceptance, but emerges from a dual-process model that combines causality and explainability. In a recent study, users' trust in AI depended on both their ability to justify and emotionally accept the outputs (causability) and their engagement in systematically evaluating why the AI made specific decisions (explainability). Based on data from 350 participants with prior experience using algorithmic services, they found that explainability and causability together account for a significant proportion (58%) of the variance in user trust and attitudes toward AI systems. When people stop asking why and move from systematic evaluation to uncritical acceptance, trust may rise, but the quality of judgment falls.[16] We risk mistaking closure for comprehension.

2nd Mechanism: Curiosity Offloading

The second mechanism runs deeper. It is not just that we accept answers too quickly, but that we begin to delegate the very act of question-formation. Instead of asking what puzzles us, we rely on the machine to suggest what we should be curious about.

One facilitator confessed during our controlled experiments: "*I found myself asking the AI what I should even be thinking about.*"[17] Recall what writer Parmy Olson noticed in her interviews with young professionals: the slow displacement of self-trust and sense of value by growing AI dependence.[18] This shift, from authoring inquiry to consuming it, marks a profound erosion. Curiosity becomes reactive rather than generative.

Teams that begin with AI-generated frameworks miss the perplexity and sense of wonder that Theaetetus experienced in dialogue with Socrates. Today, researchers identify this as curiosity's essential trigger: the productive discomfort of encountering what we don't yet understand. When algorithms pre-package the questions, they eliminate the fertile uncertainty that sparks genuine inquiry, whether prompted by probing questions or emerging organically from collaborative exploration.

Researcher Todd Kashdan and colleagues reveals what is lost when productive friction disappears from inquiry. Their comprehensive study of over 3,000 adults led to the Five-Dimensional Curiosity Scale, empirically validating five core facets (Joyous Exploration, Deprivation Sensitivity, Stress Tolerance, Social Curiosity, and Thrill Seeking). "Stress Tolerance," defined as the capacity to manage the discomfort of facing novel, uncertain, and complex problems, proved foundational to genuine curiosity.[19] This highlights that deep curiosity flourishes only where there is *persistent* engagement with ambiguity and tension, elements often eliminated by AI's instant frameworks. A tolerance for productive uncertainty proves fundamental to genuine curiosity. Yet AI's instant frameworks eliminate precisely this discomfort, short-circuiting the cognitive struggle that generates insight.

3rd Mechanism: Algorithmic Narrowing

The third mechanism is less visible but no less dangerous. By design, large language models converge on probable responses. They are built to optimize consensus, not highlight anomalies. What gets filtered out are precisely the weak signals and awkward metaphors that often trigger new thinking. Over time, the culture shifts from exploration to passive consumption, narrowing the possibilities for new ideas and innovation.

Kashdan's team demonstrated precisely what is being lost. They identified four distinctive types of curious people ("The Fascinated," "Problem Solvers," "Empathizers," and "Avoiders") each blending five curiosity facets to form unique approaches to learning, engagement, and creativity. Where open-ended discourse once relied on this person-centric diversity to spark discovery, algorithmic recommendations flatten these individual styles into statistical uniformity. The subtle cognitive friction and divergent questioning that fuelled collective insight are replaced by smooth consensus and predictable exchanges.

One Drucker Forum participant noticed this effect in her leadership practice: "*When I'm deep into the AI's suggestions, I stop watching the room. I miss signals. I lose what used to make me a good leader.*"[20] The narrowing of attention made interactions smoother but less generative.

Facilitators reported similar effects. "*The AI gives me good ideas,*" one said, "*but I lose the collaborative instinct that makes workshops come alive.*"[21] Algorithmic narrowing provides reliable prompts, but it gradually squeezes out the eccentric contributions from lived experience that spark discovery.

This narrowing is not limited to creative work using AI. It is a systemic risk documented across fields. In finance, anomaly detection algorithms are tuned for efficiency and consensus, leading institutions to screen out rare signals that could warn of new patterns in fraud or shifting market dynamics.[22] In healthcare, AI diagnostic systems learn from common presentations and may smooth away atypical findings, risking delayed recognition of rare or novel conditions.[23] Even in creative domains, recent studies show that while AI tools offer rapid suggestions, less than 0.3% of their responses match the originality of highly creative human contributors. The rest hew closely to consensus, sidelining the eccentric insights that drive discovery.[24]

These erosions are amplified by integrity gaps in the tools themselves. Features that automate reflexes and reward instant closure create what Hamilton Mann, author of *Artificial Integrity,* calls "functional alienation"; opaque decision paths create functional transparency problems; gamified rewards tip into functional addiction.[25] Together they shrink the space where perplexity can breathe and where questioning would normally take root. The result is a loss not only of questioning styles, but of the underlying psychological resources that drive innovation and well-being through curiosity.

The Combined Effect

These three curiosity-halting mechanisms rarely appear in isolation. They interact, reinforcing one another. The shallow loop reduces the depth of questioning. Offloading shifts the authorship of inquiry. Narrowing erases the anomalies that stretch imagination. Together, they create a systemic drift away from the irrational, human-authored inquiry based on lived experience that produces genuine insight.

We often do not notice the erosion at first. On the contrary, we may feel more confident. AI makes us look better, more structured, more comprehensive. But this confidence can mask a deeper loss. The intellectual muscles that once thrived on perplexity, persistence, and surprise are no longer exercised.

The organizational consequences are serious. Professionals and teams that embrace AI without discipline become efficient at refining existing strategies and ways of working but struggle to generate new ones. They can optimize current practices but falter when confronting ambiguity or unprecedented challenges. What is lost is not information but curiosity resilience, the ability to dwell in perplexity until insight emerges.

Are you authoring inquiry or consuming outputs?

The erosion of curiosity is not inevitable. Recognizing these mechanisms is the first step toward resisting them. They show us what is at stake: the apprenticeship of wonder that has always been the foundation of wisdom.

Figure 2.1 visualizes this erosion as a downward progression from deep questioning to mechanical response. As inquiry becomes shallow, offloaded, and narrowed by algorithmic shortcuts, professionals risk losing not data but their very capacity for discovery.

Amplifying Curiosity – From Anxiety to Agency

The erosion of curiosity rarely feels like an abstract intellectual issue. For professionals, it shows up as an emotional undercurrent,

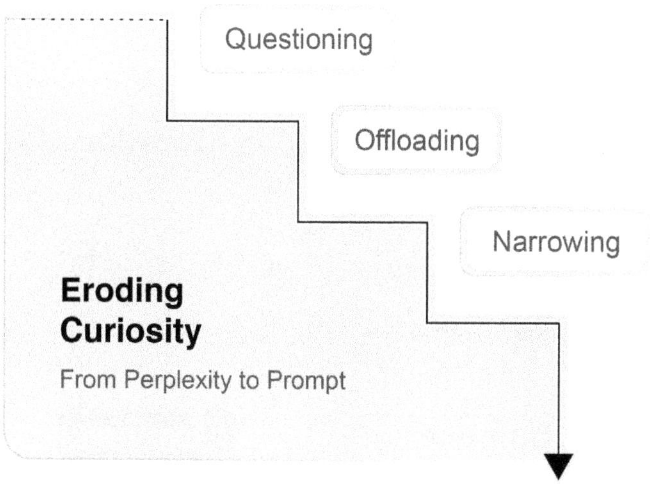

Figure 2.1 Eroding Curiosity – From Perplexity to Prompt

an unease about their role, relevance, and value creation. When questions are pre-empted by machine suggestions, they begin to feel less like explorers and more like curators of outputs they did not author.

This displacement often manifests as anxiety. The frustration of one executive we interviewed illustrates this: *"I feel less like a decision-maker and more like an AI user. Everyone expects me to ask the tool, not think for myself."*[26]

Yet anxiety does not have to signal decline. Properly channelled, it can become the very energy that powers agency. Curiosity, when practiced deliberately with AI, can transform uncertainty into momentum. Rather than being displaced by instant answers, perplexity can be harnessed as a driver of renewed engagement.

The Curiosity Amplification Cycle

This transformation unfolds through a cycle that begins with a *question*, often vague or incomplete, that sparks *exploration*. Exploration, in turn, creates opportunities for *surprise*: the unanticipated connection, the anomaly that does not fit, the unexpected voice in the room. Surprise builds higher-level *confidence* because it affirms our capacity to navigate uncertainty rather than eliminating it. Rather than closing the loop, this confidence in our questioning abilities renews curiosity about what other discoveries await us.

Figure 2.2 illustrates how curiosity amplifies through an iterative cycle: questioning sparks exploration, exploration yields surprise, surprise builds confidence, and confidence renews curiosity.

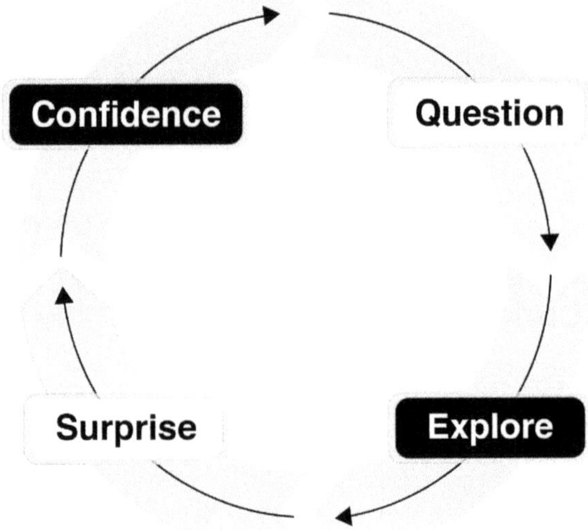

Figure 2.2 The Curiosity Amplification Cycle

Seen this way, curiosity is not a fragile spark easily extinguished by AI. It is a renewable practice that grows stronger with each iteration. Anxiety arises when the cycle is interrupted, when questions are closed too soon or delegated too quickly. Agency arises when the cycle is allowed to run its course.

We can design for this cycle. In 2024, Morgan Stanley introduced what they call "evaluation loops" in their wealth management division. Advisors must compare AI-generated recommendations with their own expertise before presenting options to clients.[27] This slows decision-making slightly but preserves the discipline of inquiry, ensuring that confidence is grounded not in algorithmic polish but in human judgment.

Similarly, the BBVA bank instructed strategy teams to draft contrarian scenarios before consulting AI forecasts. If the system predicted steady market growth, teams first had to imagine plausible downturns and identify triggers. Only then could they compare their scenarios with machine projections.[28] The practice not only preserved radar-style exploration but also increased confidence in final strategies, since leaders knew they had tested more possibilities than the machine alone supplied.

These examples from big corporations show how anxiety, the sense of being displaced, can be redirected into agency. By embedding cycles of questioning, exploration, surprise, and confidence, organizations make curiosity a renewable resource rather than a fragile faculty.

The Psychology of Agency

Neuroscience fortunately reinforces this picture of agency. Research on "productive struggle" shows that learning deepens when individuals carry unresolved questions for long enough to build anticipation before resolution.[29] When that anticipation is short-circuited, that is, when questions are outsourced prematurely to machines, the process that would have built confidence and expertise is skipped. Passive consumption replaces active inquiry, and the neural machinery designed for deep engagement remains underused.

The discomfort of not knowing is a feature that primes the brain for stronger memory and deeper insight. Dopamine responses, hippocampal activation, and robust learning effects all peak when curiosity is sustained, not instantly satisfied. Memory is strongest for answers that follow periods of wanting; insight emerges from the tension between uncertainty and closure. When we bypass this struggle by outsourcing questions to machines, we deprive ourselves of the very conditions that build confidence.

Anxiety, then, is not an enemy to be eliminated. It is a raw material for agency. When we allow ourselves to linger in uncertainty and convert each cycle of discovery into renewed curiosity, we nurture the very conditions in the brain that transform anxiety into confidence. The loop turns displacement from a threat into fuel for learning and adaptive confidence.

From Individual Habit to Collective Practice

At its best, the Curiosity Amplification Cycle scales beyond individuals to teams. In our LSP experiments, facilitators who resisted the urge to over-script workshops with AI prompts reported more unexpected group insights. One explained: "*When I let participants push through their own confusion, we found ideas none of us had anticipated. When I relied too much on AI, we moved quickly, but nothing surprising happened.*"[30] The difference lay in whether curiosity cycles were allowed to run or were short-circuited by instant prompts.

The same pattern surfaced in our interviews with executives. When managers say they stop watching the room, or heeding what is happening, group energy and insights significantly decrease. That loss of presence is not trivial. It shows how algorithmic focus can narrow attention precisely when collective awareness is most needed.

All professionals can cultivate these cycles in collective settings by protecting time for open exploration, encouraging reflection before consulting AI outputs, and explicitly rewarding the articulation of surprising insights. Such practices move anxiety about being replaced into agency to lead inquiry that no system can replicate.

Curiosity transforms anxiety into agency when we resist the comfort of instant answers.

Curiosity, then, is not simply at risk of erosion. It is also capable of amplification. The same conditions that produce anxiety, uncertainty, ambiguity, perplexity, can, when disciplined, become the raw material of agency. Professionals who understand this shift learn to treat AI not as a replacement but as a partner, ensuring that the cycle of curiosity remains alive.

The Curiosity – AI Interaction Spectrum

Curiosity and AI do not have a single relationship. In practice, professionals move among distinct patterns that either drain or strengthen their capacity to inquire. Based on our data, a four-part spectrum emerged. The spectrum is not a maturity ladder to climb once, but a diagnostic lens you can return to often.

Figure 2.3 illustrates four modes of engagement between questioning and AI. Professionals strengthen inquiry by stabilizing in the right-hand quadrants, where human-authored questions sustain deeper exploration.

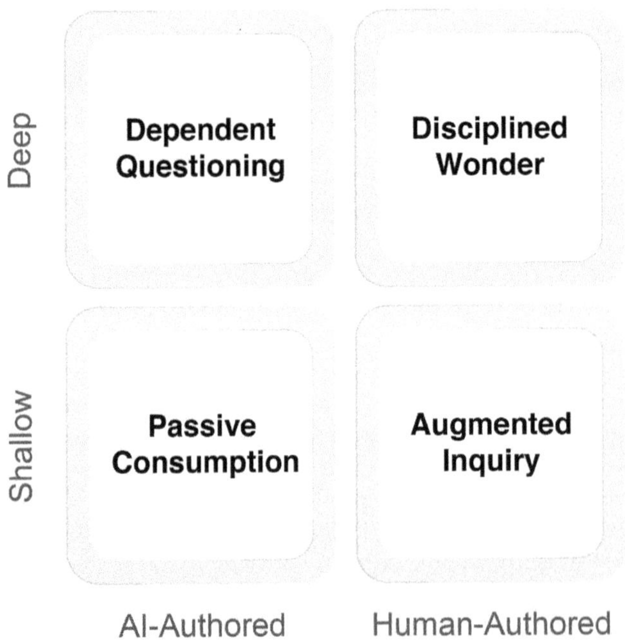

Figure 2.3 The Curiosity – AI Interaction Spectrum

1. Passive Consumption

Here, AI is treated as an answer engine. Questions are shallow and framed to extract a result quickly. You accept first outputs, replicate recommended slides or scripts, and move on. Meetings start with the AI and seldom return to human framing. It feels efficient but weakens reasoning because perplexity never takes hold. Curiosity contracts to procurement; knowledge becomes content delivery.

Organizational signature: compressed agendas, little prework, outputs that look polished yet repeat prior patterns. Typical risks include groupthink, overconfidence, and error propagation when the initial prompt or data is mis-specified. This is where the shallow questioning loop dominates.

2. Dependent Questioning

In this quadrant, you ask many questions, but most are suggested by AI. Curiosity is active, yet externally scaffolded. Your questioning can feel collaborative while quietly offloading authorship of inquiry. It is better than passive consumption because it invites iteration, but it narrows exploration and reduces surprise.

Organizational signature: thick briefing packs generated by AI, long lists of "smart questions," and decision templates that converge on conventional options. This is where algorithmic narrowing becomes normal. Novelty appears as variations on known themes.

3. Augmented Inquiry

Augmented inquiry treats AI as a partner inside a human-authored process. Teams begin by framing their own perplexities, then use AI to extend reach, to surface counterexamples, to pressure-test assumptions, to translate stakeholder language, to simulate scenarios. Professionals who work this way describe the benefit as starting "from a more advanced starting point," while keeping authorship of the path. The device is neither oracle nor afterthought; it is an instrument for widening the search without surrendering authorship.

Organizational signature: early human framing memos, deliberate prompt logs that record alternatives tried, and short reflection pauses between machine outputs and human next steps. The previously mentioned BBVA's contrarian scenario rule and Morgan Stanley's evaluation loops are practical anchors here. The discipline is to ensure the machine expands inquiry rather than deciding it.

4. Disciplined Wonder

This is the far right of the spectrum. Teams formalize practices that preserve perplexity while harnessing AI for scale. Disciplined wonder starts with experiential sensing and divergent questioning, then cycles through exploration, surprise, and renewed curiosity before closing. AI is used at specific points to accelerate search, translate across domains, and generate contrasting views, but never to replace the human struggle that builds judgment.

Organizational signature: rituals that protect attention and presence, such as "first-person field notes before prompts," "three-question pauses," and "oddity rounds" where teams surface weak signals the model is likely to miss. In the workshops we studied, facilitators who practiced disciplined wonder reported more "none of us saw that coming" moments and stronger participant engagement.

How the Spectrum Guides Action

The spectrum is descriptive and prescriptive. Descriptive, because it names the patterns you already see. Prescriptive, because it suggests how to move rightward and upwards. Yet, moving in this direction on this spectrum requires intentional design choices. The lever is inquiry discipline more than technology sophistication. Any team can build the conditions for augmented inquiry and disciplined wonder with simple guiding principles:

- **Frame first, then fetch.** Write a short human framing of the problem and initial hypotheses before consulting the system. This preserves authorship and primes better prompts.
- **Diversify the prompts.** Ask for counterfactuals, deviating viewpoints, and edge cases. Require at least one question the system fails to answer adequately, to keep radar curiosity alive.
- **Insert evaluation loops.** Compare machine outputs to experience in the room and to direct observation. Record where the AI output is strong, weak, or just in agreement.
- **Delay close.** Hold off final convergence until after an explicit "surprise scan," where the group notes anomalies and weak signals discovered along the way.

These practices echo core findings in human-AI collaboration research and what our interviewees do when they are at their best: craft better questions, hold the tension a bit longer, and use the machine to widen rather than narrow the field.

Why Positioning Matters Now

Your position on the spectrum predicts resilience in fast-change contexts. In sectors where AI agents are already becoming teammates and default operators, the temptation toward passive consumption is strong. Already OpenAI's December 2024 enterprise review noted that "98 percent of advisors now use AI daily," which means the differentiator is ow you structure the relationship, not whether you use the tools.[31] In homogenous tool environments, curiosity posture becomes a competitive advantage.

Design choices matter. When systems lack what Hamilton Mann calls "artificial integrity," users normalize dependence and mistake convenience for autonomy, a pattern he describes as a kind of "technological Stockholm syndrome" in which our own cognitive defences quietly collapse into compliance.[32] This is precisely why posture, not just access, predicts resilience.

Usage data underscores the risk. By mid-2025, ChatGPT alone accounted for 18 billion weekly messages from 700 million people, roughly 10 percent of the world's adults. More than 70 percent of these conversations were non-work related, dominated by requests for guidance, information, and writing. Even in professional contexts, over half of the messages focused on executing tasks rather than framing questions.[33] The pattern is clear: the tool is overwhelmingly used to *close* questions, not to keep them open.

Leaders at various levels often ask for a single metric to assess the organization's use of AI. I suggest three proxies that can better capture all that this chapter discussed:

1. the proportion of meetings that begin with human framing,
2. the percentage of projects that include an explicit counter-scenario, and
3. the count of documented "useful surprises" per quarter.

None are perfect, but together they *indicate* whether curiosity is being eroded or amplified. Moving right and upward on the spectrum is less about heroics and more about habit. It requires small commitments, renewed often: to notice the room before the screen, to ask one more question before closing, to treat confident outputs as beginnings, not ends. In the age of instant answers, these habits are what keep curiosity alive and kicking.

You cannot outsource authorship of inquiry and keep its benefits. Frame first, then fetch.

Returning to Theaetetus – Curiosity as Professional Power

We began this chapter with the perplexed young mathematician, Theaetetus. Pressed by Socrates, he admitted his confusion: he felt lost, unable to hold a definition of knowledge without it collapsing under friendly scrutiny. What looked like failure was in fact the seed of insight. Socrates recognized wonder and puzzlement as the birthplace of wisdom, the threshold where curiosity ceases to be idle diversion and becomes disciplined inquiry.

That insight is no less urgent today. In the age of AI, perplexity can feel like weakness. Why struggle when AI offers clarity? Why dwell in uncertainty when a confident answer based on all available text, pixels, and frames is seconds away? Yet the real professional danger is not in being perplexed but in refusing to remain there. Perplexity is capability in formation. It signals the willingness to confront the unknown, to sustain the questions that systems cannot formulate, to resist the temptation of instant closure.

Some, but far from all, AI capable professionals I meet and talk with display precisely this trait. They do not treat machine outputs as destinations but as provocations. They ask: What assumptions lie beneath this response? What voices are missing? What if we reversed the frame? They stay in the space of perplexity long enough to see beyond the obvious. Their strength lies not in competing with algorithms for speed or comprehensiveness, but in orchestrating questions that extend beyond the machine's horizon.

This is what makes curiosity a professional power rather than a personal quirk. In organizations, it sustains innovation by keeping radar-style scanning alive when laser precision dominates. It restores professional agency by transforming anxiety about displacement into disciplined wonder. It ensures that important tasks remain a process of human-authored inquiry into values, risks, and futures not yet imagined.

Yet this posture does not emerge by accident. As Hamilton Mann argues, when systems are designed without the friction, transparency, and counter-scenarios that preserve human questioning, users risk mistaking convenience for autonomy. Perplexity, then, requires not just individual courage but institutional safeguards that keep the space for inquiry open.

Theaetetus' confession of confusion was an act of courage. It acknowledged the gap between what he knew and what remained unresolved. Today, we need to demonstrate the same courage. This recognition of "not knowing" is the beginning of curiosity as civic practice. It is an attitude that once animated the *agora* and now must return to the workplace, where we dwell in uncertainty long enough for genuine wisdom to emerge.

In practice, this is a real challenge because LLMs are not designed to say, "I do not know." Instead, they are trained to respond like a multiple-choice quiz, compelled always to produce an answer, even where none may exist. This design choice is the root cause of the so-called "hallucination" problem, where AI models confidently produce information that is mistaken or entirely fabricated.[34] When we accept machine-generated certainty, we risk losing the humility that fuels curiosity and genuine learning.

Curiosity is not a fixed trait but a capability you can deliberately cultivate. By strengthening your questioning habits and resisting erosion, you prepare curiosity to function as a professional enabler rather than a private preference. It becomes the foundation that ensures AI amplifies, never replaces, the intelligence that makes you and your team distinctively human.

Your professional future depends less on how quickly you can resolve uncertainty and more on how deeply you can inhabit it. Machines will always be faster at generating answers. But only you can preserve perplexity as power, the distinctly human magic of sustaining wonder in a world saturated with certainty.

Curiosity makes professionals irreplaceable by framing questions algorithms cannot formulate. When AI offers instant answers, humans can preserve the capacity to ask what deserves inquiry in the first place. Algorithms optimize for answers. We optimize for questions worth asking. Yet questions alone remain inert without the courage to pursue what they reveal. *Wonder frames possibility; creation brings it forth.* This is where imagination enters as curiosity's natural extension. Disciplined inquiry discovers what might be explored. Creative practice transforms that possibility into what does not yet exist. Chapter 3 examines how systematic curiosity evolves into creative power when professionals learn to generate insights no algorithm can envision.

When confused, pause and explore before prompting. Confusion signals learning in progress.

Self-Assessment – From Quick Answers to Deeper Questions

This assessment helps you reflect on your current curiosity practices and their relationship to AI integration in your work. It is designed not as a test with right answers but as a tool for awareness and development.

For each dimension, consider your recent questioning patterns (past three months) and rate your typical approach using the scale below. The goal is honest self-reflection rather than idealized self-presentation.

1. Erosion Resistance: Avoiding Shallow Loops

How effectively do you resist the tendency to accept first AI outputs and close inquiry prematurely?

- ☐ **Always:** I consistently interrogate AI outputs, generate follow-up questions, and resist premature closure.
- ☐ **Often:** I usually push beyond first answers but sometimes accept outputs too quickly under pressure.
- ☐ **Sometimes:** I occasionally dig deeper but often settle for initial AI responses.
- ☐ **Rarely:** I usually accept first outputs and move on without further questioning.
- ☐ **Never:** I treat AI as an answer engine and rarely question its initial responses.

Interpretation: Shallow questioning loops collapse the exploration process that builds insight. If you lean toward quick acceptance, practice inserting pauses between AI outputs and decisions. Generate at least three follow-up questions before moving forward.

2. Question Authorship: Resisting Offloading

Do you author your own questions or delegate inquiry formation to AI systems?

- ☐ **Always:** I consistently frame my own questions and use AI to extend rather than replace my inquiry.
- ☐ **Often:** I usually start with my own framing but sometimes ask AI what I should be thinking about.
- ☐ **Sometimes:** I mix human-authored and AI-suggested questions without clear intention.
- ☐ **Rarely:** I frequently ask AI what questions I should ask.
- ☐ **Never:** I depend entirely on AI to suggest what deserves my curiosity.

Interpretation: Question authorship determines whether curiosity remains generative or becomes reactive. To strengthen authorship, write brief human framings before consulting AI. Practice asking: "What puzzles me about this?" before seeking algorithmic guidance.

3. Productive Uncertainty: Stress Tolerance

How well do you tolerate the discomfort of not knowing while exploring complex problems?

- ☐ **Always:** I embrace uncertainty as essential to discovery and resist rushing to resolution.
- ☐ **Often:** I can sit with ambiguity but sometimes seek closure too quickly to reduce discomfort.
- ☐ **Sometimes:** I tolerate uncertainty in familiar domains but avoid it when stakes feel high.

☐ **Rarely:** I prefer clear answers and find sustained uncertainty stressful.
☐ **Never:** I immediately seek AI solutions to eliminate any confusion or ambiguity.

Interpretation: Stress tolerance is fundamental to genuine curiosity. If uncertainty feels uncomfortable, practice extending exploration before seeking resolution. The productive discomfort signals that learning is occurring.

4. AI Interaction Pattern: Where You Operate
Which pattern best describes your typical relationship with AI in inquiry work?

☐ **Always:** Disciplined Wonder (I formalize practices that preserve perplexity while using AI strategically).
☐ **Often:** Augmented Inquiry (I frame problems myself then use AI to extend reach and test assumptions).
☐ **Sometimes:** Dependent Questioning (I ask many questions but most are AI-suggested).
☐ **Rarely:** Passive Consumption (I treat AI as an answer engine for quick results)
☐ **Never:** I avoid AI entirely in my inquiry work.

Interpretation: Moving rightward on this spectrum requires intentional design choices. If you operate in the left quadrants, practice "frame first, then fetch" and insert evaluation loops between AI outputs and decisions. The goal is using AI to widen rather than narrow inquiry.

Using Your Profile

When you map yourself across these four dimensions, you will see patterns. Perhaps you resist shallow loops but struggle with stress tolerance. Perhaps you author good questions but operate too often in passive consumption mode with AI. The key is deliberate cultivation of what is weak while extending what is strong. Your curiosity profile guides you toward the practices that will keep questioning alive, even as AI systems offer instant closure.

AI can extend our reach in every direction, but only humans can choose which directions are worth exploring.

Notes

1 All quotes are from Plato (1997: 155c–d; 210a–c).
2 Aristotle (1998).
3 TNM research data (2025).
4 LSP research data (2025).
5 Carruthers (2024).
6 TrendWatching (2025, October 6).
7 Berlyne (1960).
8 Harryson & Roos (2017).
9 LSP research Data (2025).
10 Litman (2005).
11 TNM research data (2025).
12 Kidd & Hayden (2015).
13 GMAC (2024).
14 TNM research data (2025).
15 Carruthers (2024).
16 Shin (2025).
17 LSP Research Data (2025).
18 Olson (2025, May 6).
19 Kashdan et al. (2018).
20 TNM research data (2025).
21 LSP Research Data (2025).
22 O'Sullivan (2025).
23 Wilhelm et al. (2024).
24 Haase et al. (2025).
25 Hamilton Mann (2025).
26 TNM research data (2025).
27 OpenAI (2025, April 11).
28 OpenAI (2025, April 11).
29 Kidd & Hayden (2015).
30 LSP research data (2025).
31 OpenAI (2024).
32 Hamilton Mann (2025).
33 Chatterji et al. (2025).
34 Tauman Kalai et al. (2025); Open AI (2025).

References

Aristotle. (1998). *Metaphysics* (H. Lawson-Tancred, Trans.). Penguin Classics. https://www.penguinrandomhouse.com/books/260885/the-metaphysics-by-aristotle/.

Berlyne, D. E. (1960). *Conflict, arousal, and curiosity*. McGraw-Hill.

Carruthers, P. (2024). The contents and causes of curiosity. *The British Journal for the Philosophy of Science, 75*(4), 871–895.

Chatterji, A., Cunningham, T., Deming, D. J., Hitzig, Z., Ong, C., Shan, C. Y., & Wadman, K. (2025). *How people use ChatGPT* (NBER Working Paper No. 34255). National Bureau of Economic Research. http://www.nber.org/papers/w34255

Cohen, W. M., & Levinthal, D. A. (1990). Absorptive capacity: A new perspective on learning and innovation. *Administrative Science Quarterly, 35*(1), 128–152.

Graduate Management Admission Council. (2024). *AI in business education: Current practices and future potential.* https://www.gmac.com/market-intelligence-and-research/research-library/curriculum-insight/ai-current-practices-future-potential

Haase, J., Hanel, P. H. P., & Pokutta, S. (2025). Has the creativity of large-language models peaked? An analysis of inter- and intra-LLM variability. *arXiv Preprint*, arXiv:2504.12320. https://arxiv.org/abs/2504.12320

Harryson, S. J., & Roos, J. (2017). *Disrupting innovation through collaborative competitions: Extreme breakthroughs solving any challenge faster better smarter.* New Insights Press.

Hult International Business School. (2024). *Faculty AI integration survey report.* Internal document.

Hutson, J. (2025). Human-AI collaboration in writing: A multidimensional framework for creative and intellectual authorship. *International Journal of Changes in Education*, 1–10. https://doi.org/10.47852/bonviewIJCE52024908

Ivancovsky, T., Ben-Moshe, T., & Shamay-Tsoory, S. G. (2024). A shared novelty-seeking basis for creativity and curiosity: Response to the commentators. *Personality and Individual Differences, 206*, 112158. https://doi.org/10.1016/j.paid.2023.112158

Kashdan, T. B., Stiksma, M. C., Disabato, D. J., McKnight, P. E., Bekier, J., Kaji, J., & Lazarus, R. (2018). The five-dimensional curiosity scale: Capturing the bandwidth of curiosity and identifying four unique subgroups of curious people. *Journal of Research in Personality, 73*, 130–149. https://doi.org/10.1016/j.jrp.2017.11.011

Kidd, C., & Hayden, B. Y. (2015). The psychology and neuroscience of curiosity. *Neuron, 88*(3), 449–460. https://doi.org/10.1016/j.neuron.2015.09.010

Litman, J. A. (2005). Curiosity and the pleasures of learning: Wanting and liking new information. *Cognition & Emotion, 19*(6), 793–814. DOI:10.1080/02699930541000101

Mann, H. (2025, September 10). Escaping technological Stockholm syndrome: The case for artificial integrity in AI design. *California Management Review* (Insight, Frontier). https://cmr.berkeley.edu/2025/09/escaping-technological-stockholm-syndrome-the-case-for-artificial-integrity-in-ai-design/

Olson, P. (2025, May 6). Addicted to ChatGPT? Here's how to reclaim your brain. *Bloomberg Opinion.* https://www.bloomberg.com/opinion/articles/2025-05-06/chatgpt-addiction-how-to-reclaim-your-brain-from-ai-bots.

OpenAI. (2025, April 11). *AI in the enterprise: Lessons from seven frontier companies.* https://cdn.openai.com/business-guides-and-resources/ai-in-the-enterprise.pdf

O'Sullivan, S. (2025). Finance & AI: Fraud detection, algorithmic trading & risk management. *American Technology Net Blog.* https://blog.american-technology.net/ai-fraud-detection-algo-trading-risk-management/

Plato. (1997). *Complete Works*, edited by John M. Cooper. Indianapolis: Hackett Publishing Company.

Roos, J. (2025). From adoption to action: GenAI as a catalyst for change at Hult. In *AI Ready: Shaping tomorrow with AI and human intelligence* (pp. 35–44). Thinkers50. https://thinkers50.com/downloads/AI-Ready.pdf

Shin, D. (2021). The effects of explainability and causability on perception, trust, and acceptance: Implications for explainable AI. *International Journal of Human-Computer Studies*, 146, 102551. https://doi.org/10.1016/j.ijhcs.2020.102551

Tauman Kalai, A., Nachum, O., Vempala, S., & Zhang, E. S. (2025). Why language models hallucinate. *arXiv Preprint, arXiv:2509.04664*. https://arxiv.org/abs/2509.04664.

TrendWatching. (2025, October 6). Anthropic's zero-slop pop-up invites New Yorkers to slow down and think. https://www.trendwatching.com/innovations/anthropics-zero-slop-pop-up-invites-new-yorkers-to-slow-down-and-think

Wilhelm, C., Steckelberg, A., & Rebitschek, F. G. (2024). Benefits and harms associated with the use of AI-related algorithmic decision-making systems by healthcare professionals: A systematic review. *The Lancet Regional Health – Europe*, *48*, 101145. https://doi.org/10.1016/j.lanepe.2024.101145

3 Creativity – From Polished Outputs to Original Insights

The Notebooks and the Algorithm

Milan, 1505. In the predawn darkness of his workshop, Leonardo da Vinci arranges a collection of bird wings across his wooden table. Starling, kestrel, crow. Each feather positioned with the precision of a master anatomist, each joint articulated to reveal the mechanics of flight. For months, he has watched the birds wheel above the Lombard countryside, sketching their movements in rapid strokes, dissecting their forms to understand the invisible forces that lift flesh into air.

His notebook lies open beside the specimens, pages dense with mirror script and detailed drawings. Leonardo observed how wind penetrates beneath a bird's wings "like a wedge," lifting it skyward. Each model taught him about the marriage of form and function. Theory and practice must work together, he argued.[1]

This is how breakthrough creativity works: through the patient accumulation of not only abstract knowledge, but embodied, "hands-on" knowledge and the willingness to fail forward through countless iterations. Leonardo's flying machine will never carry him above the rooftops of Milan, but his process of deep observation, physical experimentation, and cross-domain synthesis will eventually enable others to soar. *"Those who are passionate about practice without science are like a sailor who enters a ship without a helm or compass,"* he notes in his characteristic mirror script. *"Learning never exhausts the mind."*[2]

Leonardo's notebooks remind us that creativity is most often not the result of sudden inspiration but of deliberate cycles of observation, experimentation, and revision. His countless sketches of wings and flight mechanisms were stages in a longer journey of discovery. Each drawing, each failed prototype, each return to the aviary deepened his understanding of how air, form, and motion interact. His inefficiency was his genius: the discipline of staying with a problem long enough for something truly new to emerge.

Modern research underscores this lesson. Mitch Resnick, professor at MIT and long-time director of the Lifelong Kindergarten group at the Media Lab, describes creativity as a "learning spiral." In his formulation, creativity flourishes through repeated cycles

DOI: 10.4324/9781003732570-3

of imagining possibilities, creating prototypes, playing with them, sharing results, reflecting on feedback, and then imagining again. The spiral is not linear progress toward a fixed goal, but an ever-deepening loop that sustains engagement and opens pathways to unexpected insights.[3]

Renowned design expert Tim Brown makes a similar point from a practitioner's perspective: *"AI has become a testing tool for complex tasks. It helps generate possible scenarios and prototype the future during the design process, avoiding some of the pitfalls."*[4] His words capture what Resnick and Leonardo already intuited. Iteration matters more than instant output, and that tools, whether clay, code, or AI, are valuable only insofar as they feed the cycle of experimentation.

What Leonardo practiced instinctively in Renaissance Milan, Resnick has articulated as a principle for modern learning and innovation. His work with tools like Scratch, LEGO® robotics, and maker labs shows that genuine creativity emerges when people are encouraged to tinker, iterate, and reflect rather than rush to produce finished results. The process matters as much as the product, because it cultivates the habits of mind that allow individuals to generate, test, and refine ideas in ever more original ways.

The contrast of this creative process with today's AI tools is instructive. Generative systems can survey vast domains of prior work, remix elements in novel combinations, and deliver polished outputs in seconds. They excel at producing variety, but they do not engage in the spiral of imagining, building, sharing, and reflecting that deepens human understanding. The risk is that we begin to confuse rapid recombination with genuine innovation, mistaking the appearance of creativity for its practice.

This distinction matters greatly for professionals in the AI age. If we rely on machines to generate endless variations, we neglect the slower, sometimes frustrating, but ultimately more rewarding cycle that Resnick describes and Leonardo embodied. Creativity is not about how many ideas can be produced, but about how deeply we can engage with possibilities, refine them through iteration, and draw meaning from the process.

Understanding this distinction is where the science of creativity provides practical guidance. Scholars such as Teresa Amabile have shown that creativity depends on specific, manageable skills, processes, and motivation, which can be cultivated deliberately. Building on these foundations, we can design ways of working with AI that preserve the spiral of experimentation rather than short-circuiting it.

AI outputs are instant; creative insight takes a spiral.

The Science of Creative Practice

Modern research provides a foundation for understanding creativity as a set of identifiable, cultivable processes. Three frameworks provide a fundamental understanding of creative thought.

The Componential Model

Among the most influential contributions is Teresa Amabile's Componential Model, which provides the most practical foundation for understanding creativity in professional contexts. Unlike abstract theories that treat creativity as mysterious inspiration, her model identifies specific, manageable elements that we can influence directly. Her framework reveals creativity as the intersection of three essential components[5]:

- *Domain-relevant skills* include the technical knowledge, expertise, and talent necessary for creative work in specific fields. Leonardo possessed deep domain knowledge across anatomy, engineering, and art. All professionals similarly need foundational expertise to recognize patterns, spot opportunities, and evaluate possibilities within their fields. AI can enhance these skills by providing access to broader knowledge bases and analytical capabilities, but cannot replace the understanding that comes from direct, hands-on experience.
- *Creativity-relevant processes* encompass cognitive styles, personality characteristics, and thinking patterns that facilitate creativity. These include the ability to think differently, suspend judgment, take intellectual risks, and tolerate ambiguity.
- *Intrinsic motivation* forms the most critical component: the drive to engage in creative work for its inherent satisfaction rather than external rewards. Leonardo's notebooks reveal a mind driven by pure curiosity about how things work, not by commissions or recognition. This intrinsic engagement sustains the persistence required for breakthrough creativity. Research consistently shows that external pressures and rewards can undermine creative performance when they shift focus from intrinsic to extrinsic motivations.

Amabile's framework complements Resnick's creative spiral. Where the spiral emphasizes the *process* of continuous imagining, making, and reflecting, Amabile highlights the *conditions* that allow that process to thrive. Both perspectives converge on the same point: creativity is not a one-off event but an ecosystem of skills, practices, and motivations that can be nurtured in individuals and organizations.

Amabile's individual components interact with organizational climate factors that either support or undermine creative performance. Amabile identified key environmental influences: freedom and autonomy in how work is conducted, challenging assignments that stretch capabilities without overwhelming, sufficient time and resources, and encouragement from supervisors and colleagues.

When AI handles routine tasks, we have increased opportunity to design environments that cultivate intrinsic motivation, provide suitable challenges, and create the psychological safety necessary for creative risk-taking. Her framework suggests that AI's greatest contribution may be freeing human energy in organizations for the relational and environmental work that creativity requires.

This is a useful insight when working alongside AI. Generative systems can augment domain-relevant skills by providing fast access to knowledge, and they can accelerate certain creative processes by generating combinations at scale. But they cannot substitute for the intrinsic motivation that drives human engagement, nor can they replicate the reflective cycles of iteration that give creativity its depth. The science is clear: if we treat AI's outputs as endpoints, we risk eroding the very capabilities that make us distinctive. If we use them as inputs into our own spirals of imagining and refining, we can amplify our potential.

The Interactionist Model

Another model of creativity, Woodman and colleagues' Interactionist Model, extends Amabile's individual focus to view creativity as a systemic phenomenon emerging from the interaction of individual attributes, group dynamics, and organizational context.[6] AI may intervene simultaneously at all levels: reshaping individual workflows, altering team collaboration patterns, and embedding new organizational routines. Understanding these interactions helps us design AI adoption strategies that amplify rather than erode collective creativity.

At the individual level, AI reshapes workflows by handling routine analysis and accelerating idea generation. This capacity of AI raises questions, however, about how we sustain our individual distinctiveness and personal creative agency. At the group level, AI introduces new mechanisms for knowledge sharing and collaboration, allowing teams to test broader ranges of options but also risking homogenization when the same tools dominate discussions. At the organizational level, AI alters structures and climates by embedding new routines, standards, and decision protocols into everyday practice. This perspective proves particularly relevant when AI becomes part of the creative ecosystem, requiring new forms of coordination between human and machine capabilities.

The Embodied Dimension of Creativity

A third model of creativity that AI cannot replicate is what I refer to as the "embodied" dimension of creativity. My own research with Peter Bürgi revealed that creative breakthroughs often emerge when professionals shift between three distinct imagination roles that reveal forms of embodied intelligence no algorithm can replicate. These roles – handyman, architect, and storyteller – capture the physical, environmental, and narrative dimensions of creative practice.[7]

The *handyman* role captures the capacity to discover through doing, where hands lead thinking rather than the reverse. Physical manipulation engages different cognitive pathways than digital interaction, a fact repeatedly observed in my LSP workshop research. One participant in our recent studies described how building with bricks "*made my mental capacity much broader and much deeper at the same time.*"[8] Leonardo embodied this role through his constant sketching, dissection, and prototype construction. Each physical act of creation revealed insights not accessible through purely mental analysis.

The *architect* role concerns how environments and materials shape imagination. Creative breakthroughs often arise not just from what people think, but from the spaces, objects, and arrangements that support them. Colour, texture, spatial configuration, and physical artifacts all influence how people perceive problems and generate ideas. Leonardo understood this deeply, designing his "maker space" workshop to support both detailed observation and large-scale experimentation. In workshops, even simple objects like clay models or quick prototypes create shared reference points that enable participants to address tensions remaining invisible in purely verbal exchanges.

The *storyteller* role highlights imagination's conceptual dimension: the ability to construct narratives connecting scattered insights to larger patterns and purposes. Storytelling transforms creative fragments into meaningful visions that motivate action. While AI can generate text, images, or scenarios, weaving them into narratives that resonate with context, the sense of values, history and aspiration remain distinctly human. As one executive interviewed observed, "*AI brings the options, but humans bring the meaning.*"[9]

* * *

Together, these frameworks provide a comprehensive lens for understanding creativity that remains relevant in the AI age. Amabile's model clarifies the ingredients of individual creativity, the Interactionist Model shows how creative outcomes depend on systemic interactions, and the Imagination Roles highlight the embodied practices through which ideas take shape and gain meaning. They caution that AI's value cannot be judged by individual productivity alone but must be assessed by its impact on intrinsic motivation, collaborative dynamics, and the distinctively human capacities that no algorithm can replicate.

Modern research provides three complementary frameworks for translating creativity theory into professional practice. Together, they clarify how individual, social, and embodied processes can be intentionally designed and enhanced in the AI era, as summarized in Table 3.1.

These frameworks illustrate how theory becomes method: each links scientific understanding of creativity with actionable levers that preserve human agency while integrating AI as an amplifier rather than a substitute.

The dynamics of this melding of processes to generate creative breakthroughs are not confined to studios or workshops. They now shape scientific discovery itself. Sanjiv Patel, CEO of Relay Therapeutics

Table 3.1 From Creativity Theory to Practice Translation

Theory	*Core Principle*	*Practitioner Lever*	*AI-Era Implementation Example*
Componential Model	Creativity arises from the intersection of domain expertise, creativity-relevant processes, and intrinsic motivation.	Design work for autonomy, invest in skill growth, and nurture intrinsic motivation.	Use AI to perform routine analysis while preserving human ownership of meaning-making. Scientists can let AI handle computational exploration so they can focus their energy on genuine discovery.
Interactionist Model	Creativity emerges through continuous interaction among individuals, teams, and organizational context	Align practices across levels: equip individuals with empowering tools, form teams for cognitive and cultural diversity, and sustain climates that reward experimentation.	Integrate AI not only as a personal productivity aid but as a shared system shaping workflows and culture. Embed AI in both solo sketching and group critique sessions to enhance systemic creativity.
Embodied Dimension Model	Breakthroughs occur when professionals shift fluidly among three imagination roles: *handyman* (doing), *architect* (shaping environments), and *storyteller* (creating meaning).	Encourage hands-on exploration, design spaces that invite experimentation, and craft narratives that connect ideas to shared purpose.	Apply AI to generate early variations, then move into physical building and narrative framing to transform options into distinctive, meaningful insights.

in Boston in July 2025, told me that his company nearly abandoned AI altogether after early failures. "*Our first attempts were disasters,*" he recalled. Scientists had treated the system like a more powerful microscope, expecting sharper views of what they already knew. When that failed, frustration mounted.

The breakthrough came when one researcher reframed the relationship. Instead of demanding final answers, she began treating the AI like a highly capable prolific, fast, sometimes erratic, research intern, but able to generate possibilities she alone could not. That reframing preserved her scientific judgment while opening a new mode of collaboration. The AI multiplied her option space, generating countless molecular variations, but only her intuition could sense which might yield a breakthrough compound. The machine produced the possibilities; the human found the meaning.

This shift from expecting solutions to exploring possibilities mirrors what I have seen repeatedly in executive workshops. When professionals first encounter unfamiliar intelligence, their instinct is to retreat to familiar tools, treating the new partner as a faster version of the old. Genuine creativity emerges only when they reclaim leadership of the process and invite AI into the exploration.

"AI can suggest what to create; only humans can decide what's worth creating."

Eroding Creativity

Creativity rarely vanishes dramatically. Like curiosity it erodes slowly, alike to riverbanks carved by steady currents, shaped by daily concessions to efficiency. The danger is not collapse but drift: feeling more productive while gradually losing the capacities that make work distinctive. Leonardo understood this instinctively.

Leonardo's notebooks reveal a mind willing to linger in uncertainty, to return repeatedly to unsolved problems, to let ideas develop through extended observation and experimentation. He pursued what seemed inefficient because he recognized that potential newness emerges not from speed but from depth. Today we face a different challenge: AI tools that promise to accelerate every aspect of creative work while quietly undermining the very processes that make innovation possible.

Through research across industries and professional practices, three primary mechanisms of erosion have become visible. Each targets a different dimension of human creativity, capacity, voice, and presence, often below conscious awareness. Together they explain why we may generate more outputs with AI but fewer new ideas that matter.

1st Mechanism: Generative Atrophy

The first mechanism strikes at creativity's core: the weakening of generative capacity through over-reliance on algorithmic assistance. This manifests in two interconnected ways: premature closure and confidence crisis.

Creative work depends on tolerance for uncertainty, yet AI outputs arrive sharp, refined, and ready for use. They create the illusion of completion, tempting us to stop searching once a plausible solution appears. Neuroscience shows that new ideas often arise in mental states where the brain lingers in ambiguity, allowing connections between previously unrelated ideas.[10] By collapsing uncertainty too soon, AI short-circuits this process.

An architect in our research noted, "*AI can generate floorplans faster than I can sketch them. But when I use those as starting points, I never discover the spatial relationships that emerge from drawing by hand.*"[11] Research finds that AI reduces writers' creative self-efficacy even as it raises productivity, creating a cycle where reduced confidence leads to more reliance on the tool. It seems reactivity in stories is strongly linked to rich perceptual (including tactile and spatial) details and narrative imagination, which are areas where AI still frequently still falls short.[12]

Professional facilitators report this tension directly. They rated their agreement with the phrase, "AI has streamlined my preparation process," significantly higher than with "AI makes me more self-efficacious in my facilitation role."[13] One executive in our interviews summarized the concern starkly: "*We're becoming a generation of creative middle managers. We can optimize and make machine outputs look great, but we're losing the courage and conviction to bet on our own wild ideas.*"[14] This is the wide gulf between AI's potential and the modest gains most users achieve. By settling for "good enough" outputs rather than pushing for variation and iteration, professionals unintentionally sacrifice originality for speed.[15]

"Speed kills creativity when it prevents the productive struggle that drives insight."

2nd Mechanism: Creative Displacement

The second mechanism operates more subtly, gradually displacing human creative voice with algorithmic and converging patterns. As AI handles more creative load, we shift from authors to curators, becoming editors of machine output rather than originators of ideas.

AI systems excel at recombining patterns from their training data, but underlying structures remain tethered to existing norms (in the training data). Those who rely heavily on these outputs begin to follow similar grooves in their thinking, resulting in e-mail messages, LinkedIn posts, and memos increasingly written with the same style, voice, tones, emojis, and where commas are replaced with the "em" dash character. This narrowing is often invisible to creators. People believe they are working with diverse ideas, and being creative, when their and outputs from others share deep similarities.

As one executive interviewed observed, "*Sometimes we let the tool do everything, and other times we collaborate in a way where they get the best of the human and the best of the AI. It's a huge learning phase.*"[16] What appears as creative choice is often unconscious alignment with algorithmic patterns. Design leaders we interviewed noticed the same effect in their work. One admitted, "*I realized I hadn't sketched anything truly weird in months. All my designs looked sophisticated and professional, but they also looked like they came from the same AI aesthetic rather than my own mind.*"[17]

Researchers have demonstrated that creative distinctiveness declines by almost a full standard deviation when professionals rely on AI, even as technical novelty rises.[18] This erosion impacts ownership, crucial for creative persistence. As AI-generated prompts become starting points, people report lower creative confidence, heightened anxiety without AI support, and weaker connection to their final outputs.

"When AI becomes your creative voice, whose ideas are you implementing?"

3rd Mechanism: Presence Dissolution

The third mechanism strikes at creativity's deep embodied dimension. Ideas often surface through engagement with materials, gestures, and spaces, but when creativity becomes confined to screens and algorithms, even in meetings, this physical dimension is diminished or lost, dissolving the holistic attention that creative work requires.

Leonardo's genius emerged through constant physical engagement with the world. His anatomical studies required dissection, his engineering insights came through building prototypes, his artistic breakthroughs arose from mixing pigments and experimenting with surfaces. Each physical act of creation revealed insights not accessible through mental analysis alone. Participants in serious play workshops repeatedly rediscovered this truth: "*For me, it was the use of physical bricks that really stayed with me. How using something physical can make our mental capacity much broader and much deeper at the same time.*"[19]

When AI replaces physical engagement, embodied processes disappear. We lose the unexpected insights that come from tactile exploration, especially though our hands,[20] the shared sensemaking that arises when groups manipulate the same materials, and the visceral grounding that connects ideas to lived experience. My early research on the impact of object-mediated communication demonstrated how artifacts help people know differently, agree differently, and cope differently.[21] Outputs may be technically proficient but lack the embodied understanding that makes ideas resonate.

Equally problematic is the presence paradox: AI proves useful during preparation but disruptive during live creative engagement.

The Compound Effects of Erosion

Individually these mechanisms are concerning. Together they are corrosive. Generative atrophy weakens the capacity to produce original ideas and the confidence to trust them. Creative displacement substitutes algorithmic patterns for human voice and dilutes personal ownership of creative outcomes. Presence dissolution removes the embodied engagement and live attention that creative work requires. Each mechanism reinforces the others, creating a cycle of dependence that feels like progress while masking fundamental erosion.

The compounding effect is difficult to detect because it mimics advancement. Faster preparation, smoother processes, impressive outputs all appear to be signs of improvement. Teams generate more options, meet deadlines more easily, and produce technically sophisticated work. Yet the very ease that feels like progress masks the erosion of deeper capacities. Only when we face challenges that demand genuine originality, like breakthrough innovation, unprecedented problems, or contexts where existing patterns fail, does the cost become visible. By then the habits may already be ingrained. Recall Parmy Olson's observation about the young professional substituting their creativity for compelling AI outputs and gradually developing a feeling of the imposter syndrome at work.[22]

Leonardo's workshop would have seemed inefficient by modern standards. Years spent studying bird flight, countless sketches that led nowhere, prototypes that never flew. Yet this apparent inefficiency was deep learning, building the embodied understanding and creative confidence that enabled him to envision possibilities others could not imagine. The question facing us now is not whether to use AI's enormous computational power, but how to preserve Leonardo's discipline of discovery while doing so.

Figure 3.1 visualizes this decline. As creative energy shifts from intrinsic exploration to external automation, imagination gives way to imitation. Generative vitality weakens, ownership drifts toward the machine, and coherence dissolves into scattered fragments.

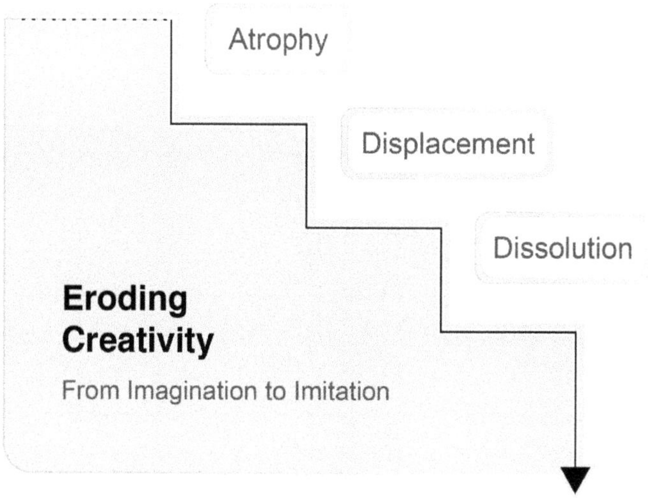

Figure 3.1 Eroding Creativity – From Imagination to Imitation

The Creative Partnership Cycle

Erosion is not destiny. The three mechanisms of erosion describe tendencies, not inevitabilities. Those who recognize them can counteract the drift by designing practices that preserve intrinsic motivation, creative ownership, and embodied engagement. The challenge is not whether to use AI in creative work but how to use it in ways that amplify rather than erode the distinctly human capacities that no algorithm can replace.

A key principle of amplification is simple but easily overlooked: let AI *augment* rather than *replace*. This is a fundamental orientation more than a semantic distinction. Leonardo would have embraced AI's computational power while preserving his discipline of direct observation and physical experimentation.

You can do the same by adopting what I call the "Creative Partnership" cycle. This is a systematic approach that leverages AI's advantages while preserving human creative capacity. The notion of this cycle emerged from my research studying successful facilitators, designers, and managers who use AI extensively yet maintain creative confidence and distinctiveness. Their cycle passes through five interconnected phases:

1. Expand the options space
2. Generate with independence
3. Evaluate with perspective
4. Embody for depth
5. Integrate for impact.

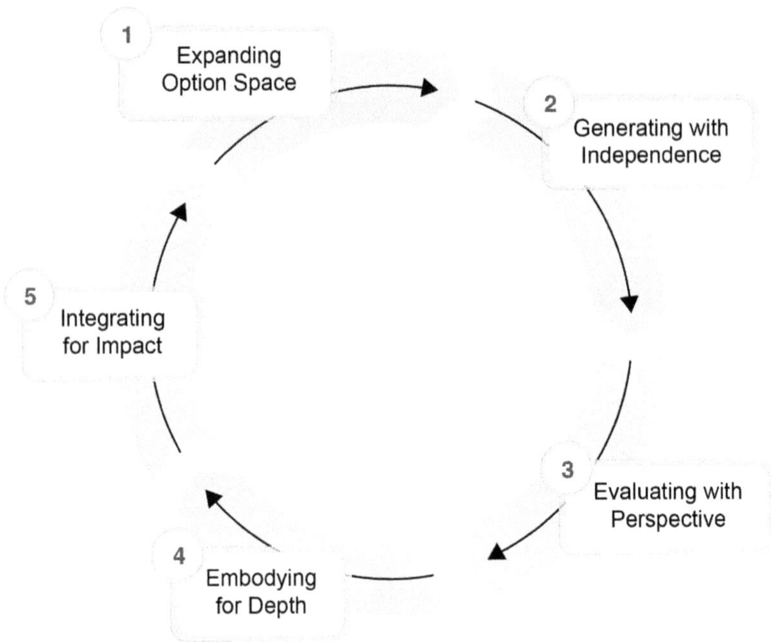

Figure 3.2 The Creative Partnership Cycle

Each phase serves a specific function, and together they ensure that AI amplifies rather than replaces the creative capacities that matter most.

This is about strategic deployment, not about restricting AI use. As one experienced facilitator discovered, "*The AI tool created the most value to me as part of the preparation for the workshop rather than in the workshop.*"[23] The key insight is to honour the temporal separation: intensive AI engagement during preparation phases, protected human space during creative execution, then strategic AI re-engagement for evaluation and refinement.

Phase 1: Expanding the Option Space

The cycle begins with intensive AI engagement during preparation phases. This is where algorithms excel: rapidly surveying possibilities, generating variations, providing computational depth that would take humans weeks to achieve. Leonardo spent years studying existing knowledge about flight before attempting original insights. Using multiple rounds of AI interaction, we can compress this research phase while expanding its scope.

- Start with broad exploratory prompts: "Generate 20 approaches to [challenge]."

- Follow with refinement requests: "Expand option 7 with implementation details."
- Push for unusual perspectives: "What would someone from [different field] suggest?"

The goal is to map the landscape of possibilities so thoroughly that human creative work can focus on breakthrough rather than baseline. Consider an example. Modern product design teams use AI to speed up research and find innovative packaging ideas. Studies show that AI tools help teams assess environmental impacts and discover recycled materials faster, supporting bigger sustainability goals.[24] Generative AI scans global patents and research, quickly revealing new options like bio-air pillows, water-soluble films, and packages made from mushroom, coconut, bamboo, or algae. One group created 20 new sustainable packaging solutions in hours using Midjourney, a process that would normally take weeks. They say AI helps them create and test new products quickly and gather feedback from consumers, pushing *"the limits of our creativity, create unique and innovative products quickly, and bring concepts to live so we can render them and gather quick consumer feedback."*[25]

This computational breadth creates what practitioners describe as creative confidence through preparation depth. One manager interviewed captured the psychological shift: "*I spend the first hour of any creative project in intensive dialogue with AI. I ask it to surface approaches I haven't considered, challenge my assumptions, and provide variations on my initial ideas. By the time I start actual creation, I've explored the territory so completely that my mind is free to focus on genuine innovation.*"[26]

The preparation phase also builds what facilitators in our research refer to "scaffolding security," because knowing that AI has helped explore the landscape thoroughly reduces anxiety about missing obvious solutions and thus the process frees mental energy for original thinking. As one workshop participant noted, "*AI support reassured me in planning*" allowing for more creative risk-taking during execution.[27] When a design team had AI map sustainable material options across continents and industries, they entered human ideation not wondering if they had considered enough, but ready to synthesize surprising combinations.

Critical to this phase is maintaining clear ownership of the creative challenge. Use AI to explore the landscape but frame the questions yourself. Define success criteria in human terms: what would make this solution meaningful to [someone or a segment], not just technically competent? The preparation phase should expand our creative resources, not replace our creative aspiration.

Creativity researcher Jeremy Utley underscores that this phase succeeds when we treat AI not as a tool but as a teammate. This is

Use AI to map the landscape so completely that your mind is free to focus on breakthrough rather than baseline.

when we engage in dialogue, iterating repeatedly, and resisting the shortcut of the first plausible answer. His FIXIT method (Focused, Individual, Context, Iterative, Team) offers a practical discipline for ensuring AI expands option space without collapsing originality.[28]

Phase 2: Generate with Independence

The second phase requires deliberate separation from AI assistance. This is where original insights emerge, where human creativity operates without algorithmic influence during uninterrupted thinking time and space. After saturating with AI during preparation, deliberately disconnect from digital tools and engage in pure human creative work. This might involve sketching by hand, building physical prototypes, writing without AI suggestions, or simply thinking without prompts. The goal is preserving the cognitive conditions that enable genuine originality.

This independence phase connects directly to Leonardo's approach. His inventions came from direct engagement with phenomena, not only from combining existing knowledge. Physical engagement proves particularly important: using hands to sketch, build, or manipulate materials activates different cognitive pathways than screen-based interaction, mobilizing not just visual ideation but also tactile, emotional, and spatial intelligences outside how LLM works.[29]

Reflecting over the impact on AI on her work, a designer explained her practice: "*After using AI to explore hundreds of visual references and design patterns, I close the laptop and spend at least an hour sketching with pencil and paper. That's where my actual ideas emerge . . .not combinations of what I've seen, but something that comes from my own aesthetic sensibility and the specific challenge I'm solving.*"[30]

Some design teams have already formalized this principle into workflow architecture. For example, some deliberately schedule "offline creative sprints" where designers handle physical samples, draw custom forms, and test shapes outside the digital environment.[31] One cosmetics brand reports breakthrough only happened after sketching packaging by hand and experimenting with unusual folding techniques, which later informed the AI-assisted refinements. These teams describe this phase as the moment where the "why" of the design is fused into the "how," ensuring that human values, not just technical novelty, drive downstream choices.

Time boundaries matter here. Set specific durations for independent creative work, for example, 30 minutes and longer for complex challenges. During this time, resist the temptation to quickly check AI suggestions. The goal is sustaining the mental state where unexpected connections emerge, where personal creative voice develops without algorithmic influence. This independence phase prevents algorithmic patterns from constraining creative exploration while building the personal ownership that sustains persistence through inevitable implementation challenges.

Your best ideas emerge not from combining algorithmic suggestions but from sustained engagement without digital interruption.

Phase 3: Evaluate with Perspective

After generating ideas independently, the cycle returns to AI engagement, but with a different purpose. Rather than seeking more options, this phase uses algorithmic analysis to evaluate, refine, and strengthen human-generated concepts. AI's extraordinary pattern recognition power proves invaluable for stress-testing ideas, identifying weaknesses, and suggesting improvements that human judgment alone might miss.

Effective evaluation involves structured prompts that preserve human ownership while leveraging AI. Rather than asking "Is this idea good?" ask "What are three potential weaknesses in this approach?" or "How might someone from [relevant field/perspective] critique this solution?" The framing maintains creative agency while gaining analytical depth. This phase also leverages AI's unmatched pattern recognition capabilities: ask it to identify similar approaches, benchmark against existing solutions, or highlight what makes your idea distinctive. The goal is informed refinement, not replacement of our lived human reasoning fuelled by senses.

Leading design teams now routinely employ digital twins and simulation tools to rigorously test the durability, manufacturability, and environmental compliance of promising concepts. Teams in sustainability pilots simulate thousands of real-world scenarios, from temperature shifts to logistics stresses, cycling between virtual iteration and hands-on modification. Design teams in Nestlé, for example, validated package durability and recyclability through advanced simulation before committing to mass production, avoiding expensive errors that manual testing alone would have missed.[32]

These teams bring AI back to expose strengths and flaws in human-generated concepts, enabling refinement that moves ideas past both human bias and machine-generated limitations. One manager we interviewed described this approach: "*I bring my rough concepts back to AI not for validation but for challenge. I want it to poke holes, suggest risks I haven't considered, point out implementation challenges. But the ideas themselves remain mine. AI helps me make them stronger, not different.*"[33]

This evaluation phase demonstrates AI's value as analytical partner rather than creative director. Teams maintain control over which concepts deserve development while leveraging algorithmic capabilities to stress-test assumptions and reveal hidden constraints. The result is more robust innovation grounded in both human insight and computational analysis, informed refinement rather than replacement of lived human judgment.

Stress-test your thinking with AI, while keeping creative ownership.

Phase 4: Embody for Depth

The fourth phase moves ideas from digital concepts into physical, sensory, and narrative dimensions. This is where creativity gains the embodied grounding that makes it memorable, meaningful, and actionable. Leonardo's ideas worked because they emerged from direct physical engagement with materials and phenomena. We need to preserve this dimension even when working with AI tools.

Embodiment in creativity spans far beyond mere technical prototypes. It's a multidimensional phenomenon. Physical prototyping, whether building models or crafting mock-ups, remains a cornerstone of creative exploration, fostering hands-on insight and resilience through tangible iteration.

Embodiment may also thrive in narrative development: story crafting that aligns abstract ideas with human values, lived experience, and emotional resonance. Spatial thinking, too, brings essential realism to solutions, allowing us to imagine how innovations operate within actual environments with their unique constraints.

Our workshop research consistently shows that ideas developed through physical manipulation prove more robust and memorable than those remaining purely conceptual. As one participant noted, "*using something physical can make our mental capacity much broader and much deeper at the same time.*"[34] The physical engagement reveals insights not accessible through mental analysis alone.

Design teams have formalized this principle into workflow discipline. Building on insights from evaluation, teams move into rapid prototyping using 3D printers, cardboard folding, or assembly from recycled substrates. Several electronics firms quickly transitioned from

AI-generated digital models to low-fidelity cardboard and 3D-printed prototypes, catching usability issues and aesthetic missteps invisible to digital-only analysis, often reversing or reshaping original concepts before manufacturing scale-up. Physical embodiment exposes how packages feel in hand, how they perform in transport, and how they align with customer contexts, enabling adjustments that preserve both technical feasibility and human meaning.

Even as practitioners deepen embodied practice, AI systems are advancing toward simulating physical reality. Tech companies, most notably NVIDIA, have accelerated progress in creating "World Models," the sophisticated simulators trained on immense datasets of real-world sensory inputs to mimic aspects of reality including gravity, spatial reasoning, and physical causality. The 2025 launch of NVIDIA's Cosmos World Foundation Models represents a leap toward democratizing physical AI development, offering open-source platforms for robotics, autonomous systems, and embodied agents.[35] These models can generate physics-aware synthetic data, enabling faster, safer, and more scalable training across domains.

Yet even as such world models grow more realistic, leading research and technology analysts still emphasize their fundamental limitation: synthetic data, however refined, cannot capture the richness, irreducibility, and unpredictability of lived human experience. Real-world data grounds solutions in the complexity of real environments and supports the contextual, value-driven judgment essential for making changes and decisions. The gap shows the enduring power of human creativity rooted in touch, story, and spatial imagination over physical AI, like humanoid robots, trained on synthetic data. To date, physical AI cannot emulate deep engagement with materials, contexts, and sensory feedback in the same way humans do. Even the most advanced AI would fail what some call the "Embodied Turing Test," today and in the foreseeable future.[36]

Physical prototyping reveals insights that digital analysis cannot access, catching fatal flaws before expensive mistakes.

Phase 5: Integrate for Impact

The final phase combines human insights with AI efficiency to create value. This is where creative work transitions from possibility to reality, where breakthrough ideas gain the systematic support needed for valuable and lasting impact.

Integration leverages AI's strengths in project planning, risk analysis, and resource optimization while preserving the human creativity that drives the work. Use AI to develop implementation timelines, anticipate obstacles, and design feedback mechanisms. But maintain human ownership of the creative direction and strategic direction. This phase moves beyond individual innovation to embed creative insights into supply chains, branding, and customer experience, translating breakthrough concepts into repeatable organizational practice.

Leading design teams form joint taskforces with sustainability officers, manufacturing partners, and marketing specialists early in the implementation process. Teams observed in sustainability pilots began partnering with marketing and logistics during integration rather than after launch, establishing continuous data feedback and market testing cycles that ensure creative insights translate to market performance. This cross-functional collaboration prevents the common failure mode where brilliant ideas lose coherence as they move through organizational handoffs.

Research on ChatGPT-4 and Stable Diffusion as creative agents in iterative design cycles confirms that project success depends on structured feedback, ongoing critique, and adaptive revision processes between humans and AI.[37] Rather than treating AI outputs as final solutions, teams design workflows for iterative improvement throughout the lifecycle, using algorithmic capabilities to monitor performance while maintaining human judgment about strategic adjustments.

This phase also involves designing systems that nurture creativity over time. How will you preserve the insights gained through this cycle? How will you avoid falling back into erosion patterns? Share insights gained through the creative process, document what worked and what didn't, build learnings across teams. The goal is ensuring that individual creativity contributes to collective creative capacity, that today's breakthrough becomes tomorrow's foundation rather than a one-time achievement.

* * *

Together, these five phases form a cycle that preserves Leonardo's creative discipline while leveraging AI's computational advantages. The approach requires conscious design but enables us to maintain creative agency while benefiting from algorithmic assistance. Most importantly, it ensures that speed never compromises depth, efficiency never undermines meaning, and assistance never replaces authorship.

AI outputs are starting points for improvement, not final solutions.

The Cycle in Practice

The five phases of the Creative Partnership Cycle reflect an emerging best practice among teams successfully navigating human-AI creative collaboration. Research by Board of Innovation documenting over 20 packaging breakthroughs in 2025 reveals a consistent pattern: teams that systematically moved through all five phases achieved both enhanced creative outcomes and preserved human creative confidence.[38]

Consider how the pattern manifests across industries. One beverage company used AI to identify compostable composites during the Expanding phase, generating material options that would have taken weeks to surface manually. But they only discovered critical consumer handling challenges after building physical models in the Embodying phase. This was a clear demonstration that algorithmic suggestions require human creative judgment grounded in tangible reality. Cosmetic brands leveraged digital twins to simulate shelf-life during Evaluating, then conducted in-person "retail stress tests" to adjust point-of-sale integration, moving fluidly between computational analysis and lived experience. Across sectors, project journals highlight Integrating processes where cross-disciplinary teams managed launch complexity and gathered post-deployment feedback to refine the next cycle.

These implementations reveal the Creative Partnership Cycle exemplifies a disciplined approach to creative collaboration that preserves human agency while leveraging AI capabilities. The pattern appears across industries and scales, from individual projects to organizational transformation initiatives. Most significantly, teams following this approach report sustaining the creative confidence essential for breakthrough work rather than experiencing the erosion patterns documented earlier.

"Prepare like a machine, create like a human, implement like a team."

Leonardo's Timeless Creative Cycle

Return to that Milan workshop in 1505. Leonardo arranges his bird specimens with methodical precision, but his process reveals something more sophisticated than simple observation. His approach anticipates by five centuries what modern research validates as optimal creative practice.

Consider how Leonardo naturally embodied the Creative Partnership Cycle. His preparation phase involved exhaustive research including studying every available text on mechanics, hydraulics, and natural philosophy. He saturated himself with existing knowledge until he could confidently map the boundaries of current understanding. Had AI existed, he would have used it intensively during this phase, generating countless variations on wing designs, analysing aerodynamic principles, and exploring mechanical possibilities others had never considered.

Yet Leonardo's amazing insights emerged during periods of independent observation and experimentation. Away from books and authorities, he sat for hours watching birds in flight, sketching with his own hands, building prototype mechanisms. This independence phase allowed his unique perspective to develop without interference from existing patterns. His famous mirror writing itself reflects this principle: a deliberately separate space where his thoughts could develop without external influence.

The evaluation phase appears throughout his notebooks, where he returned to test insights against principles, critique his own assumptions, and refine approaches based on systematic analysis. He constantly asked: Where might this fail? What haven't I considered? How do the mechanics work in practice? This wasn't self-doubt but strategic scepticism that strengthened rather than weakened his creative drive.

The embodiment phase defined Leonardo's entire methodology. He never remained satisfied with theoretical understanding but always moved ideas into physical form, like sketches, models, prototypes. Each physical iteration revealed insights invisible in purely mental analysis. His flying machine designs worked not because he imagined flight, but because he built his understanding through direct engagement with materials and mechanisms.

Finally, integration appeared in his systematic documentation and teaching. Leonardo preserved insights in forms others could use, connected individual discoveries to broader principles, and designed his knowledge to outlive his own work. His notebooks survive as testament to creative discipline that preserved breakthrough insights for future implementation.

Leonardo understood intuitively that genuine innovation requires both intensive preparation and protected independence, both sceptical analysis and embodied exploration, both individual insight and systematic preservation. We can learn from his example by using AI tools with the same strategic discipline Leonardo brought to every resource available in his time.

Leonardo surely would have embraced AI's computational and pattern recognition power while preserving the human creative qualities that made his work irreplaceable. The Creative Partnership Cycle offers modern professionals a way to do exactly that.

Creativity makes professionals valuable by imagining possibilities algorithms cannot envision. When AI recombines patterns at scale, humans preserve the capacity to envision what matters beyond metrics. Algorithms optimize for novelty. Leaders choose for value. Yet creative abundance creates its own problem: how do we determine which possibilities deserve pursuit? *Creation generates options; human reasoning evaluates them.* This is where critical thinking enters as its completion, not a constraint. Creative practice explores possibilities through disciplined imagination. Critical thinking evaluates them through disciplined analysis. Chapter 4 examines how professionals preserve their reasoning even as algorithms increasingly do our analysis, distinguishing between what machines suggest and what contexts demand.

AI can multiply ideas endlessly, but only you can decide which ideas are worth creating.

Self-Assessment – From Polished Outputs to Original Insights

This assessment helps you reflect on how you currently cultivate creativity in an AI-supported work environment. It is not a test of talent but a tool for self-awareness and deliberate development.

For each dimension, consider your recent creative practices (past three months) and rate your typical approach using the scale below. The aim is honest reflection over where AI may be expanding your imagination and where it may be narrowing it, so you can strengthen what keeps your creativity distinctively human.

1. Creative Independence: Preserving Original Voice

How effectively do you maintain creative autonomy while using AI assistance?

- ☐ **Always:** I generate original ideas first and use AI only to expand, test, or refine them.
- ☐ **Often:** I start with my own framing but sometimes rely on AI to accelerate idea generation.
- ☐ **Sometimes:** I mix my ideas with AI outputs without clear boundaries between the two.
- ☐ **Rarely:** I depend heavily on AI to initiate ideas and only adjust its results.
- ☐ **Never:** I use AI outputs almost as-is, with little sense of my own authorship.

Interpretation: When AI becomes the starting point rather than the support, creative ownership erodes. Protect the early, formative stage of ideation for yourself before consulting the machine.

2. Embodied Creative Practice: Thinking Through Doing

How consistently do you engage in physical, sensory creative work?

- ☐ **Always:** I regularly sketch, build, or prototype to test ideas beyond the screen.
- ☐ **Often:** I include hands-on steps in most projects, knowing they deepen insight.
- ☐ **Sometimes:** I experiment physically when time allows but default to digital tools.
- ☐ **Rarely:** I seldom translate ideas into tangible form.
- ☐ **Never:** My creative process happens entirely through screens and prompts.

Interpretation: Physical exploration activates forms of intelligence that AI cannot replicate. If your work stays purely digital, re-introduce hands, space, and materials to recover depth and confidence.

3. Creative Partnership Strategy: Directing the Collaboration

How deliberately do you orchestrate the relationship between human and AI contributions?

- ☐ **Always:** I use AI intensively for preparation, then switch to human creation before re-engaging it for evaluation and integration.
- ☐ **Often:** I treat AI as a partner – never a director – and maintain clear decision ownership.
- ☐ **Sometimes:** I balance roles inconsistently, letting AI lead parts of the process.
- ☐ **Rarely:** I let AI shape outcomes more than intended.
- ☐ **Never:** I delegate creative work to AI with little human intervention.

Interpretation: High-quality collaboration depends on timing and boundaries. Use AI where it adds analytical power, but reserve direction and meaning making for yourself.

4. Intrinsic Motivation: Sustaining Meaning and Joy

How well do you preserve personal satisfaction and purpose in creative work?

- ☐ **Always:** My projects remain deeply engaging and purposeful, regardless of AI use.
- ☐ **Often:** I stay connected to the meaning behind my work, though efficiency sometimes distracts me.
- ☐ **Sometimes:** AI makes tasks easier but less fulfilling.
- ☐ **Rarely:** My creative work feels mechanical or externally driven.
- ☐ **Never:** I complete projects efficiently but feel little sense of personal value or joy.

Interpretation: Intrinsic motivation fuels originality. If your creative energy feels flat despite productivity, reconnect with why the work matters to you, not just completion.

Using Your Profile

When you map yourself across these four dimensions, patterns emerge. You might preserve strong creative independence yet neglect embodied practice. You may partner effectively with AI but feel your intrinsic motivation slipping. The task is not perfection but balance to deliberately strengthening what is underdeveloped while protecting what is already generative.

Research shows that three practices preserve and strengthen creative ownership:

- **Temporal separation** – protecting moments of AI-free creation, where ideas can take shape without premature optimization.
- **Physical engagement** – building or sketching by hand, which anchors imagination in confidence and discovery.
- **Personal connection** – remembering why a project matters beyond efficiency metrics, which sustains intrinsic motivation.

Your creative profile points to where deliberate boundaries, physical engagement, and renewed meaning can turn efficiency into genuine originality.

Notes

1 Richardson (2019).
2 Da Vinci (in Richter, 1970, §1161).
3 Resnick (2017).
4 Personal communication, Munich Design Week, April 13, 2025.
5 Amabile (2018); Amabile & Pratt (2016).
6 Woodman et al. (1993).
7 Bürgi & Roos (2006).
8 LSP research data (2025).
9 Drucker Forum Transcript (2025).
10 Beaty et al. (2016).
11 LSP research data (2025).
12 Doshi & Hauser (2023); Orwig et al. (2024).
13 LSP research data (2024).
14 TNM research data (2025).
15 Utley (2025).
16 TNM research data (2025).
17 LSP research data (2025).
18 Zhang et al. (2025)
19 LSP research data (2025).
20 Wilson (1998).

21 Roos (2006).
22 Olsen (2025).
23 LSP research data (2025).
24 Ma et al. (2025); Yu et al (2025).
25 https://www.boardofinnovation.com/blog/20-sustainable-packaging-solutions-developed-with-ai/
26 TNM research data (2025).
27 LSP research data (2025).
28 Utley (2025).
29 Liu (2025).
30 LSP research data (2025): post-survey feedback following I workshop I led in conjunction with the 2025 *Munich Design Week*.
31 Miranda (2025, March 26).
32 Nestlé (2025).
33 TNM research data (2025): post-survey feedback following I workshop I led in conjunction with the 2024
34 TNM research data (2025).
35 Agarwal et al. (2025); NVIDIA (2025); Liu et al. (2025).
36 Zador (2023); Orwig et al. (2025).
37 Liu (2025).
38 Board of Innovation (2025).

References

Aquinas, T. (1265–1274/1947). *Summa theologica* (Fathers of the English Dominican Province, Trans.). Benziger Bros.

Aristotle. (1984). *The Organon*. In J. Barnes (Ed.), *The complete works of Aristotle: The revised Oxford translation* (Vols. 1–2). Princeton University Press. (Original works published ca. 350 BCE.)

Bailin, S., Case, R., Coombs, J. R., & Daniels, L. B. (1999). Conceptualizing critical thinking. *Journal of Curriculum Studies, 31*(3), 285–302. https://doi.org/10.1080/002202799183133

Chatterji, A., Cunningham, T., Deming, D. J., Hitzig, Z., Ong, C., Shan, C. Y., & Wadman, K. (2025). How people use ChatGPT (NBER Working Paper No. 34255). National Bureau of Economic Research. https://www.nber.org/papers/w34255

Ciatto, G., Agiollo, A., Magnini, M., & Omicini, A. (2025). Large language models as oracles for instantiating ontologies with domain-specific knowledge. *Knowledge-Based Systems, 298*, 110935. https://doi.org/10.1016/j.knosys.2024.110935

ComplyAdvantage. (2024, November 25). *Enhancing AML efforts with explainable AI*. https://complyadvantage.com/insights/enhancing-aml-using-explainable-ai/

DigGrowth. (2025, August 6). *Transforming business analytics with AI-driven reporting and dashboards*. https://diggrowth.com/blogs/analytics/ai-driven-reporting-and-dashboards/

D'Northwood, G., & Rattray, J. (2024, online first). What is this thing called critical thinking? Perspectives from business school academics. *Innovations in Education and Teaching International*. https://doi.org/10.1080/14703297.2024.2422310

Dwyer, C. P., Hogan, M. J., & Stewart, I. (2014). An integrated critical thinking framework for the 21st century. *Thinking Skills and Creativity, 12*, 43–52. https://doi.org/10.1016/j.tsc.2013.12.004

Ennis, R. H. (2011). *The nature of critical thinking: An outline of critical thinking dispositions and abilities*. University of Illinois. https://education.illinois.edu/docs/default-source/faculty-documents/robert-ennis/thenatureofcriticalthinking_51711_000.pdf

Facione, P. A. (2000). The disposition toward critical thinking: Its character, measurement, and relationship to critical thinking skill. *Informal Logic, 20*(1), 61–84. https://informallogic.ca/index.php/informal_logic/article/view/2254/1698

Gerlich, M. (2025). AI tools in society: Impacts on cognitive offloading and the future of critical thinking. *Societies, 15*(1), Article 6. https://doi.org/10.3390/soc15010006

Goh, E., Gallo, R., Hom, J., et al. (2024). Large language model influence on diagnostic reasoning: A randomized clinical trial. *JAMA Network Open, 7*(10), e2440969. https://doi.org/10.1001/jamanetworkopen.2024.40969

GSC Online Press. (2025). *The role of AI in preventing financial fraud and enhancing compliance*. https://gsconlinepress.com/journals/gscarr/sites/default/files/GSCARR-2025-0086.pdf

Haefner, N., Wincent, J., Parida, V., & Gassmann, O. (2021). Artificial intelligence and innovation management: A review, framework, and research agenda. *Technological Forecasting and Social Change, 162*, 120392. https://doi.org/10.1016/j.techfore.2020.120392

Hello Operator. (2024, December 31). *How AI dashboards simplify engagement analysis*. https://www.hellooperator.ai/blog/how-ai-dashboards-simplify-engagement-analysis

Herodotus. (2008). *The Histories* (R. Waterfield, Trans.; C. Dewald, Ed.). Oxford University Press. (Original work published ca. 440 BCE.) https://global.oup.com/academic/product/the-histories-9780199535668.

Huang, L., & Liaw, M. L. (2011). The application of critical thinking in teaching English reading. *Theory and Practice in Language Studies, 1*(2), 158–164. https://www.academypublication.com/issues/past/tpls/vol01/02/03.pdf

Ji, Z., Lee, N., Frieske, R., Yu, T., Su, D., Xu, Y., . . . & Wang, W. Y. (2023). Survey of hallucination in natural language generation. *ACM Computing Surveys, 55*(12), 1–38. https://doi.org/10.1145/3571730

Kolbjørnsrud, V. (2024). Designing the intelligent organization: Six principles for human–AI collaboration. *California Management Review, 66*(2), 44–64. https://doi.org/10.1177/00081256231211020.

Kuhn, D. (2019). Critical thinking as discourse. *Human Development, 62*(3), 146–164. https://doi.org/10.1159/000500171

Means, T. (2025, May 23). The AI microscope: How AI can enhance critical thinking and creativity in education. LinkedIn. https://www.linkedin.com/pulse/ai-microscope-how-can-enhance-critical-thinking-creativity-means-h1juc.

Moore, T. (2013). Critical thinking: Seven definitions in search of a concept. *Studies in Higher Education, 38*(4), 506–522. https://doi.org/10.1080/03075079.2011.586995

Muller, J. Z. (2018). *The tyranny of metrics*. Princeton University Press.

Mulnix, J. W. (2012). Thinking critically about critical thinking. *Educational Philosophy and Theory, 44*(5), 464–479.
Nisbett, R. E., & Wilson, T. D. (1977). The halo effect: Evidence for unconscious alteration of judgments. *Journal of Personality and Social Psychology, 35*(4), 250–256.
Nguyen, A., & Welch, K. (2025). Generative AI and the erosion of interpretive authority in qualitative data analysis. *Qualitative Inquiry, 31*(7), 873–889. https://journals.sagepub.com/doi/10.1177/10944281251377154
Nofal, H. A., Mohamed, A. E., Almadani, N., Mahfouz, R., Bahri, H. A., Ali, H. T., & Elrafey, D. S. (2025). The impact of an artificial intelligence enhancement program on healthcare providers' knowledge, attitudes, and workplace flourishing. *Frontiers in Public Health, 13*, 1639333. https://www.frontiersin.org/journals/public-health/articles/10.3389/fpubh.2025.1639333/full
Nowotny, H. (2021). *In AI we trust: Power, illusion and control of predictive algorithms*. Polity Press.
OECD. (2023). *AI language models*. Organisation for Economic Co-operation and Development. https://www.oecd.org/en/publications/ai-language-models_13d38f92-en.html
OpenAI. (2025, April 11). *AI in the enterprise: Lessons from seven frontier companies*. https://cdn.openai.com/business-guides-and-resources/ai-in-the-enterprise.pdf
Paul, R., & Elder, L. (2021). *Critical thinking: Tools for taking charge of your learning and your life* (4th ed.). Rowman & Littlefield.
Petress, K. (2004). Critical thinking: An extended definition. *Education, 124*(3), 461–466.
Roberts, N., & Candi, M. (2024). AI-driven innovation: How artificial intelligence shapes organizational creativity. *Journal of Business Research, 158*, 113670. https://doi.org/10.1016/j.technovation.2024.103081
Roos, J. (2025, June 11). Expire or evolve? Rethinking how we frame our future. *AACSB Insights*. https://www.aacsb.edu/insights/articles/2025/06/expire-or-evolve-rethinking-how-we-frame-our-future
The Stoiverse. (2025, August 10). *Why critical thinking is disappearing: The rise of collective stupidity* [Video]. YouTube. https://www.youtube.com/watch?v=5NDotKQUqvc
Thorndike, E. L. (1920). A constant error in psychological ratings. *Journal of Applied Psychology, 4*(1), 25–29.
Toulmin, S. (1958). *The uses of argument*. Cambridge University Press.
von Krogh, G., & Roos, J. (1996). Arguments on knowledge and competence. In G. von Krogh & J. Roos (Eds.), *Managing knowledge: Perspectives on cooperation and competition* (pp. 97–119). Sage Publications.
Wang, L. W. (2025). Impact of generative artificial intelligence on the professional qualities curriculum and reflection essays during physician training. *Internal Medicine Journal, 55*(5), 739–742. https://pmc.ncbi.nlm.nih.gov/articles/PMC12240007/

4 Critical Thinking – From Shallow Reasoning to Clear Judgment

The Oracle and the Questioner

In 550 BCE, Croesus, the wealthiest king of his age, stood before a choice that could possibly destroy his kingdom. The Persian Empire's armies pressed at his border. His advisors counselled war. His treasuries overflowed with gold to fund any campaign. Yet something made him pause. Like any prudent leader facing strategic uncertainty, he sought external validation. He sent emissaries to the Oracle at Delphi, whose pronouncements shaped kingdoms.

The Oracle's response arrived in perfect hexameter verse: "*If Croesus crosses the Halys River, a great empire will fall.*"[1]

The poetry was exquisite. The claim absolute. The king heard what he wanted to hear: victory foretold by divine authority. His war council saw confirmation of their strategic analysis.

But no one asked the essential question: *which empire*?

Croesus crossed the Halys. Within months, his kingdom was in ashes, his wealth seized, his name a cautionary tale about misreading oracular pronouncements. The Oracle hadn't lied. A great empire had indeed fallen, his own. The fault lay not in the prophecy but in the failure to interrogate it.

A century later, in that same Greek landscape, another man faced his own oracular moment. The Oracle at Delphi had declared Socrates the wisest man in Athens. Unlike Croesus, who accepted divine pronouncement as strategic guidance, Socrates treated it as a puzzle demanding investigation. He questioned politicians who claimed to understand justice but couldn't define it. He interrogated craftsmen who knew their trade but mistook narrow expertise for universal wisdom. One by one, their certainties crumbled under scrutiny.

Socrates concluded that if he possessed wisdom, it lay only in knowing the boundaries of his knowledge. This relentless questioning would ultimately cost him his life. In 399 BCE, Athens forced him to drink hemlock, charging that his systematic interrogation corrupted youth and threatened social order. The city that birthed democracy could not tolerate a man who questioned every assumption.

The contrast between Croesus and Socrates illuminates our present moment with unsettling clarity. The pattern persists today. Today's

DOI: 10.4324/9781003732570-4

oracles don't inhale vapours in stone temples. They operate in giga data centres, summoned by prompts and queries. Their pronouncements arrive not in cryptic verse but in confident paragraphs, beautiful images, and videos inseparable from reality. Yet the danger is the same: mistaking the authority of form for the substance of reasoning.

Scholars describe this as the "oracle effect" – the tendency to treat outputs from large language models as authoritative simply because they are fluent and well-structured. AI generates *associations*, not *interpretations*. Its outputs may resemble careful analysis, but they lack the logical "because" that links evidence to conclusion. They cannot explain *why* a claim follows from data. In qualitative research, this effect is especially corrosive. The danger is not only inaccurate answers but the gradual erosion of our interpretive muscle.[2]

Our research confirms this pattern of AI outputs appearing like reasoned conclusions but missing the inferential link. One executive, reflecting on his use of AI admitted: *"I realized during a presentation that I had the data and the conclusion. But the why in between? That had become a black box I'd stopped trying to open."*[3]

This is Croesus at Delphi, resources at hand but interpretive authority surrendered. The parallel is unmistakable. Just as the ancient king accepted the Oracle's authority without examining the *why* or *because*, many now accept algorithmic authority without tracing the reasoning from data to decision. The LLM's probabilistic association becomes the interpretation of meaning we rely on.

Research documents the consequences across numerous domains. In medicine, physicians with AI support felt more confident but were less likely to elaborate their decision-making process or scrutinize clinical uncertainties. Teams that delegate problem-framing to AI converge around machine-generated categories, losing the pluralism of perspectives that strategy requires. The conclusion is that GenAI, based on current transformer architectures, is unsuitable for qualitative data analysis.[4]

A year before the arrival of ChatGPT, in 2021 Helga Nowotny foresaw this risk. In her book, *In AI We Trust*, she argued that our faith in predictive systems seduces us into an illusion of control, shrinking both our agency and our openness to uncertainty. The challenge, as she framed it, is to resist the spell of technological certainty and maintain space for distinctly human interpretive plurality. The real danger of uncritically using predictive systems is an *illusion of understanding* and *surrender of agency*.[5]

Ask before you trust; the strength of any system depends on the questions you pose.

Why We Believe Oracles (Even When We Know Better)

Why do well-trained, experienced professionals still lean toward oracles? Not because they are gullible, but because specific frictions push them there.

First, speed compresses scrutiny. When an answer arrives with confidence and tidy summary, it feels unkind to the calendar to ask for the "because." We are all busy at work. The cost of giving it more attention becomes invisible until judgment thins.

Second, authority diffuses accountability. In our interviews, a seasoned executive admitted deferring to a model despite industry instincts: *"I don't understand the mathematics behind the prediction, but this doesn't smell right."*[6] Nevertheless, he took it as a recommendation. The oracle offers cover, an escape hatch from owning the *Because*.

Third, design flatters compliance. Facilitators in our 2025 LSP study praised AI for impeccable workshop structures in preparation agendas, yet several reported feeling thinner in live sessions when pressed to explain why a particular design choice served the learning goal. As one put it, *"I knew what to do, but not why."*[7] In the room, authority returns to the human: reading energy, pacing, safety, and meaning. Those are warrants in motion, things the AI tool cannot hold for us.

Fourth, fluency mimics understanding. Researchers show how generative systems can reproduce the form of qualitative insight while skipping the warrant, the logical connection, entirely. What looks like interpretation is often association arranged to resemble it. Correlation among millions of data points in the past is mistaken for causation in living, adaptive systems. A senior executive told me she had dismissed data analysis until AI changed her mind: *"Now I love it – these are undeniable facts."* When I asked if the past reliably predicted the future in her industry, she had no answer.[8] We sense this dissonance but, under pressure, we accept algorithmic fluency as a proxy for reason.

Finally, the halo effect amplifies these vulnerabilities. The halo effect is a classic cognitive bias: a single positive trait, such as fluency, structural consistency, or even visual beauty, unjustifiably elevates all other attributes, including perceived trustworthiness and authority.[9] In the hands of scientists, consultants, and managers alike, this means radiant AI-generated prose can blind us to what is missing: solid interpretive grounding, or an explanation of how meaning is made.

Slow down the rush to decide – urgency kills judgment faster than error.

These frictions do not indict AI *per se*. They indict our habits under constraint.

The Science of Critical Thinking

Croesus mistook certainty for guidance; Socrates treated an oracle's riddle as the beginning of inquiry. Their contrast captures the spirit of critical thinking, but to move from parable to practice we need firmer ground. What, exactly, is this capability that separates untested belief from reasoned assessment?

Critical thinking is not about knowing facts. It is about how we challenge information, dig for meaning, and make judgments under pressure, in real decisions where the stakes are high. At its core, critical thinking is purposeful, reflective judgment that applies reasoned and logical standards to guide belief and action.[10] The mark of expertise lies not in how much we know, but in how deliberately we pause, question, and apply those standards before moving forward.

Strong critical thinkers pair analytical skills with habits of mind: open-mindedness, self-regulation, professional courage.[11] In practice, critical thinking is less about intelligence and more about the willingness to scrutinize our own thinking when momentum, group consensus, or authority tries to sweep it away.

Four Pillars of Critical Thinking

Critical thinking in professional practice rests on four essential disciplines, each validated across decades of research in education, business, medicine, and public policy.

1. **Purposeful reflection.** Speed and complexity define professional life, but critical thinking begins when we intentionally slow down, recognize the thinking process, and stay alert to possible blind spots. Most professionals admit these pauses are rare, yet they are the shield against error and assumption. This absence of reflection is precisely what the discipline seeks to prevent.
2. **Application of standards.** Reasoning is evaluated by clarity, sufficiency, relevance, fairness.[12] These standards distinguish an argument that merely sounds right from one that can withstand questioning in the boardroom, classroom, or meeting room. We know how quickly a finished-looking report or slide deck can bypass true scrutiny. But a critical thinker asks: Is this grounded in fact? What are the hidden assumptions? What perspectives has it omitted?
3. **Analysis and synthesis.** Critical thinking disassembles claims into components and then reconstructs them into warranted conclusions.[13] It is the craft of tracing how evidence leads, or fails to lead, to action. This is where validated frameworks become indispensable, because they force the *Because* into view. Without this connective tissue, we have data and conclusions, but no reasoning.

4. **Skills and dispositions together.** Training in logic means little without the disposition to persist and question, especially under pressure or when authority discourages dissent. Research emphasizes that critical thinking requires both cognitive ability and habits of mind: persistence, systematicity, open-mindedness.[14] Without these inclinations, skills remain brittle. This explains why some professionals trained in logical frameworks still defer to algorithmic outputs. They know how to analyze but lack the reflexive courage to interrupt the momentum of group thinking.

Critical Thinking as Dialogue

Critical thinking thrives in dialogue, not solitude. We develop this capability through argument and counterargument, by testing claims against peers, surfacing assumptions, and allowing our reasoning to be examined publicly.[15] In professional practice, critical thinking becomes inherently social, made stronger when reasoning is shared, debated, and refined. Participants in strategy workshops consistently report that the strongest insights emerge when people must explain and defend their thinking to others. As one observed: "*When I had to explain my build, I realized what I was really assuming.*"[16]

In 2025, I staged for 1,300 leaders in business schools from all over the world an Oxford Union-style debate where two teams of leaders had to debate a motion, suffer my cross examination to qualify their claims, articulate their warrants, and offer rebuttals to each other.[17] Before the debate began, I polled the audience on the motion. The results revealed a sharp division: 59 percent agreed, 41 percent objected. What followed was not consensus-building but structured yet friendly confrontation. Opening statements collided with cross-examinations. Rebuttals forced both sides to strengthen their reasoning under pressure. The format created what I intended: a head-on collision of viewpoints that made thinking visible and testable.

By the debate's end, I polled the audience again. The sharp division had dissolved into an almost perfect 50/50 split. Minds had not been closed by argument; they had been opened, challenged, and enriched through it. As one participant reflected afterward: "*This wasn't just a novel format. It showed us a process we could adapt for our classrooms.*" Another added: "*It's given me ideas for how to structure difficult conversations at our next faculty retreat.*"

The debate revealed a truth often obscured in professional settings: critical thinking deepens not through individual analysis alone, but through the friction of structured disagreement. The format itself becomes the teacher, demonstrating that when we design processes that require people to qualify claims, defend reasoning, and respond to counterargument, we create conditions where critical thinking must emerge. The shift in audience opinion was not evidence of wavering conviction. It was evidence of minds engaging with complexity, weighing competing evidence, and refining judgment through collective reasoning.

This dialogic dimension proves essential because it surfaces what individual reflection might miss. A consultant's private analysis may contain hidden biases; peer challenge exposes them. A physician's diagnostic reasoning may skip steps; explaining it to colleagues reveals gaps. A leader's decision may rest on unstated warrants; board questions force them into view.

Eroding Critical Thinking

The habits that once anchored critical thinking – reflection, standards, analysis, and dialogue – now face subtle erosion. From Aristotle's logic to Aquinas's disputation, from Socrates' disciplined questioning to modern cognitive science, we have refined ways to distinguish sound reasoning from surface persuasion. These methods have long protected professional judgment against bias, haste, and dogma. Yet the foundations that once held under pressure now weaken quietly under the weight of automated reasoning.

The oracle effect described earlier exposes not a single failure but three interconnected fractures. Each undermines one of the pillars of critical thought: the ability to trace *because*, sustain dialogue, and practise reflective self-questioning. Together they explain how interpretive authority slips away, not through ignorance, but through habits that feel efficient and sophisticated until the connective tissue between evidence and claim thins to breaking point.

1st Mechanism: Warrant Unmooring

Critical thinking depends on surfacing the *Because* that connects evidence to conclusion. In argumentation, this is the warrant. Without it, arguments become only claims or assertions. In AI-supported settings, warrants weaken through three habits that we rarely notice forming.

The first is **metric substitution**. Numbers begin to replace reasoning. Reviews of business analytics outputs show that teams routinely treat changes in key metrics as explanations in themselves, mistaking numeric correlation for causal logic.[18]

The second is **confidence laundering**. Probabilities are mistaken for reasons. In finance, health care, and education, researchers have shown that users often accept statistical likelihoods as self-justifying.[19] The numeric veneer conceals that no explanation has been given, only a prediction.

The third is **proxy drift**. Professionals optimize what is easiest to count rather than what matters. A large-scale usage study of generative AI found that people rely on chatbots precisely for tasks most prone to proxy thinking. Output length and formatting displace substance; what is measurable substitutes for what is meaningful.[20]

The research on the oracle effect is supported by other empirical studies that show how heavy reliance on algorithmic advice reduces the habit of warrant-checking.[21] Medical research confirms the same pattern: doctors using diagnostic AI felt more confident but interrogated causal reasoning less.[22] They became faster and more assured, but shallower in justification.

These shortcuts feel like competence. More than ever, we can cite figures, quote scores, and display dashboards with conviction. Yet when pressed for the reasoning in between, we falter. Warrant erosion fractures the standards pillar of critical thinking. Clarity, relevance, and sufficiency fade when the *Because* remains invisible.

2nd Mechanism: Algorithmic Deference

If warrant erosion corrodes analysis, algorithmic deference corrodes dialogue. This mechanism describes how LLMs simulate interpretation so fluently that their outputs command unearned authority. Once a refined answer appears, critique feels redundant or impolite.

Three dynamics reinforce this habit.

Compelling output discourages dissent. Teams often anchor discussions on the AI-generated summary before any human framing occurs. International policy reports the same effect at national level: the more sophisticated the AI briefing, the less likely leaders are to introduce alternative frames.[23] The system's surface appearance invites consent, quietly closing the space for questioning.

Convergence to templates compounds the problem. Experiments in AI-assisted brainstorming reveal that groups rapidly align to the categories or framings offered by the machine.[24] Consensus emerges not from genuine synthesis but from alignment to the default patterns of the model.

Finally, **expert syndrome** extends a long-standing human bias toward authority. Studies of workplace decision-making show that professionals increasingly defend AI-generated recommendations even when they privately doubt them.[25] The social instinct once reserved for recognized experts is now triggered by the smooth competence of AI.

This is the fracture of the dialogic pillar. Instead of debate, there is convergence. Instead of interpretive pluralism, we get rapid consensus. The loss is not merely the risk of error, but the fading of the habit of raising alternatives at all. The oracle has spoken, and the group falls silent.

3rd Mechanism: Reflexive Complacency

The third erosion cuts deeper still. Reflexive complacency refers to the decline of deliberate self-questioning. The discipline of examining one's own assumptions recedes as professionals shift from meaning-makers to operators of AI tools.

Two dynamics illustrate the process.

Split attention undermines presence. Facilitators, educators, and managers report losing awareness of group dynamics as focus drifts to the AI display rather than the human interaction unfolding before them. One facilitator described this loss succinctly: "*The AI helped me in planning, but in the room I lost responsiveness. I wasn't fully present.*" The cost is not efficiency but situational awareness – the very capability that defines effective leadership and facilitation.[26]

Identity outsourcing compounds the effect. Surveys show that as professionals depend more on AI-generated narratives, they feel less like interpreters and more like intermediaries.[27] Their authority to frame and evaluate diminishes. A participant in a Drucker Forum discussion captured this sensation well: "*My team has become brilliant at finding AI-powered solutions. The problem is, we've stopped asking whether we're solving the right problems.*"[28]

This is a fracture in the dispositions pillar of critical thinking. Traits such as open-mindedness, systematicity, and intellectual courage weaken when reflection is delegated. Reflexive complacency is an existential erosion because it touches the habits of mind and integrity at the heart of professional judgment.

The Compounded Erosion Effect

These three erosions rarely act in isolation. *Warrant unmooring* fractures analysis and standards. *Algorithmic deference* silences dialogue. *Reflexive complacency* dulls the disposition to examine one's own assumptions. Each may seem minor, yet together they form a slow collapse of interpretive authority.

Croesus lost his empire not because the Oracle lied, but because he failed to question what it meant. Professionals risk the same fate when they surrender warrants, silence dissent, and neglect reflection. The science of critical thinking shows what the pillars should be. These erosions show what happens when they weaken.

The consequence reveals a single pattern beneath the surface differences: each weakness feeds the others. When speed replaces deliberation, when authority replaces dialogue, and when fluency replaces understanding, the scaffolding of reasoning begins to collapse.

Figure 4.1 depicts this downward drift – from grounded judgment to compliant acceptance. As justification unmoors, authority replaces

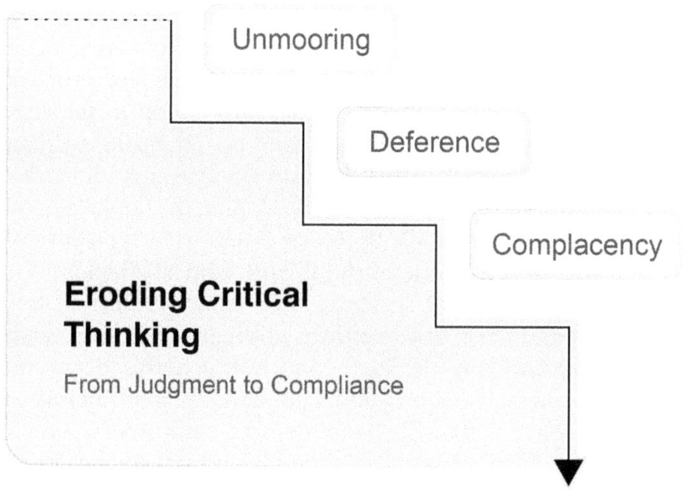

Figure 4.1 Eroding Critical Thinking – From Judgment to Compliance

inquiry, and reflexive capacity weakens, reasoning descends step by step toward dependence on the machine.

Rebuilding Critical Thinking

Recovering these lost capacities is not about nostalgia for slower times or suspicion of AI tools. It is about re-anchoring professional reasoning in practices that algorithms cannot perform: questioning meaning, weighing warrants, and holding uncertainty long enough to gain perspective.

The task ahead is to rebuild this structure, to restore integrity to how we reason, decide, and act under the pressure of accelerated intelligence systems. Only by repairing the cracks can professionals ensure that critical thinking remains the keystone of sound judgment in an AI-driven world. This means reviving standards, re-opening dialogue, and renewing reflection.

Challenge one assumption in every meeting – that's how thinking stays alive.

An Apprenticeship of Doubt

To stop the erosion, we need more than awareness. We need disciplines strong enough to restore the connective tissue of reasoning. This requires an "apprenticeship of doubt." Like any apprenticeship, it is not mastered in a moment but cultivated over time, through habits, routines, and structures. Socrates practiced this apprenticeship in dialogue, constantly testing claims against assumptions and occasionally driving people to be perplexed, frustrated, and sometimes even hostile. For professionals today, the challenge is not philosophical conversation in the agora or risking a cup of hemlock or polonium tea, but systematic evaluation in boardrooms, classrooms, and workshops awash with algorithmic outputs.

Many helpful frameworks exist for developing the doubt required by critical thinking. Robert Ennis, Professor Emeritus at the University of Illinois and founding director of the Illinois Critical Thinking Project, developed the foundational structure that defines critical thinking as two essential parts: core abilities, like clarifying questions, analyzing arguments, and checking evidence; and indispensable dispositions.[29] These dispositions include open-mindedness, intellectual courage, and a systematic approach that insists on following a clear process, even when the answers appear obvious or a machine claims mathematical certainty.

The Paul-Elder framework, created by Richard Paul (founder of the Foundation for Critical Thinking) and Linda Elder (the Foundation's President), has become the standard business tool for systematic analysis, used in companies and professional development programs worldwide. It builds a practical checklist for dissecting any analysis, human or machine, asking professionals to break thinking down into its essential parts: purpose, questions, assumptions, data, and implications.[30] Both remain invaluable for professionals navigating AI-augmented decision-making.

Frameworks like these two hold us accountable when convenience trumps doubt. They are more than academic scaffolds. They are ways of slowing our impulse toward closure. They force us to externalize what might otherwise remain tacit. Without them, the erosions described earlier creep in unnoticed. Warrant unmooring thrives when we skip the bridge between evidence and claim. A framework obliges us to articulate it. Algorithmic deference thrives when silences dissent. A framework provides language for challenge without hostility. Reflective complacency thrives when assumptions go unexamined. A framework makes assumptions visible and therefore debatable.

We know that critical thinking requires both persistence and courage. But as many executives confessed in our interviews, courage fades under the pressure of AI's confident outputs. The standards urge us to test reasoning for clarity and depth. But as interviewees testify, managers, consultants, and even educators too easily converged on AI-provided categories that seem complete.

The Supreme Architecture of Reasoning

For me, the most powerful and enduring framework for critical thinking is Stephen Toulmin's model of argument, published almost seven decades ago.[31] His model of argumentation draws deeply from and modernizes ancient models of reasoning, especially those of Aristotle and the medieval work of Thomas Aquinas.

Ennis gives us the soil in which doubt can take root. Paul and Elder give us the shears to prune sloppy reasoning. But standing on the shoulders of ancient and medieval giants, Toulmin gives us the architecture that makes reasoning visible. If dispositions anchor the will to doubt and standards sharpen its quality, Toulmin provides the structure in which disciplined doubt can grow. His model does not pretend to deliver absolute truth. It makes arguments testable and exposes assumptions. And it allows us to monitor our own reasoning with the same rigor we demand of others.

Since my early career as a management researcher, I have relied on Toulmin's framework as both an analytical method and a practical tool. In my early organizational research with Georg von Krogh, we used argument mapping to uncover the implicit theories driving executive reasoning and decisions about knowledge management.[32] As an academic leader, Managing Director, President, Dean, and Chief Academic Officer, I have applied the framework to structure presentations and clarify strategic thinking for myself, in presentations to peers in leadership teams and to boards of directors. Most recently, I have used it as the underlying design in AI voice assistants that conduct systematic interviews for The Next Management and other initiatives. This progression from analyzing human reasoning to programming algorithmic reasoning over decades demonstrates why Toulmin's architecture proves essential for contemporary professionals: it works equally well for examining human arguments and for evaluating AI outputs.

Aristotle's foundational work on logic established the structure and validity of deductive reasoning: arguments proceed from major and minor premises to a necessary conclusion.[33] While inspired by ancient models of reasoning, Toulmin argued that these are too rigid to capture the messy, field-dependent character of everyday and professional arguments. His model is a response to the limitations of abstract formal logic, offering instead a scheme that makes visible the links that make arguments hold together in actual practice. The key component is the warrant, comparable to the major premise of Aristotelian reasoning. Toulmin also takes inspiration from medieval scholasticism, including the renowned scholar-monk Thomas Aquinas, by emphasizing that good arguments require not just formal correctness but *practical justification*.[34] How can reasons, supported with backing, be defended, challenged, or qualified in a specific field?

Toulmin's model of argument looks deceptively simple. Yet it remains one of the most useful tools for professionals who must reason amid uncertainty. Rather than insisting on formal logic, it maps how real arguments unfold. Toulmin identified six interdependent elements present in any serious claim:

1. **Claim:** the conclusion or decision proposed.
2. **Grounds:** the evidence or reasons offered.
3. **Warrant:** the reasoning principle connecting grounds to claim.
4. **Backing:** additional support for the warrant.
5. **Qualifier:** an indication of strength or scope.
6. **Rebuttal:** explicit recognition of exceptions or counterarguments.

At first glance, this may seem like another checklist. Its genius lies in how it captures the messiness of real reasoning without abandoning rigor. In practice, these six elements act less like a formula and more like an architecture of thought. This is a structure that keeps claims, evidence, and assumptions in dialogue.

Figure 4.2 visualizes this architecture as a reasoning bridge that makes the *Because* of every argument visible. It shows how sound judgment emerges when claims, grounds, warrants, backing, qualifiers, and rebuttals work together in balance.

The main bridge – *Grounds* → *Warrant* → *Claim* – shows how reasoning moves from evidence to conclusion. *Backing* strengthens the bridge from below, while *Qualifier* and *Rebuttal* guard its limits above. Together, they form a practical compass for professionals navigating complex, ambiguous decisions.

The model is both *diagnostic* and *developmental*. It exposes where an argument is thin – where warrants are missing or claims overreach, and provides a disciplined way to rebuild them. As reasoning gains

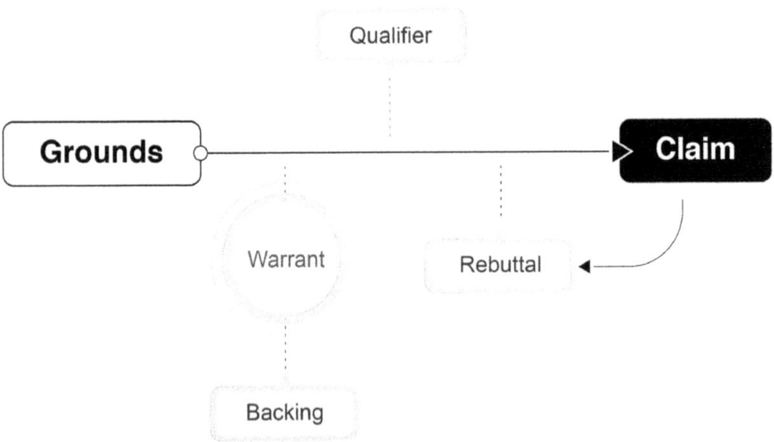

Figure 4.2 Toulmin's Model

backing, qualifiers, and counterarguments, it also gains resilience. In this way, Toulmin's architecture directly counteracts the erosions of critical thinking described earlier: it restores warrants, re-opens dialogue, and reactivates reflection.

Let us illustrate how it works in practice by returning to Andrew Jassy's email to Amazon staff in July 2025 from Chapter 1: *"Technologies like Generative AI come about once-in-a-lifetime, and completely change what's possible for customers and businesses."* He went on to predict that AI agents would act as teammates, allowing people to focus less on rote work and more on strategic thinking.

If we break this claim down using Toulmin's framework, the structure becomes visible (Table 4.1).

By mapping these six elements, we can see where the reasoning is strong but also where it is fragile. Arguments stop being black boxes and become transparent structures. What appeared as natural authority in Jassey's message to his employees is revealed as an incomplete chain, an assertion.

Toulmin as Antidote to the Three Erosions

Each erosion identified earlier finds its antidote in Toulmin's architecture.

- **Warrant unmooring** thrives on cognitive fracture. Toulmin forces the warrant into view. Professionals can no longer present claims with data alone; they must articulate the "because" that links them.

Table 4.1 Mapping Toulmin's Model to a Corporate Leadership Claim

Toulmin Element	*Example from Passage*	*Comment*
Claim	AI agents are a once-in-a-lifetime shift that will transform business and leadership.	Strong, bold vision
Grounds	Rapid Fortune 500 adoption; productivity and cost gains	Cited evidence, but presented selectively
Warrant	(Assumed) If a technology is adopted widely and yields measurable gains, it must be transformative	Unstated, causal connection presumed, but not examined
Backing	Industry surveys, executive testimony	Thin; specifics and counterpoints are lacking
Qualifier	"Completely," "once-in-a-lifetime"	Absent; no hedging or recognition of limits
Rebuttal	None	Ignores questions, risks, or dissent

- **Algorithmic deference** thrives on cultural fracture. Toulmin shifts group discussion from admiring confident statements to debating warrants, backing, and rebuttals. It legitimizes dissent by providing a common vocabulary.
- **Reflective complacency** thrives on identity fracture. Toulmin requires us to declare our own assumptions and scope limitations. By making qualifiers and rebuttals explicit, we reclaim authorship rather than outsourcing frames.

Our data confirms the need for these antidotes. Those who defend AI outputs without understanding the reasoning suffer warrant unmooring. The facilitator whose workshop converged too quickly around AI outputs experienced algorithmic deference.[35] The leader who admitted missing signals when immersed in AI exemplified reflexive complacency. In each case, Toulmin's six elements would have forced reasoning back into the open.

Apprenticeship of Doubt Grows in Phases

One does not become a master without an apprenticeship, and it proceeds in three phases:

1. **Beginner:** Identify claim and grounds. Even this step slows closure and exposes assumptions of relevance.
2. **Intermediate:** Add warrant and backing. This surfaces the connective *Because* and the supports behind it.
3. **Advanced:** Integrate qualifiers and rebuttals. This acknowledges limits and prepares for exceptions.

Most professionals already operate at the beginner level since they often can state claims and cite data. The real work lies in advancing toward intermediate and advanced practice, where assumptions, scope, and vulnerabilities become explicit.

In practice, this means embedding Toulmin traces into professional routines: project proposals, board submissions, client recommendations, AI-generated outputs. People that map arguments this way naturally stop debating personalities and start debating reasoning. Doubt becomes disciplined and constructive, not destructive.

Algorithmic scepticism demands only loyalty to reasoning itself. The goal is not neatness, but developing a habit. By making warrants, qualifiers, and rebuttals routine, we ensure that AI outputs are not accepted as elegant endpoints but tested as provisional claims.

Socrates never let an oracle's pronouncement close inquiry. Toulmin gives us the modern grammar to do the same. In an age of algorithmic fluency, this is our apprenticeship of doubt.

Two Examples of Corporate AI Doubt

Two short, real-world walkthroughs applying a Toulmin lens show how this looks in practice.[36]

Example 1: A company added short "why" explanations to its job-matching AI assistant, sort of mini-warrants that linked the match claim to evidence. The result: a 20% increase in started applications and a 13% increase in successful placements.

A Toulmin reading clarifies why this worked. The claim: This job is a good match for you. The grounds: Your profile shows skills X and Y; this posting requires X and Y. The warrant: When a candidate's skills align with job requirements, the job is likely suitable. The backing: Internal placement data; recruiter expertise; historical conversion rates. The qualifier: Likely or strong fit. The rebuttal: Fit may fail if location, culture, or schedule misalign.

The leverage point is obvious: by making the warrant and backing visible, the AI assistant turned a vague suggestion into a reasoned argument. Surfacing the *Because* didn't just build trust; it changed behaviour. More people applied, and more applications succeeded. Warrants are behavioural instruments.

Example 2: In another case, a service firm introduced an AI assistant for its advisors. But before deploying it widely, they subjected it to structured evaluations on tasks like summarization, translation, and advice quality. Only after the system passed these tests did they roll it out. The results: 98% of its advisors now use the assistant daily; document access jumped from 20% to 80%; and client responsiveness improved.

A Toulmin reading clarifies the governance logic. The claim: This AI assistant's output is reliable enough for client-facing work. The grounds: It performed well on carefully designed internal evaluations. The warrant: If a system meets performance thresholds on tasks that simulate real work, its outputs can be trusted with professional oversight. The backing: The evaluation design itself, with benchmarks, thresholds, red team stress tests, ongoing monitoring, and human review protocols. The qualifier: Reliable within defined guardrails. The rebuttal: May fail with new document types, domain shifts, or unexpected client contexts.

In this example, the backing is institutional, not rhetorical. The warrant doesn't rest on personal conviction but on structured tests and thresholds. This is how organizations stop the "because" from dissolving into opinion in AI outputs: they bind it to evidence generated through deliberate evaluation.

Before you argue, draw your "because" since clarity wins over confidence.

Practicing Algorithmic Scepticism

Frameworks matter, but they only protect judgment if they are practiced. Dispositions remain abstract unless expressed in behaviour. Standards risk becoming slogans if not tested against real outputs. Structures remain theoretical unless mapped onto actual arguments. What transforms these into lived capability is practice: repeated routines that keep reasoning visible even when convenience tempts us to close inquiry.

This is the work of algorithmic scepticism. It is not mistrust of machines but loyalty to reasoning itself. If Toulmin's framework gives us the architecture of doubt, these practices are how we live in that architecture daily. They operationalize the claim, grounds, warrant, backing, qualifier, and rebuttal in meetings, strategy sessions, and workshops.

Three practices stand out. Each counters a different erosion, each makes a different element of Toulmin visible, and together they form the culture of disciplined doubt. Let us speculate how these practices look like in Amazon after Jassy's email about agents becoming teammates.

Pause. A team of Amazon employees hearing Jassy's declaration might pause before moving directly to implement his vision. They would explicitly identify his core claim, AI agents will redefine professional work, and then ask, "On what grounds is this claim based?" By doing so, they avoid conflating his confidence and presentation with reasoning, instead demanding clarity of both claim and evidence before taking the next step.

Review. Suppose an Amazon manager drafts a recommendation in response to Jassy's speech. Rather than simply echoing the CEO, the manager sketches all six Toulmin elements: the clear claim, the data presented, the unstated warrant, the limited backing, the scope of the claim, and any possible rebuttals. When the backing is thin and qualifiers are omitted, gaps become visible. This transparency moves debate away from mere authority and toward substantive argument where people see what's missing or assumed, not just what's confidently claimed by the boss.

Counter. At a follow-up strategy meeting, let us assume that Amazon managers could challenge the given framing. If Jassy predicts agents will increase productivity, someone is assigned to present at least one credible alternative, say, that productivity gains will plateau because of diminishing marginal return effects, or create new complexities. By surfacing counter-frames and scenario alternatives, they can bring rebuttal and qualifier elements into routine use. This practice ensures strong assertions are not taken as the only story and that multiple perspectives shape the conversation.

Use AI as a sparring partner, not a judge, and stay loyal to your own reasoning.

Practicing What I Preach: A Toulmin Analysis of This Book

To remain valuable partners with AI systems, working professionals should *systematically* cultivate the five essential human capabilities, Curiosity, Creativity, Critical Thinking, Communication, and Collaboration, as well as the integrative meta-capability, Practical Wisdom.

The Core Argument Under Analysis

Claim: Working professionals should systematically cultivate the five essential human capabilities, Curiosity, Creativity, Critical Thinking, Communication, and Collaboration, and the integrative meta-capability of Practical Wisdom, to remain irreplaceable strategic partners with AI systems.

Grounds: The evidence supporting this claim comes from multiple converging sources. Research demonstrates that AI users exhibit measurably lower brain engagement and weakened independent thinking. Next Management findings show executives report they feel more like AI concierges rather than strategic decision-makers. Facilitator survey data about AI use before, during, and after client engagements reveal how AI affects professional confidence and embodied presence. Enterprise AI case studies document daily AI usage among advisors with mixed collaboration results. Recent reports testify how billions of people use LLMs. Interview transcripts capture professional anxiety about algorithmic decision-making displacing human judgment.

Warrant: If AI demonstrably erodes human cognitive engagement and independent reasoning, as the grounds testify to, while organizations increasingly rely on algorithmic outputs, then systematically developing uniquely human capabilities will preserve professional relevance, effectiveness, and responsibilities in hybrid human-AI environments.

Backing: This warrant rests on several foundational supports: classical wisdom traditions demonstrating these capabilities have driven human progress for millennia; empirical research on cognitive offloading effects and the neuroscience of reasoning under AI assistance; three decades of organizational research across hundreds of companies documenting capability development outcomes; successful large-scale AI integration experience demonstrating practical implementation challenges.

Qualifiers: The claim applies to:

- AI-anxious and AI-excited working professionals in organizational contexts.
- Primarily Western professional environments, acknowledging cultural specificity.
- Roles requiring strategic judgment rather than routine task execution.

- Timeframes where AI remains tool rather than autonomous agent.
- Contexts where human capabilities become more critical.

Rebuttals: The argument will require reconsideration if:

- AI develops genuine practical wisdom and contextual judgment capabilities.
- Organizational efficiency demands complete algorithmic decision-making.
- Professional roles become so automated that human capabilities prove economically irrelevant.
- Cultural shifts devalue embodied presence, creative distinctiveness, or collaborative meaning-making.

***

What does this analysis reveal? First, the warrant behind this book is strong, but also vulnerable: it assumes organizations will continue to value human reasoning and judgment, an assumption that could shift. Second, the backing is substantial but uneven, relying heavily on early-stage evidence that may need updating as AI evolves. Third, the qualifier narrows the scope more than I initially acknowledged. Fourth, the rebuttals are not remote possibilities but plausible scenarios that demand ongoing monitoring.

However, by exposing these weaknesses, Toulmin's framework does not weaken my argument; it strengthens it by clarifying conditions, assumptions, and vulnerabilities. If I expect you, the reader, to analyze AI-supported outputs systematically, I must model the same discipline.

Critical thinking makes professionals irreplaceable by evaluating what analysis means beyond algorithmic output. When AI delivers confident recommendations, humans preserve the capacity to determine whether conclusions serve purposes that transcend optimization. Algorithms deliver outputs. Professionals, leaders included, provide judgment. Yet reasoning and judgments that remains private accomplishes nothing. Critical thinking strengthens individual reasoning, but unless that reasoning becomes visible through dialogue, it cannot shape collective action. *Judgment becomes wisdom only when it learns to speak.* This is where communication enters as critical thinking's necessary expression. Disciplined analysis ensures conclusions rest on sound warrants. Communication makes those warrants available for others to understand, test, and trust. Chapter 5 examines how professionals create authentic influence through embodied presence no algorithm can replicate.

Voice your doubt, change begins with the question you dare to ask.

Self-Assessment

This assessment helps you reflect on how you practise critical thinking when working with AI. It is not a test of intelligence but of habits and the attitudes, standards, and disciplines that keep reasoning visible and interpretation alive.

For each dimension, consider your recent professional decisions (past three months), especially those involving AI support, and select the option that best describes your typical approach.

1. Dispositions of Doubt: Cultivating the Mindset of Inquiry

How consistently do you embody the attitudes that anchor critical thinking – open-mindedness, systematicity, and intellectual courage?

☐ **Always:** I question confidently, resist premature closure, and challenge both AI outputs and my own assumptions, even under pressure.
☐ **Often:** I sustain these dispositions in most situations but occasionally revert to faster patterns when time is tight.
☐ **Sometimes:** I notice when I slip into convenience reasoning and try to restore critical-thinking habits.
☐ **Rarely:** I recognize the value of doubt but find it difficult to sustain when algorithmic outputs arrive clear and certain.
☐ **Never:** I usually defer to AI conclusions, treating doubt as inefficiency rather than discipline.

Interpretation: High scores signal intellectual courage, i.e. readiness to question authority, including your own. Low scores suggest creeping deference to machine certainty; practising deliberate questioning restores autonomy of thought.

2. Reasoning Standards: Testing Quality Beyond Appearance

How effectively do you apply intellectual standards – clarity, accuracy, relevance, depth, fairness, and logic – to your reasoning and to AI outputs

☐ **Always:** I consistently apply standards across decisions and can explain which matter most in each context.
☐ **Often:** I usually test clarity, accuracy, and logic but sometimes skip deeper checks under time pressure.
☐ **Sometimes:** I know the standards but apply them inconsistently, especially when outputs appear clear.

☐ **Rarely:** I sense when something lacks rigor but lack systematic methods to evaluate it.
☐ **Never:** I accept surface fluency as substance, rarely probing beyond coherence or style.

Interpretation: Applying standards transforms judgment from impression to discipline. If you rely on polish as proof of quality, slow down – ask whether the reasoning, not the rhetoric, truly holds.

3. Argument Mapping: Making Warrants Visible

How well do you make claims, grounds, warrants, backing, qualifiers, and rebuttals explicit in your reasoning?

☐ **Always:** I habitually map arguments using Toulmin's framework and teach others to do the same.
☐ **Often:** I identify claims and warrants in most important decisions, adding qualifiers when time allows.
☐ **Sometimes:** I apply the framework selectively, especially for complex cases, but not as a daily reflex.
☐ **Rarely:** I can distinguish evidence from conclusion but struggle to articulate the reasoning that connects them.
☐ **Never:** I accept claims without tracing warrants, letting AI supply logic I never examine.

Interpretation: Visibility is the safeguard of reasoning. When you make warrants explicit, you prevent algorithmic deference; when you skip them, you outsource judgment to the machine.

4. Systematic Practice of Doubt: Turning Reflection into Routine

How consistently do you follow the three disciplined practices – Pause, Trace, Counter?

☐ **Always:** I have embedded these practices into my work and team protocols, adapting them across contexts.
☐ **Often:** I usually apply them, inserting pauses, tracing arguments, and surfacing counter-frames, though I sometimes rush.
☐ **Sometimes:** I use the practices irregularly, experimenting with ways to make them habitual.
☐ **Rarely:** I apply only fragments, moving from AI output to decision without full evaluation.
☐ **Never:** I default to algorithmic recommendations; reflection feels like unnecessary friction.

Interpretation: Routine scepticism protects clarity. Practise deliberate pauses and counters until they become instinct, so doubt is no longer hesitation but strength.

Using Your Profile

When you map yourself across these four dimensions, patterns emerge. You may sustain strong dispositions but lack systematic methods. Or perhaps you trace arguments well but fail to apply standards consistently under pressure.

What matters is not the score but the pattern – the shape of your apprenticeship of doubt. Research shows that three disciplines preserve and strengthen critical thinking in AI-rich environments:

- **Frameworks make reasoning visible** – Toulmin's architecture exposes warrants, qualifiers, and rebuttals, preventing warrant erosion and algorithmic deference.
- **Systematic practices counter convenience** – the *Pause, Trace, Counter* routine turns reflection into muscle memory.
- **Dialogic accountability sustains courage** – explaining your reasoning aloud and inviting challenge keeps doubt alive even when AI discourages it.

Your profile is not a verdict on ability but a map of development. It highlights where deliberate practice can move you from Croesus's error of trusting oracular certainty toward Socratic wisdom, treating every answer as the start of inquiry.

Notes

1 Herodotus (2007).
2 Nguyen & Welch (2025).
3 TNM research data (2025).
4 Gerlich (2025).
5 Nowotny (2021).
6 TNM research data (2025).
7 LSP Survey Data (2025).
8 Author interview (January 2026).
9 Thorndike (1920); Nisbett & Wilson, (1977).
10 Dwyer et al. (2014); Bailin et al. (1999).
11 Moore (2013); D'Northwood & Rattray (2024).
12 Petress (2004); Paul & Elder (2021).
13 Mulnix (2012).
14 Falcione (2010); Ennis (2011); Dwyer et al. (2014).
15 Kuhn (2019); Verma et al. (2022).
16 LSP research data (2025).
17 Roos (2025).
18 Muller (2018).

19 Gerlich (2025).
20 Chatterji et al. (2025).
21 Nguyen & Welch (2025); Gerlich (2025).
22 Goh et al. (2024); Wang (2025).
23 OECD (2023).
24 OpenAI Research (2024).
25 Kolbjørnsrud (2024).
26 TNM research data (2025).
27 Means (2025).
28 TNM research data (2025).
29 Ennis (2011).
30 Paul & Elder (2021).
31 Toulmin (1958).
32 von Krogh & Roos (1996).
33 Particularly the classical deductive reasoning that is built on a major premise, a minor premise, and a conclusion (syllogism), and reasoning where the pemise is implied rather than explicitly stated so that the audience will fill in the missing information (enthymeme). See Aristotle (1984).
34 Aquinas' approach in the seminal *Summa Theologiae* states objections, presents a principle, and apply it to a case, anticipates Toulmin's use of warrants, backing, and rebuttal. Aquinas was carefully balancing between science and faith, arguing that faith without reasoning was blindness, and that reason was faith was arrogance.
35 Roberts & Candi (2024).
36 Both examples extracted from OpenAI (2024).

References

Aquinas, T. (1265–1274/1947). *Summa Theologica* (Fathers of the English Dominican Province, Trans.). Benziger Bros.

Aristotle. (1984). *The Organon*. In J. Barnes (Ed.), *The complete works of Aristotle: The revised Oxford translation* (Vols. 1–2). Princeton University Press. (Original works published ca. 350 BCE.)

Bailin, S., Case, R., Coombs, J. R., & Daniels, L. B. (1999). Conceptualizing critical thinking. *Journal of Curriculum Studies, 31*(3), 285–302. https://doi.org/10.1080/002202799183133

Chatterji, A., Cunningham, T., Deming, D. J., Hitzig, Z., Ong, C., Shan, C. Y., & Wadman, K. (2025). How people use ChatGPT (NBER Working Paper No. 34255). National Bureau of Economic Research. https://www.nber.org/papers/w34255

Ciatto, G., Agiollo, A., Magnini, M., & Omicini, A. (2025). Large language models as oracles for instantiating ontologies with domain-specific knowledge. *Knowledge-Based Systems, 298*, 110935. https://doi.org/10.1016/j.knosys.2024.110935

ComplyAdvantage. (2024, November 25). *Enhancing AML efforts with explainable AI*. https://complyadvantage.com/insights/enhancing-aml-using-explainable-ai/

DigGrowth. (2025, August 6). *Transforming business analytics with AI-driven reporting and dashboards*. https://diggrowth.com/blogs/analytics/ai-driven-reporting-and-dashboards/

D'Northwood, G., & Rattray, J. (2024, online first). What is this thing called critical thinking? Perspectives from business school academics. *Innovations in Education and Teaching International*. https://doi.org/10.1080/14703297.2024.2422310

Drucker Forum Transcripts. (2025). *Executive leadership discussions on AI integration and strategic decision-making*. Global Peter Drucker Forum.

Dwyer, C. P., Hogan, M. J., & Stewart, I. (2014). An integrated critical thinking framework for the 21st century. *Thinking Skills and Creativity, 12*, 43–52. https://doi.org/10.1016/j.tsc.2013.12.004

Ennis, R. H. (2011). *The nature of critical thinking: An outline of critical thinking dispositions and abilities*. University of Illinois. https://education.illinois.edu/docs/default-source/faculty-documents/robert-ennis/thenatureofcriticalthinking_51711_000.pdf

Facione, P. A. (2000). The disposition toward critical thinking: Its character, measurement, and relationship to critical thinking skill. *Informal Logic, 20*(1), 61–84. https://informallogic.ca/index.php/informal_logic/article/view/2254/1698

Gerlich, M. (2025). *AI tools in society: Impacts on cognitive offloading and the future of critical thinking. Societies, 15*(1), 6.

Goh, E., Gallo, R., Hom, J., et al. (2024). Large language model influence on diagnostic reasoning: A randomized clinical trial. *JAMA Network Open, 7*(10), e2440969. https://doi.org/10.1001/jamanetworkopen.2024.40969

GSC Online Press. (2025). *The role of AI in preventing financial fraud and enhancing compliance*. https://gsconlinepress.com/journals/gscarr/sites/default/files/GSCARR-2025-0086.pdf

Haefner, N., Wincent, J., Parida, V., & Gassmann, O. (2021). Artificial intelligence and innovation management: A review, framework, and research agenda. *Technological Forecasting and Social Change, 162*, Article 120392. https://doi.org/10.1016/j.techfore.2020.120392

Hello Operator. (2024, December 31). *How AI dashboards simplify engagement analysis*. https://www.hellooperator.ai/blog/how-ai-dashboards-simplify-engagement-analysis

Herodotus. (2008). *The histories* (R. Waterfield, Trans.; C. Dewald, Ed.). Oxford University Press. (Original work published ca. 440 BCE). https://global.oup.com/academic/product/the-histories-9780199535668

Huang, L., & Liaw, M. L. (2011). The application of critical thinking in teaching English reading. *Theory and Practice in Language Studies, 1*(2), 158–164. https://www.academypublication.com/issues/past/tpls/vol01/02/03.pdf

Ji, Z., Lee, N., Frieske, R., Yu, T., Su, D., Xu, Y., . . . & Wang, W. Y. (2023). Survey of hallucination in natural language generation. *ACM Computing Surveys, 55*(12), 1–38. https://doi.org/10.1145/3571730

Kolbjørnsrud, V. (2024). Designing the intelligent organization: Six principles for human–AI collaboration. *California Management Review, 66*(2), 44–64. https://doi.org/10.1177/00081256231185032

Kuhn, D. (2019). Critical thinking as discourse. *Human Development, 62*(3), 146–164. https://doi.org/10.1159/000500171

Means, T. (2025, May 23). The AI microscope: How AI can enhance critical thinking and creativity in education. LinkedIn. https://www.linkedin.com/pulse/ai-microscope-how-can-enhance-critical-thinking-creativity-means

Moore, T. (2013). Critical thinking: Seven definitions in search of a concept. *Studies in Higher Education, 38*(4), 506–522. https://doi.org/10.1080/03075079.2011.586995

Muller, J. Z. (2018). *The tyranny of metrics*. Princeton University Press.

Mulnix, J. W. (2012). Thinking critically about critical thinking. *Educational Philosophy and Theory, 44*(5), 464–479.

Nguyen, A., & Welch, K. (2025). Generative AI and the erosion of interpretive authority in qualitative data analysis. *Qualitative Inquiry, 31*(7), 873–889. https://doi.org/10.1177/10778004251 34567

Nisbett, R. E., & Wilson, T. D. (1977). The halo effect: Evidence for unconscious alteration of judgments. *Journal of Personality and Social Psychology, 35*(4), 250–256.

Nofal, H. A., Mohamed, A. E., Almadani, N., Mahfouz, R., Bahri, H. A., Ali, H. T., & Elrafey, D. S. (2025). The impact of an artificial intelligence enhancement program on healthcare providers' knowledge, attitudes, and workplace flourishing. *Frontiers in Public Health, 13*, 1639333. https://www.frontiersin.org/journals/public-health/articles/10.3389/fpubh.2025.1639333/full

Nowotny, H. (2021). *In AI we trust: Power, illusion and control of predictive algorithms*. Polity Press.

OECD. (2023). *AI language models*. Organisation for Economic Co-operation and Development. https://www.oecd.org/en/publications/ai-language-models_13d38f92-en.html

OpenAI. (2024). *Enterprise AI deployment and adoption patterns*. OpenAI.

Paul, R., & Elder, L. (2021). *Critical thinking: Tools for taking charge of your learning and your life* (4th ed.). Rowman & Littlefield.

Petress, K. (2004). Critical thinking: An extended definition. *Education, 124*(3), 461–466.

Roberts, N., & Candi, M. (2024). AI-driven innovation: How artificial intelligence shapes organizational creativity. *Journal of Business Research, 158*, 113670.

Roos, J. (2025, June 11). Expire or evolve? Rethinking how we frame our future. *AACSB Insights*. https://www.aacsb.edu/insights/articles/2025/06/expire-or-evolve-rethinking-how-we-frame-our-future.

The Stoiverse. (2025, August 10). *Why critical thinking is disappearing: The rise of collective stupidity* [Video]. YouTube. https://www.youtube.com/watch?v=5NDotKQUqvc

Thorndike, E. L. (1920). A constant error in psychological ratings. *Journal of Applied Psychology, 4*(1), 25–29.

Toulmin, S. (1958). *The uses of argument*. Cambridge University Press.

Verma, A., Thompson, L., & Li, J. (2022). Dialogic critical thinking in organizations: Evidence from collaborative teams. *Journal of Organizational Behavior, 43*(5), 731–748. https://doi.org/10.1002/job.2639.

von Krogh, G., & Roos, J. (1996). Arguments on knowledge and competence. In G. von Krogh & J. Roos (Eds.), *Managing knowledge: Perspectives on cooperation and competition* (pp. 97–119). Sage Publications.

Wang, L. W. (2025). Impact of generative artificial intelligence on the professional qualities curriculum and reflection essays during physician training. *Internal Medicine Journal, 55*(5), 739–742. https://pmc.ncbi.nlm.nih.gov/articles/PMC12240007/

5 Communication – From Data Dashboards to Hybrid Authority

The Senate's Silence

On the morning of November 8, 63 BCE, Marcus Tullius Cicero rose to address the Roman Senate with words that would echo through millennia. Before him sat Lucius Sergius Catilina, the conspirator whose plot to overthrow the Republic had been uncovered. The tension in the chamber was palpable. The fate of Rome itself hung in the balance.

Cicero began not with a scroll of prepared remarks, but with presence. He positioned himself deliberately in the Senate chamber, using spatial dynamics to establish authority before uttering a single word. His gaze swept the assembled senators, reading their expressions and gauging the room's energy, before fixing directly on Catalina, known in English as Catiline. The physical confrontation was unmistakable. When he finally spoke, his opening words – *Quo usque tandem abutere, Catilina, patientia nostra?* (How long, O Catiline, will you abuse our patience?) – were delivered with an intensity that transformed the Senate floor into a theatre of moral judgment.

What followed was not merely a speech, but an embodied performance of rhetorical authority. Cicero employed strategic movements across the floor, not pacing randomly but positioning himself to maximize visual dominance. His calculated pauses allowed accusations to resonate while he observed their effect on individual senators. His gestures followed the prescribed Roman vocabulary of embodied communication, including hand movements signalling aversion, grief, wonder, and righteous anger in choreographed sequence. His direct eye contact with specific senators was not general audience engagement but targeted visual pressure, building alliances and isolating opponents in real time.[1]

The words were powerful, but it was Cicero's embodied delivery that moved the Senate to action. He utilized what we now recognize as gestural synchrony, the coordination of movement and attention that forms the neurological foundation of trust and collective purpose. The senators' bodies swayed subtly in response to his stance. Their breathing patterns aligned with his vocal rhythms. Brain-to-brain

DOI: 10.4324/9781003732570-5

coupling transformed intellectual argument into visceral conviction. Recognizing his fate, Catiline fled Rome that very night.

Two millennia later, contemporary neuroscience substantiates what the ancients intuited. Research demonstrates that effective communication in dynamic environments depends on what Romans called *eloquentia corporis* (the eloquence of the body), where perception, decision, and action are inseparable. Professionals, leaders included, must continuously act and decide while acting, reading emergent cues and adapting in real time.[2] This mirrors Cicero's rhetorical genius. He engaged the Senate not with words alone, but by sensing and responding to the shifting mood of his audience moment by moment, employing his body as much as his intellect to shape meaning and influence.

Research on embodied communication reinforces this understanding. Authentic human interaction occurs through parallel and highly interactive couplings between communication partners. People synchronize their body sway, mimic each other's posture, and unconsciously align gestures, facial expressions, and rhythms of speech. This synchrony provides the foundation for trust, persuasion, and collective action.[3] Cicero anticipated in practice what science now confirms: meaning making is irreducibly embodied.

Yet here lies our contemporary predicament. Twenty centuries after Cicero moved the Senate through presence, we live in an era where AI can generate sophisticated text, craft compelling arguments, and even mimic conversational rhythm. AI has solved the problem of producing words. But it has inherited a fundamental limitation: it cannot participate in the embodied synchrony of voice and movement that research identifies as essential for authentic human communication.

The Vanderbilt Moment

In February 2023, following a tragic shooting that killed three students at Michigan State University, administrators at Vanderbilt University's Peabody College sought to express support to their sister community. Instead of composing a personal message of condolence, they turned to ChatGPT to generate what they hoped would be an appropriate statement. On February 16, the Office for Equity, Diversity and Inclusion distributed the AI-drafted email to their own students and staff.

The message was grammatically correct, structurally sound, and contained all the conventional elements of crisis communication. It expressed sympathy for the victims, acknowledged the community's pain, and emphasized inclusivity and togetherness. By computational standards, it was flawless. But then the email cited a note at the bottom: "*Paraphrase from OpenAI's ChatGPT AI language model, personal communication.*"

By human standards, the message was devastating. When Vanderbilt students discovered that their leaders had delegated a vulnerable moment to an algorithm, the response was immediate and visceral. Student publications described the message as "disgusting" and "automated hypocrisy." The university was forced to apologize not for the content of the message, but for the process of its creation. Administrators apologized the next day, acknowledged poor judgment, and stepped back during a formal review.[4]

The problem was not the words themselves, but the absence of embodied presence. These administrators failed to signal genuine emotional presence at a moment of shared grief. Audiences expect communication that emerges from lived experience, not statistical prediction of the next token. When we outsource their voice to algorithms, we risk what the ancient Romans would have recognized as the collapse of *auctoritas* itself. What Vanderbilt violated was not a rule of rhetoric, it was a threshold of humanness.

AI can write your words, but only you can make them matter.

The Science of Communication

For most of human history, communication research treated message transmission as if bodies were incidental containers for words. The engineering model dominated: a sender encodes information, transmits it through a channel, and a receiver decodes it. This framework, borrowed from telecommunications, presumed that meaning resided in the message itself, independent of how it was delivered or who delivered it. The body, in this model, was noise to be filtered out.

If communication is simply information transfer, then the challenge becomes optimizing the signal, minimizing static, and ensuring accurate reception. Bodies become inconvenient biological equipment through which pure information must flow. This view explains why early email champions celebrated the elimination of physical presence as liberation from bias, why virtual meetings were assumed equivalent to face-to-face gatherings, and why organizations embraced remote coordination as frictionless efficiency.

Communication research reveal how fundamentally wrong this assumption was . . . and still is. Studies confirm that embodied presence enables dynamic adaptation, physical affordances, and synchrony systems that no machine can reproduce.[5] *Communication is not information transfer through passive vessels. It is the embodied creation of shared meaning through synchronized movement, mirrored gestures, and aligned rhythms.*

Science helps explain why.

Four Factors of Communication

The boundaries between where human and machine communication begins and ends are critical. Communication scholars call it the "authenticity threshold" of human-machine communication. When people interact with communicative technologies, they distinguish between human and computer communication on four factors: origin of being, degree of autonomy, emotional capability, and authenticity of response.[6] In routine exchanges, these boundaries may blur without consequence. But in moments that matter, like crisis, grief, conflict, celebration, we enforce these boundaries with instinctive intensity.

An algorithm, regardless of its eloquence, cannot grieve. It has no being from which authentic sympathy might emerge, regardless of kinds words. It possesses no emotional capability to genuinely feel loss. Its responses, however well-crafted, lack the authenticity that can only arise from lived experience. When leaders delegate crisis communication to AI, they violate the expectation that in moments of shared vulnerability, communication must originate from a human being who can authentically share in that vulnerability.

This is where the contemporary challenge comes into sharp focus. Research on communication impact reveals that most influence comes from embodied elements rather than verbal content. While precise percentages vary by context, studies rooted in theatrical training adapted for business contexts demonstrate a clear conclusion: body language and physical presence carry most of the communicative weight, with vocal dynamics contributing significantly, and verbal content playing a smaller role than commonly assumed. How we stand, how we move, how we modulate our voice, and how we make eye contact shape how our respective audiences trust us, believe us, and follow us. This is why leadership communication programs systematically develop physical embodiment, vocal presence, and cognitive architecture as distinct competencies.[7]

The implication is striking. If most communication impact resides in embodied presence, then AI's greatest strength – language generation – addresses only the smallest slice of the communicative challenge. A beautifully crafted algorithmic message delivered without embodied presence is like a musical score without its performance. The notes may be perfectly written, but the music is absent. Conversely, a message prepared with AI assistance but delivered with authentic embodied presence

Communication is not information transfer – it is embodied meaning-making that no algorithm can replicate.

can combine cognitive clarity with emotional resonance, leveraging the best of both human and machine capabilities.

This creates both danger and opportunity. The danger is that we mistake eloquence for effectiveness, outsourcing communication to AI and wondering why our influence erodes. The opportunity is that those who understand the science of embodied communication can use AI strategically to strengthen the structure and clarity of their messages while preserving their unique capacity for credibility and emotional resonance through embodied presence.

The foundation is now clear. *Communication is embodied meaning-making and eloquentia corporis still matters.* Modern science validates what classical rhetoric and cross-cultural understanding have long taught: authentic influence requires physical presence that no algorithm can simulate, today. The question becomes how this understanding dissolves in practice, and how leaders can resist that erosion.

Text Box 5.1: The Science of Mirroring

Our brains contain mirror neurons that fire when we observe authentic human gestures, creating the neurological foundation for trust. The discovery of mirror neuron systems provides the neurological foundation for understanding why bodies matter profoundly in communication. These neural networks fire not only when we perform actions ourselves but also when we observe others performing them. When you watch someone gesture emphatically, lean forward with interest, or recoil in surprise, specific neurons in your brain activate as if you were performing those actions yourself. Communication becomes possible because our brains are designed to resonate with the embodied actions of others.[8]

Research demonstrates that people communicating face-to-face engage in parallel and highly interactive couplings that range from low-level motor systems to higher-level cultural symbol interpretation. The traditional signal transmission model cannot account for what really happens when humans create meaning together. Based on what is currently known about how our speech and gesture influence each other, computational models to mimic this have a long way to go.[9]

This resonance extends beyond individual gestures to encompass whole-body synchrony. Research shows that during live interactions, people unconsciously coordinate their movements in ways that strengthen connection and facilitate understanding. Body sway synchronization occurs when conversation partners subtly mirror each other's postural adjustments. Gestural alignment emerges as people unconsciously adopt similar hand movements and facial expressions. Even breathing patterns and speech rhythms synchronize during engaged dialogue. These systems of synchrony reduce cognitive load, facilitate information flow, and enhance mutual understanding by creating brain-to-brain coupling between speakers and listeners.[10]

The implications of this extend beyond passive reception to active decision-making in communication. Most of us must work in situations where perception, decision, and action are inseparable. We must decide while acting, reading emergent cues and adapting in real time.[11] Like many others, I have learnt through decades of practice to notice a furrowed brow mid-presentation and make a split-second adjustment, slowing pace, adding an example, changing position, initiating short discussions among pairs, inviting questions. Most of these micro-adaptations happen too quickly for conscious deliberation. They emerge from embodied judgment honed through thousands of hours of physical presence with audiences.

Communication science transforms how we must think about professional communication in the age of AI. LLMs can generate flawless text, images, and videos. It can structure arguments with perfect logic. It can even analyze sentiment and suggest rhetorical strategies. But it cannot participate in embodied synchrony or experience the sense of collective virtuosity and beauty that emerges, as it does in orchestras when the musicians simultaneously become performer and audience.[12] AI tools have no mirror neurons to activate in observers or participants. They have no body to sway, no gestures to align, no physical presence to create resonance: no *eloquentia corporis*. The very mechanisms that science identifies as foundational for authentic communication remain categorically beyond algorithmic reach.

Eroding Embodied Communication

When leaders delegate communication to AI, they do not simply save time or gain efficiency. They trigger a systematic erosion of the very capabilities that make influence possible. This decline follows a familiar loop: reduced presence weakens authenticity, which increases reliance on AI, which further erodes presence. What feels like progress is, in fact, a feedback spiral of disembodiment.

Figure 5.1 visualizes this downward pattern – from presence to disconnection. Each step represents a weakening of embodied influence: as physical presence fades, affordances disappear, and synchrony breaks, communication becomes technically efficient but humanly hollow.

Understanding this decline matters because it makes the invisible visible. What feels like increased efficiency is, in fact, a feedback system

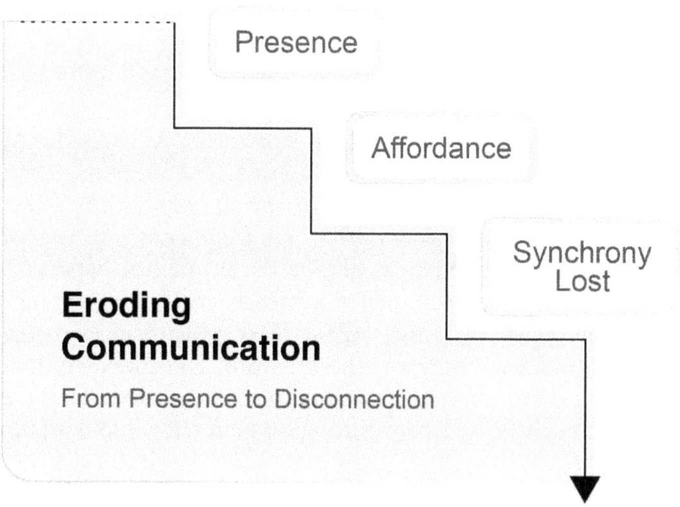

Figure 5.1 Eroding Communication – From Presence to Disconnection

that steadily weakens embodied authority. Recognizing the pattern is the first step toward reversing it.

1st Mechanism: Losing Embodied Decision-Making

Leadership communication has always been more than words. It is a living act of reasoned judgment, expressed not only through what is said but how it is said, when it is said, and to whom it is delivered. Research confirms what Cicero and every seasoned leader have learnt: communication is an embodied decision. In dynamic environments, perception, decision, and action are inseparable. Professionals must act while deciding and decide while acting, reading emergent cues and adapting in real time. Our body is not a vessel carrying the message. It is part of the message itself.

In the 1960s, Marshall McLuhan observed that "the medium is the message," meaning that the form of communication, at that time print versus television, shapes experience as much as content does.[13] In the era of AI-mediated leadership, the shift from living, embodied acts to algorithmic messages signals not simply a new channel, but a new reality. When generative AI assumes the task of communication, we risk amputating more than our words; we sacrifice the embodied dynamics that carry meaning and presence: our tone, pace, spontaneity, and responsiveness.

When we hand this function to algorithms, we reduce part of our communicative capacity. The AI-generated memo, however correct, cannot sense the pause that should be held a heartbeat longer, the audience silence that signals disapproval, or the rising energy in a room that calls for urgency rather than caution. Communication becomes frozen text rather than a living act.

Our research on professional facilitators using AI tools during live workshops reveals this erosion in stark terms. One facilitator described the experience precisely: "*I had split attention between the room, and the interactions with the AI tool.*"[14] This fragmentation of attention proved consequential. When cognitive focus divides between algorithmic consultation and audience presence, leaders might miss out on important group dynamics. What these practitioners recognized is what neuroscience confirms: the attention consumed by machine interaction weakens the leader's ability to scan the room, adapt in real time, and sense the subtle cues through which trust and commitment are negotiated.

The cost shows up in what gets lost. Effective facilitation requires observing the room and adapting with experience and knowledge. This real-time observation and adaptation depend on undivided attention. When our gaze drops to a screen to consult AI suggestions, we break the embodied connection with our audience. Mirror neurons that would fire in response to sustained eye contact remain dormant. Gestural synchrony that would emerge from mutual attention fails to develop. The micro-adjustments that skilled communicators make in response to subtle audience feedback, such as a furrowed brow, a slight lean forward, a collective exhale, go unnoticed.

Multiple facilitators in our research emphasized that they needed to be present all the time, managing dynamics, listening, and keeping people on track. This continuous presence and undivided attention cannot be divided. You are either fully attending to the humans in the room, or you are not. The algorithmic support, however sophisticated, could not match the value of embodied attention in real-time.

This fragmentation of attention has consequences beyond any single moment. Over time, professionals who habitually consult AI during communication begin to lose confidence in their own embodied judgment. They start to trust the algorithm's suggestions more than their own reading of the room. The very instincts that once made them effective communicators atrophy from disuse. What is an excellent tool for preparation and follow-up becomes a crutch for delivery, and eventually a replacement for embodied presence itself.

When you're reading the AI's script, you're not reading the room.

2nd Mechanism: Eliminating Physical Affordances

Communication is enacted through physical affordances: the way we enter a room, how we position ourselves in space, the gestures that emphasize key points, the vocal dynamics that signal conviction or uncertainty. Cicero's confrontation of Catiline succeeded not only through words but through the embodied performance of those words. His physical stance, his sustained gaze and controlled vocal intensity created the rhetorical force no written text could generate.

AI-generated messages eliminate these affordances entirely. Recent empirical research reveals a fundamental flaw: even when AI-generated text is grammatically perfect and logically sound, recipients perceive it as significantly less authentic than human-authored communication. Even despite anthropomorphic cues, in controlled experiments, authenticity ratings dropped precipitously when messages were revealed as AI-authored, while messages known to come from human senders increased in perceived authenticity.[15]

While people can detect AI-generated text at only slightly better than chance levels, they unconsciously respond differently to AI generated communication. Messages feel, in the precise language one study used, "technically adequate but hollow or insufficient." The words may be appropriate, the structure sound, the tone calibrated. Yet something essential is missing. The consequence is reduced authenticity and even moral disgust.[16]

That missing element is, unsurprisingly, embodied authorship. When we delegate communication to AI, we surrender our gestural emphasis, embodied timing, and vocal dynamics, i.e., what makes our passion and conviction becomes visible. Research confirms that AI cannot reproduce the influence of embodied, real-time human communication: vocal modulation that signals emotional states, spontaneous adaptation to audience response, and the physical synchrony that builds trust.[17] The Vanderbilt managers discovered this when their ChatGPT-generated condolence message felt complete but hollow, technically correct but humanly insufficient. So far, LLMs struggle to match human stylistic variation.

What makes this erosion particularly insidious is that it undermines perceived sincerity and moral presence even when recipients cannot articulate exactly what feels wrong. Human authorship, especially when relational closeness exists, elevates sincerity, trust, and affective resonance. To date, these are qualities that algorithmic generation categorically cannot provide.[18]

The physical building process that participants undertake in LSP workshops reveals what AI communication lacks. Participants typically say that the physical construction revealed more than they were thinking to put in it. The hands-on engagement serves as a diagnostic and developmental tool when it surfaces insights expressed as colour, size, shape that purely verbal or written communication would have missed. AI can generate text describing insights, but it cannot enact the embodied discovery through which those insights become personally meaningful.

3rd Mechanism: Disrupting Synchrony Systems

The most critical erosion mechanism lies in the disruption of synchrony systems. Research reveals that authentic communication is dynamic coordination of bodies and minds. People unconsciously synchronize their gestures, postures, and even micro-movements during live interaction. This gestural synchrony and body sway synchronization forms the neurological foundation of trust and collaboration.[19]

These synchrony systems activate neural pathways associated with empathy, shared attention, and cooperative behaviour. They explain why we feel rapport when conversation flows smoothly, why trust deepens when eye contact is held, and why teams align when their movements unconsciously mirror each other. The coordination happens below conscious awareness but generates conscious effects: we emerge from synchronous interactions feeling understood, connected, and aligned.

AI-generated communication, however sophisticated, cannot participate in this dance. It has no body to sway, no rhythm to align, no presence to synchronize. The result is disembodied communication that may achieve compliance but cannot generate the trust, empathy, and shared energy that sustain collaboration.

Our workshop research provides striking evidence of this disruption. Practitioners recognized that AI sometimes lacks the emotional intelligence needed to fully engage participants or adapt to subtle shifts in group energy. This limitation matters because effective communication depends on sensing and responding to these subtle shifts. The success was more related to the facilitator and engagement from participants than the AI, multiple workshop evaluations confirmed.[20]

What emerged from the research was a clear pattern: effective integration requires what practitioners called a delicate balance between leveraging technology and maintaining the essential human touch. This balance proves difficult to maintain during live communication. However, facilitators reported that confidence grows not from algorithmic support but from engaging authentically with the group in real time. Authentic engagement requires undivided presence. Synchrony fractures when attention divides.

Workshop participants confirmed this disruption from their perspective. When AI use remained invisible, the process flowed smoothly. But participants noted that visible AI consultation would disturb the flow of the workshop. The consensus pointed to a clear principle: effective communication requires invisible integration. When facilitators used AI in a discreet way, such as preparation support that remained backstage, synchrony could develop. When AI became visible or demanded significant attention during live moments, synchrony fractured.

The Loop Closes Off Trust and Influence

These three mechanisms reinforce each other in a circular pattern. Those who lose touch with embodied presence become less confident in their own judgment, which increases their reliance on AI-generated content. This increased reliance further reduces opportunities to practice embodied communication, which weakens the very skills needed for impactful physical presence. As physical affordances erode, leaders lose the ability to create embodied synchrony with the people they talk with. Without synchrony, they cannot build the deep trust needed for real influence. The loss of influence drives them back to AI for ever-more-sophisticated textual solutions, completing the loop.

The pattern mirrors what we saw in earlier chapters with curiosity, creativity, and critical thinking. Just as AI answers can short-circuit inquiry and AI suggestions can undermine creative agency, AI communication can short-circuit embodied presence. We feel efficient producing more messages faster, reaching wider audiences, maintaining consistent tone, but the quality of connection erodes. What was gained in productivity is lost in authentic influence.

This erosion is particularly stealthy because it remains invisible in conventional metrics. Email response rates, message clarity, and distribution reach may all improve while authentic influence quietly dissolves. Teams may comply with directives while losing commitment to shared purpose. The organization runs smoothly on paper while the bonds of trust that make it resilient in crisis slowly weaken.

Efficiency in message production does not equal effectiveness in meaning creation.

The Disembodied Leadership Loop represents the communication equivalent of cognitive offloading[21] in earlier capabilities. When we outsource thinking to algorithms, we erode our capacity to *think independently*. When we outsource communication to algorithms, we erode our capacity to *connect with our fellow humans*. The tool designed to amplify becomes the force that diminishes.

Yet this erosion is not inevitable. The same technologies that threaten embodied connection can, when positioned wisely, become powerful amplifiers of authentic human communication. The question is not whether AI will shape our communication, but whether we will learn to integrate AI without surrendering our embodied authority

Hybrid Authority: The Amplification Path

The challenge lies in distinguishing what machines do well and what only humans can provide. This requires a framework for hybrid communication intelligence.

Ironically, the clearest framework remains Aristotle's map of the domains of influence. He understood that persuasion operates through three distinct modes: logos, the appeal to logic; ethos, the appeal to credibility; and pathos, the appeal to emotion. These are not mere rhetorical categories; they map onto the fundamental architecture of human communication and reveal where AI can contribute and where it categorically cannot.

- **Logos** represents argument structure, evidence gathering, and logical scaffolding, what we also discussed in Chapter 3. This is computational territory. Algorithms excel at organizing information, identifying patterns in data, surfacing claims, grounds, and counterarguments, and stress-testing logical consistency. AI tools can rapidly help us do all that, faster and better. The machine handles synthesis and structure with efficiency humans cannot match.

Yet logos alone rarely changes minds. We know that when people assess communication effectiveness, they respond overwhelmingly to presence, not propositions. The most rigorous argument delivered without embodied authority fails where weaker reasoning delivered with authentic presence succeeds. Great arguments only become actions when it learns to speak.

- **Ethos** emerges from earned credibility, which cannot be generated by AI. When a leader stands before a team and accepts accountability for a failure, ethos builds through vulnerability made visible. When a facilitator navigates conflict with calm authority, ethos strengthens through composure under pressure. These moments require physical presence, sustained eye contact, vocal steadiness, and gestural congruence. No algorithmic output, however eloquent, creates this dimension of influence. On the contrary, it can do real damage.
- **Pathos** depends on emotional resonance created through shared presence. When Cicero faced Catiline, his words mattered, but his physical embodiment carried the charge. The pause before speaking. The controlled anger in his voice. The direct gaze that held Catiline accountable before the Senate. These embodied elements created

emotional impact no written text could generate. Gesture provides perceptual-motor information that shapes how listeners understand and respond to messages. Prosody, the musical quality of speech, signals emotional states that words alone cannot convey. These dimensions of communication operate through embodied presence, not algorithmic generation.

The three modes map cleanly onto both AI and human domains. *Logos is where AI amplifies.* Use algorithms intensively for preparation: research stakeholder positions, model objections, refine structure, build confidence through thorough exploration. *Ethos and pathos are where humans remain vital.* Trust, credibility, and emotional connection emerge only through sustained physical presence.

Once more, this creates a clear division of labour. AI handles the cognitive architecture that supports communication. Humans provide the embodied performance that creates influence. The error lies in conflating domains, in believing that algorithmic eloquence can replace the eloquence of human presence, or that preparation alone ensures impact.

The complementary pattern to the Disembodied Leadership Loop is its antidote: *the Amplification Path.* Figure 5.2 illustrates how embodied authority emerges when humans and AI share clear domains of work. The framework maps Aristotle's modes of persuasion onto modern hybrid communication, showing where technology enhances and where humanity must lead.

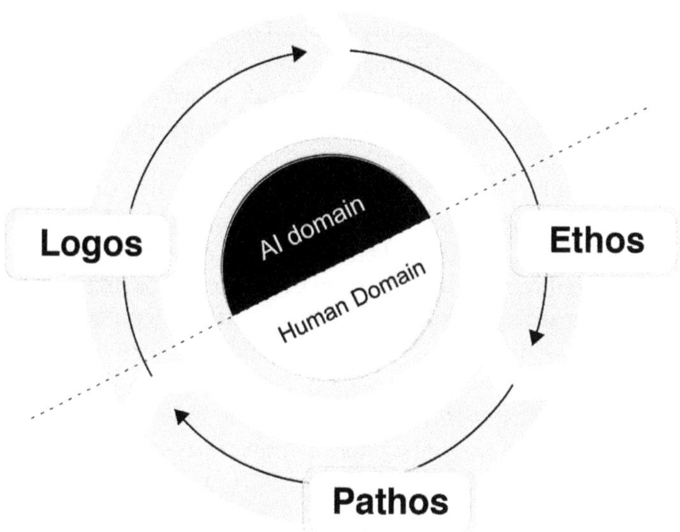

Figure 5.2 Hybrid Authority – AI and Human Domain

The Amplification Path demonstrates how authority regains authenticity when AI and humans work in concert. AI supports *logos*, the logical and structural core of communication, while humans embody *ethos* and *pathos* through credibility, presence, and emotion. Together, they form hybrid authority, in which influence arises from complementarity rather than substitution.

This framework restores balance. When we let machines handle *logos* and reserve *ethos* and *pathos* for embodied expression, communication regains integrity. The outcome is not disembodied leadership but hybrid intelligence, efficient in architecture, authentic in presence, and capable of genuine influence.

AI builds the argument. Only you can make it resonate.

The Theatrical Disciplines to Develop Presence

Understanding that ethos and pathos depend on embodied presence raises a practical question: What specific elements create communicative authority?

Theatre arts provide the answer, through learnable skills that can enhance influence. Institutions like the renowned Royal Academy of Dramatic Art and the National Institute of Dramatic Arts regularly train business leaders in communication competencies through theatrical techniques. These are not esoteric performance skills but learnable disciplines that enhance everyday communication.

Theatrical skills are neither magical nor mysterious. "All the world's a stage," as Shakespeare famously noted. Theatrical-like training offers highly studied processes for making and sharing meaning through embodied practice.[22] The techniques break down into six elements, each of which can be developed through deliberate practice:

- **Space** determines how physical positioning creates or undermines authority. Standing while others sit. Moving toward the audience during emphasis. Creating distance during reflection. These spatial choices signal relationship and power before words arrive. Speakers who remain seated behind desks during difficult conversations surrender spatial authority. Those who stand with teams during crisis claim shared presence.
- **Voice** carries vast communicative weight independent of verbal content. Research on voice pitch demonstrates that vocal qualities influence perceived leadership capacity regardless of message substance.[23] Lower-pitched voices are perceived as more authoritative and physically stronger. But pitch is only one dimension. Pace signals confidence or uncertainty. Volume commands attention or

invites intimacy. Tone conveys emotion that words alone cannot express. Skilled communicators modulate all these dimensions intuitively, adjusting to context and audience response.

- **Body** provides the visible architecture of presence. Postural alignment signals confidence or defensiveness. Gestural emphasis reinforces key points. Facial expression reveals or conceals emotion. Eye contact establishes connection or creates distance. Studies of embodied communication show that listeners are sensitive to subtle differences in action dynamics, using bodily cues to interpret meaning beyond words.[24] When a speaker's gestures align with verbal content, credibility strengthens. When they conflict, audiences trust the body over the words.
- **Structure** organizes content for maximum impact. This is where preparation meets performance. Theatre teaches that effective communication requires narrative arc, strategic pacing, and clear transitions between ideas. AI can help build this architecture during preparation. But delivery requires human sensitivity about when to pause, when to accelerate, when to circle back to reinforce a point.
- **Awareness** means reading room energy in real time and adjusting accordingly. This is the discipline that AI consultation during live communication most severely disrupts. When leaders check devices mid-conversation, awareness fractures. An experienced facilitator captured this precisely: "*It takes you out of the moment.*"[25] Another noted that tuning out of the dynamics around you is not good practice, recommending AI use only during scheduled breaks. Room awareness requires undivided attention. The moment one's focus shifts to a screen, presence dissolves.
- **Spontaneity** distinguishes performance from recitation. Prepared content provides foundation, but impact emerges through real-time adaptation. When an audience member asks an unexpected question, or when energy shifts mid-presentation, spontaneous response maintains connection. People who rigidly follow scripts regardless of audience response demonstrate competence without authority. Those who adapt fluidly to emerging needs demonstrate both.[26]

These six elements operate in concert. Effective communication requires using them in our authentic, coherent daily life performance. Research demonstrates that such theatre strategies systematically develop emotional intelligence skills essential for business communication.[27] The techniques are not ornamental but foundational. They distinguish communication that simply *informs* from communication that *influences*.

Understanding these six elements requires practice. Theatre director Scott Handy demonstrated this in a session we organized for professional facilitators at the 8th International LEGO® Serious Play®

Conference in 2024.[28] Through engaging exercises, Handy helped participants experience how actors make performances interesting rather than boring. What stops us in our tracks? What draws us toward something and makes us want to reach out? That's what's interesting.

What makes communication interesting? Moving toward the edge of personal capabilities. What's hidden beneath the surface. Interruptions and incompleteness. For most audiences, perfection is boring. Handy's insights reinforce what the theatrical disciplines reveal: audiences respond to authentic presence, not flawless performance.

Handy showed how actors turn these insights into small adjustments in their practices to make their work more engaging. After participating, facilitators realized they too could make their work even more interesting. Handy concluded that methods like LSP help professionals tell the truth. Like the arts, such methods move participants from generalities to specifics. The method, by design, makes seemingly boring conversations interesting.

The theatrical framework also reveals why AI consultation during live communication proves so disturbing. Each element depends on sustained embodied attention, while AI disrupts it. Space awareness fractures when checking a device. Vocal modulation weakens when reading algorithmic suggestions on an iPad. Gestural authenticity disappears when cognitive focus splits between audience and screen. Awareness of room energy vanishes entirely. Spontaneity becomes impossible.

Facilitators in our 2025 research about the impact of AI tools on facilitators' self-efficacy confirmed this pattern. Some noted feeling less present at the workshop while trying to use the AI tool. Others reported that using the tool distracted from engaging with the workshop and would not use it in future sessions. Yet others observed that if reliance on AI became too visible, it could present as a barrier to establishing rapport and credibility with participants.

However, the same research revealed where AI does amplify. The AI tool created the most value as part of preparation for the workshop rather than in the workshop itself, as one facilitator reported. Another appreciated the support, noting that AI helped during planning but had limited use during live facilitation. The pattern points to a clear principle: prepare and follow up with AI intensity, perform with human presence. I refer to this as "sequential amplification."

When you're reading the AI's script, you're not reading the room.

The Sequential Amplification

Here is an example of using sequential integration. At the 2025 conference for 1,300 leaders in business schools I mentioned in Chapter 4,

I structured the plenary session in two phases: first, the classical Oxford-style debate with no AI involvement; second, an AI-enhanced dialogue building upon the foundation the first debate had established. The task: Argue for or against the motion that traditional business school models have expired.

The debate unfolded in rigorous confrontation, adhering to the principles of critical thinking discussed in Chapter 4. But the debate also enhanced argumentation in ways that plain analysis did not address: embodied authority through physical presence. The four debaters delivered opening statements using voice modulation, gestural emphasis, sustained eye contact, and spatial positioning to create credibility. During my cross-examination, their body language signalled confidence or uncertainty as powerfully as words. The physical staging mattered. Debaters stood while the audience sat, claiming spatial authority. They moved toward the audience during key points, using proximity to emphasize urgency. They paused for effect, letting silence create anticipation.

The pre-debate poll showed 59 percent of participants agreed that traditional business school models have expired. After the embodied debate, this division had narrowed to 51/49. The shift occurred entirely through the debaters' physical and vocal authority, their capacity to embody competing visions with equal conviction. No AI participated. The influence came from human presence.

Then the architecture shifted. Without leaving the hall, the same audience moved into conversation with "Astrid," an AI voice assistant I had designed as a real-time dialogue partner using the latest research about the sector as "her" primary knowledge base. Astrid operated through two distinct personas: The Pragmatist, focused on institutional constraints and near-term realities, and The Futurist, exploring possibilities five years ahead.

When I asked how faculty roles should evolve in an AI-rich environment, Astrid responded that faculty will shift from content delivery to experience architecture, focusing on what situations students should navigate rather than what they should know. The AI was drawing from curated knowledge about educational innovation, synthesizing patterns I had loaded into its knowledge base. When challenged about whether rapid technological integration would compromise business schools' social mission, Astrid offered pragmatic perspective: technology without purpose becomes mere efficiency, so institutions should start by clarifying their why, then integrate AI as a means, not an end.

The exchange that generated the strongest response came when I asked Astrid to predict what business education might look like by 2030 if schools embrace a startup founder mindset. The response was visionary: "*By 2030, the most innovative business schools won't have courses, they'll have challenges. Students won't listen to lectures on venture capital; they'll raise actual funding. The classroom becomes an incubator, accreditation becomes outcomes-based, and the business school transforms from knowledge provider to ecosystem orchestrator.*"

After several exchanges, I polled the audience whether Astrid's insights made sense. The room (some 90%) overwhelmingly confirmed the quality. Post-session data revealed that 54% found the experience reinforced the importance of AI integration in their work, 23% said it raised new questions about educational futures, and 20% reported it changed their perspective on institutional strategy. Only 4% found it "not my cup of tea."

This experiment demonstrated sequential amplification. The human debate established embodied authority and emotional connection through ethos and pathos. Participants trusted the debaters because they witnessed physical commitment to competing visions from known leaders. The AI dialogue then provided analytical depth and cognitive amplification, enhancing logos without requiring embodied presence. Astrid synthesized research, modelled scenarios, and provoked strategic thinking in ways that would have taken human preparation weeks to achieve.

Crucially, I remained physically present throughout the AI dialogue, alone on-stage mediating between Astrid's responses and the audience's needs, using embodied judgment to decide which threads to pursue, whom to invite for questions, when to ask for quick reactions by show of hands, and when to redirect.

The experiment validated what workshop research had shown: AI's greatest contribution comes through preparation and analytical support, while human presence creates the influence that makes ideas matter. Reverse the sequence and effectiveness collapses. Lead with AI, and audiences perceive disembodiment. Remember the research that shows how when communication is known to be AI-generated, perceived authenticity drops precipitously, undermining trust and emotional resonance before any human connection can form.[29]

Sequential amplification requires discipline precisely because convenience tempts violation. The boundary between preparation and performance demands conscious maintenance across every high-stakes communication context.

Before a crucial board presentation, use AI to explore scenarios, structure arguments, and refine language. Spend hours in dialogue with algorithms, testing assumptions and building confidence. But when the board convenes, the device stays off. All attention flows to reading room energy, adapting to emerging concerns, and embodying the conviction that thorough preparation has built.

Before a difficult conversation with a struggling team member, use AI to model different approaches, anticipate emotional responses, and clarify desired outcomes. Prepare intensively. But when the conversation begins, algorithmic support becomes distraction. The challenge requires reading subtle body language, adjusting tone in real time, and providing the authentic human presence and empathy that builds trust.

When professionals reverse this sequence, or attempt to maintain AI consultation during performance, they fracture attention, sacrifice presence, and undermine the very authority they seek to project. Hybrid communication intelligence requires honouring categorical boundaries. AI amplifies preparation. Humans provide presence. Mix these domains and both risks erode.

The path from erosion to amplification is not mysterious. It requires recognizing what machines do well and what only humans can provide. Modern neuroscience, classical rhetoric, theatrical training, and workshop research all point to the same truth: communication influence emerges from embodied presence, not algorithmic eloquence. Professionals who master this distinction, who use AI to build unshakeable preparation then deliver with complete human focus, create the hybrid intelligence the AI age demands.

Communication makes professionals irreplaceable by creating authentic influence through embodied presence that algorithms cannot replicate. When AI crafts eloquent messages instantly, humans preserve the capacity to read rooms, modulate voice in response to energy, and establish trust through physical coordination. Algorithms optimize content. Humans create connection. Sequential amplification honours this distinction. Prepare with AI intensity, perform with human presence.

Yet even the most authentic communication proves insufficient when individuals cannot coordinate effectively. The presence that influences individuals must now scale to coordinate groups. Voice becomes chorus through coordinated action. Communication transforms individual excellence into shared meaning. Collaboration transforms shared meaning into emergent capability where the whole exceeds the sum of parts. Chapter 6 examines how professionals preserve the human dynamics essential for breakthrough thinking even as AI accelerates workflow efficiency.

The art of AI integration is knowing when to set it aside.

Self-Assessment – From Data Dashboards to Hybrid Dialogue

This assessment helps you evaluate how effectively you integrate AI support with embodied communication authority. The goal is not perfection but awareness where hybrid intelligence strengthens your practice and where erosion threatens.

Rate your recent practices over the past month across five dimensions. There are no wrong answers, only honest reflections that guide development.

1. Logos Integration: Preparing with AI, Performing with Presence

Do you maintain clear boundaries between AI-supported preparation and embodied delivery?

- ☐ **Always:** I use AI intensively during preparation for argument structure, evidence gathering, and scenario modelling, then set it aside completely during live communication. My device stays off; my full attention flows to the audience.
- ☐ **Often:** I usually prepare with AI and deliver with presence, though I occasionally check devices during communication when uncertain. The boundary feels intentional but requires discipline.
- ☐ **Sometimes:** I prepare with AI but sometimes bring algorithmic suggestions into live moments. I notice this splits my attention but have not developed consistent separation practices.
- ☐ **Rarely:** I frequently consult AI during live communication, reading suggestions while speaking. My attention divides between algorithmic outputs and audience response.
- ☐ **Never:** I use AI-generated content during communication moments without distinguishing preparation from performance. I have not established boundaries between domains.

Interpretation: Sequential amplification requires categorical separation. Use AI to build unshakeable preparation, then deliver with undivided human focus. The Vienna experiment demonstrated this: AI dialogue amplified only after embodied debate established foundation.

2. Ethos Preservation: Owning Rhetorical Authority

Do you embody authentic authorship or become a curator of algorithmic eloquence?

- ☐ **Always:** I own every message I deliver, using AI to explore options but authoring final content myself. When I speak, audiences encounter my conviction, not algorithmic polish. I consciously build credibility through embodied presence.

- ☐ **Often:** I usually adapt AI suggestions substantially before delivery, making them my own. I sometimes rely more heavily on algorithmic language than I intend, but I recognize when authenticity weakens.
- ☐ **Sometimes:** I mix AI-generated and human-authored content without clear intention. I notice that some communications feel less authentic but am uncertain how to strengthen ownership.
- ☐ **Rarely:** I frequently deliver AI-generated content with minimal adaptation. My communications may be eloquent but feel disconnected from my embodied experience and values.
- ☐ **Never:** I delegate communication authorship to AI, trusting algorithmic eloquence to create influence. I measure success by message polish rather than embodied authenticity.

Interpretation: Research shows authenticity ratings drop dramatically when recipients perceive AI authorship. Ethos emerges only through embodied presence and earned credibility. Even adversaries can respect authenticity when it's embodied.

3. Pathos Cultivation: Embodying Emotional Resonance

Do you create emotional connection through physical presence or rely on algorithmic sentiment?

- ☐ **Always:** I consistently use embodied elements – voice modulation, gesture, eye contact, spatial positioning – to create emotional resonance. I read audience energy in real time and adapt presence accordingly. People report feeling genuinely connected, not just informed.
- ☐ **Often:** I deliberately attend to embodied communication during important moments. I notice audience energy and sometimes adjust voice, gesture, and pacing in response. I am developing confidence in creating emotional connection through presence.
- ☐ **Sometimes:** I recognize when communication lacks emotional resonance but default to delivering prepared content. I know I should adjust tone or presence but am uncertain how to strengthen pathos systematically.
- ☐ **Rarely:** I focus primarily on verbal content, giving limited attention to voice, gesture, or physical presence. My communication may be clear but fails to create emotional connection or move people beyond compliance.
- ☐ **Never:** I treat communication as information transmission, ignoring embodied dimensions. I rely on well-crafted words to create influence, assuming content alone suffices.

Interpretation: Physical embodiment and vocal presence dominate communication impact. Pathos cannot be algorithmic. Practice the six theatrical elements: space awareness, voice modulation, body positioning, structural thinking, audience awareness, and spontaneous response.

4. Situational Authority: Reading Context and Adapting

Do you adapt communication fluidly to context or deliver generic messages universally?

☐ **Always:** I read context before and during communication, adapting approach to specific audience needs, energy levels, and emerging dynamics. I balance preparation with spontaneous response, using embodied judgment to sense what moments require. People experience my communications as responsive to their actual situations.

☐ **Often:** I deliberately assess context before important communications and adjust accordingly. I can read when to emphasize logic versus emotion, when to speak versus listen. My adaptations feel intentional if not yet intuitive.

☐ **Sometimes:** I recognize that different contexts require different approaches but rely heavily on prepared content. I sometimes notice when communication misses the mark but am uncertain how to adapt in the moment.

☐ **Rarely:** I trust AI-generated content to work universally across contexts. I rarely adjust to specific audience concerns or energy. I measure success by message delivery, not meaning created.

☐ **Never:** I deliver the same message regardless of context, audience, or emerging concerns. Flexibility feels like inconsistency; I value preparation over adaptation.

Interpretation: Situational authority distinguishes masterful from adequate communication. This requires the awareness and spontaneity that AI consultation during delivery destroys. When you're reading the AI's script, you're not reading the room.

5. Synchrony Systems: Building Embodied Connection

Do you create synchrony through sustained presence or fracture it through algorithmic consultation?

☐ **Always:** I maintain undivided attention during communication, creating conditions for embodied synchrony. I notice when connection forms and when it breaks. I use the invisible integration standard: AI remains backstage while human presence stays primary.

- ☐ **Often:** I usually maintain presence during communication but occasionally consult devices. I recognize this disrupts synchrony but have not made invisible integration completely habitual.
- ☐ **Sometimes:** I consult AI during live communication when uncertain, noticing that this divides attention. Participants sometimes observe me checking devices, which they interpret as distraction rather than support.
- ☐ **Rarely:** I regularly use AI during communication moments, believing it enhances rather than disrupts effectiveness. I have not recognized that visible AI consultation fractures rapport and undermines credibility.
- ☐ **Never:** I treat AI as a real-time communication partner, consulting it freely during exchanges. I have not distinguished between preparation support and presence-destroying distraction.

Interpretation: Synchrony requires sustained embodied attention – something algorithmic consultation categorically destroys. Practice invisible integration until it becomes instinct: prepare intensively with AI, then perform with complete human presence.

Using Your Profile

Map yourself across these five dimensions. Patterns will emerge. You may integrate logos well but struggle with pathos cultivation. You may preserve ethos but fracture synchrony. The task is not perfection but balanced development.

Three disciplines preserve hybrid communication intelligence:

- **Sequential amplification** – Use AI to compress months of preparation into hours, then deliver with undivided presence.
- **Invisible integration** – Keep AI backstage during performance; let audiences encounter only human authority.
- **Embodied authorship** – Internalize content through your memory until delivery becomes authentic expression.

Your profile reveals where deliberate practice can move you from erosion risk toward modelling mastery, from algorithmic dependence toward hybrid intelligence.

Notes

1 Roman oratory in Cicero's era was fundamentally embodied performance, integrating sophisticated gestural systems with vocal delivery to create what classical rhetoricians understood as the unity of message and messenger (Cicero, 1976). Historians agree that Roman orators employed an extraordinarily sophisticated system of hand and body gestures that

conveyed specific emotions and amplified verbal arguments through conventional sign language (Aldrete, 1999; Dyck, 2008). The idea was that all emotional appeals necessarily lose their force if they are not accompanied by the voice, facial expression, and demeanour of the entire body. The enduring power of this speech lay not merely in its verbal content but in Cicero's mastery of *eloquentia corporis* (the eloquence of the body), demonstrating why physical presence remained irreplaceable in Roman political communication.

2 Gordon et al. (2021).
3 Kopp et al. (2008).
4 Vanderbilt Hustler (2023).
5 Gordon et al. (2021); Kopp et al. (2008).
6 Guzman (2020).
7 Johnston (2021).
8 Dickerson et al. (2017).
9 Kopp et al. (2008).
10 Hoehl et al. (2020).
11 Gordon et al. (2021).
12 Marotto et al (2007).
13 McLuhan (1994).
14 LSP research data (2025).
15 Dorigoni et al. (2025).
16 Kirk & Givi (2025).
17 Reinhart et al. (2025).
18 Kirk & Givi (2025); Dorigoni et al. (2025).
19 Hoehl et al. (2020).
20 LSP research data (2025).
21 Gerlich (2025), also discussed in Chapter 4.
22 Johnston (2021, p. 340)
23 Klofstad et al. (2012).
24 Cook & Tanenhaus, (2009).
25 LSP research data (2025).
26 At the 9th International LEGO® Serious Play® Conference in Billund, Denmark, October 1, 2025, executive coach Kate Walker Miles from Royal Academy of Dramatic Arts in London demonstrated this principle through improvisation exercises with professional facilitators. Participants experienced how moving from "No, but..." to "Yes, and..." responses creates collaborative momentum. The progression illustrated what spontaneity requires in professional communication: trusting the moment, acknowledging contributions, and adapting in real time, what Miles described as requiring both the right state of mind and body.
27 Munro et al. (2015).
28 8th International LEGO® Serious Play® Conference, October 2–3, 2024, Billund, Denmark.
29 Dorigoni et al. (2025).

References

Aldrete, G. S. (1999). *Gestures and acclamations in ancient Rome*. Johns Hopkins University Press.

Cicero, M. T. (1976). *In Catilinam 1–4. Pro Murena. Pro Sulla. Pro Flacco* (C. Macdonald, Trans.; Loeb Classical Library No. 324). Harvard University

Press. (Original speeches delivered 63 BCE.) https://www.hup.harvard.edu/books/9780674993587
Cook, S. W., & Tanenhaus, M. K. (2009). Embodied communication: Speakers' gestures affect listeners' actions. *Cognition, 113*(1), 98–104. https://doi.org/10.1016/j.cognition.2009.06.006
Dickerson, K., Gerhardstein, P., & Moser, A. (2017). The role of the human mirror neuron system in supporting communication in a digital world. *Frontiers in Psychology, 8,* 698. https://doi.org/10.3389/fpsyg.2017.00698
Dorigoni, A., & Giardino, P. L. (2025). The illusion of empathy: Evaluating AI-generated outputs in sensitive communication contexts. *Frontiers in Psychology, 16,* 1568911. https://doi.org/10.3389/fpsyg.2025.1568911
Dyck, A. R. (Ed.). (2008). *Cicero: Catilinarians.* Cambridge University Press.
Gerlich, M. (2025). AI tools in society: Impacts on cognitive offloading and the future of critical thinking. *Societies, 15*(1), Article 6. https://doi.org/10.3390/soc15010006
Gordon, J., Maselli, A., Lancia, G. L., Thiery, T., Cisek, P., & Pezzulo, G. (2021). The road towards understanding embodied decisions. *Neuroscience & Biobehavioral Reviews, 131,* 722–736. https://doi.org/10.1016/j.neubiorev.2021.09.034
Guzman, A. L. (2020). Ontological boundaries between humans and computers and the implications for human–machine communication. *Human–Machine Communication, 1,* 37–54. https://doi.org/10.30658/hmc.1.3
Hoehl, S., Fairhurst, M., & Schirmer, A. (2021). Interactional synchrony: Signals, mechanisms, and benefits. *Social Cognitive and Affective Neuroscience, 16*(1–2), 5–18. https://doi.org/10.1093/scan/nsaa024
Johnston, D. (2021). Inside the theatre of business: Performance and corporate presentation training. *Journal of Business Anthropology, 10*(1), 138–160. https://doi.org/10.22439/jba.v10i1.6187
Kirk, C. P., & Givi, J. (2025). The AI-authorship effect: Understanding authenticity, moral concern, and advocacy in consumer response. *Journal of Business Research.* https://doi.org/10.1016/j.jbusres.2024.114984
Klofstad, C. A., Anderson, R. C., & Peters, S. (2012). Sounds like a winner: Voice pitch influences perception of leadership capacity in both men and women. *Proceedings of the Royal Society B, 279*(1738), 2698–2704. https://doi.org/10.1098/rspb.2012.0311
Kopp, S., Bergmann, K., & Wachsmuth, I. (2008). Multimodal communication from multimodal thinking: Towards an integrated model of speech and gesture production. *International Journal of Semantic Computing,* 2(1), 115–136. https://doi.org/10.1142/S1793351X08000361
Marotto, M., Roos, J., & Victor, B. (2007). Collective virtuosity. *Journal of Management Studies, 44*(3), 388–413. https://doi.org/10.1111/j.1467-6486.2007.00682.x
McLuhan, M. (1994). *Understanding media: The extensions of man.* MIT Press. (Original work published 1964).
Munro, M., Munro, A., Lemmer, K., & Pretorius, M. (2015). Theatre strategies to develop emotional intelligence skills in business communication: An exploratory study. *Southern African Business Review, 19*(2), 1–26. https://www.ajol.info/index.php/sabr/article/view/121698

Reinhart, A., Markey, B., Laudenbach, M., Pantusen, K., Yurko, R., Weinberg, G., & Brown, D. W. (2025). Do LLMs write like humans? Variation in grammatical and rhetorical styles. *Proceedings of the National Academy of Sciences, 122*(8), e2422455122. https://doi.org/10.1073/pnas.2422455122

Vanderbilt Hustler. (2023, February 17). *Peabody EDI Office responds to MSU shooting with email written using ChatGPT.* https://vanderbilthustler.com/2023/02/17/peabody-edi-office-responds-to-msu-shooting-with-email-written-using-chatgpt/

6 Collaboration – From Human Teams to Bionic Collaboration

The Cathedral Builders

In the autumn of 1178, William of Sens stood atop scaffolding sixty feet above Canterbury Cathedral's stone floor, directing the installation of ribbed vaulting across the choir. Four years earlier, fire had consumed the cathedral's east end, reducing centuries of Romanesque architecture to ash and rubble.

William, a French master mason renowned across Europe for his innovations in the new vaulted Gothic construction, had accepted what seemed an impossible commission: rebuild the choir using pointed arches and flying buttresses that would soar higher than any structure England had yet seen. The design demanded engineering calculations no English mason had attempted. Load-bearing forces would flow through stone in revolutionary patterns. The vaulting alone required precise coordination among French stone carvers who understood Gothic techniques, English quarrymen who knew local limestone's properties, and carpenters who could construct scaffolding to support unprecedented heights.[1]

The timber cracked. William fell.

When he struck the stone floor, the master mason who held the architectural vision lay paralyzed, unable to continue. The mathematics of thrust and counter-thrust, the knowledge about precise angles where flying buttresses would channel forces away from thin walls, the intricate sequencing of vault installation existed partly in William's broken head and his scattered sketches, and partly in the collective memory of craftsmen who spoke different languages and practiced distinct traditions. The choir stood half-finished, its Gothic ambitions suspended. Without the master, the cathedral could remain incomplete, another monument to failed ambition.

What happened next revealed collaboration as a capability that transcends individual genius. William the Englishman, the master's closest associate, stepped forward not to replace the paralyzed master mason but to embody what the team had systematically developed over four years of intensive coordination. The project continued through what the team had built together: robust knowledge transfer systems

DOI: 10.4324/9781003732570-6

and established problem-solving protocols. It was what organizational theorist Karl Weick would centuries later term "collective mind" – the dynamic, heedful coordination that emerges when specialists contribute their unique expertise while maintaining continuous awareness of others' roles, constraints, and evolving needs.[2]

Each morning in the mason's lodge, the team gathered to share observations from the previous day's work, troubleshoot emerging challenges, and adjust techniques in real time. French masons offered expertise in rib vault construction. English quarrymen explained how local Caen stone behaved differently under compression than Continental limestone. Carpenters innovated scaffolding systems that could support loads no structure had previously demanded. Glaziers developed methods for fitting enormous windows into frameworks one-third thinner than traditional Romanesque walls required.[3] They coordinated across language barriers through physical models, careful observation, and shared understanding forged through sustained work on problems no guild had encountered before.

Modern structural analysis reveals what this collaboration achieved. Canterbury's vaults, flying buttresses, and load-bearing systems exhibit engineering complexity that required systematic collaboration among specialists, with continuous adaptation to technical challenges that emerged only during construction.[4] When stress cracks appeared in vaulting, when buttress angles proved insufficient for England's wind loads, when Gothic techniques encountered English limestone's unfamiliar properties, the team solved problems through collective intelligence, mutual monitoring, adaptability, and lived trust. Senior craftsmen would debate structural solutions, test approaches on secondary elements, and adjust the design based on what the stone itself revealed about forces flowing through it.

The rebuild would span decades, involving multiple generations of craftsmen. The traveling masons who worked on Canterbury were mobile specialists operating across Europe from the 12th through 16th centuries. They pioneered project-based collaboration that anticipated modern professional networks.[5] Unlike town guilds that protected local interests and restricted knowledge transfer, these cathedral builders created systems for sharing innovations, training apprentices, and maintaining quality standards across regional boundaries. They established lodges at construction sites where masters taught techniques to journeymen who would carry that knowledge to the next cathedral, the next kingdom, the next generation.[6]

Original workers trained apprentices who would complete arches their masters designed but would never see finished. Knowledge and skills passed not through embodied practice, not written documentation: the correct angle for a pointed arch learned by feeling the stone's resistance under the mason's chisel, the proper buttress placement understood by observing how structures responded to wind and settling across seasons, the rhythm of collective problem-solving internalized through years of morning lodge meetings where French, English, and German craftsmen negotiated solutions to challenges no manual anticipated.[7]

When the choir was completed in 1184, Canterbury Cathedral was a living demonstration of collaborative principles that these traveling masons would carry across Europe for centuries.[8] Teams could accomplish what no individual could conceive alone when they developed shared mental models, maintained space for dissent and innovation, and preserved the capacity to adapt under genuine uncertainty.

When procedures fail, heedful interrelating – not hierarchy – saves the mission.

Collaboration in the New Era

Eight centuries after Canterbury, collaboration faces a different test. Operations in corporations everywhere coordinate under a different logic. When Amazon manages logistics across hundreds of its fulfilment centres, multi-agent AI swarms allocate inventory, optimize robotic pick paths, and route packages in real time: the agents-as-teammates paradigm introduced in Chapter 1.[9]

Beyond logistics, enterprises deploy agent swarms for customer service orchestration, supply chain optimization, and financial modelling.[10] Research demonstrates that these systems coordinate tasks with unprecedented speed and consistency.[11]

The efficiency gains prove substantial. Coordination happens faster, errors decline, and workflows optimize continuously. Yet something else changes too. As agents assume coordination responsibilities, the micro-collaborative practices through which humans develop team capability begin to fade. Accountability gaps emerge when human oversight proves inadequate. As organizations rely on agent swarms for coordination, human collaboration risks atrophying not through neglect, but through disuse.

Multi-agent swarms excel at real-time optimization, but research identifies risks today that no organization has ever faced: over-dependency on autonomous systems, reduced human situational awareness, and difficulty integrating ethical judgment at scale.[12] When agents become misaligned or encounter situations outside their training background, system-wide coordination can break down rapidly. Accountability gaps emerge when human oversight proves inadequate. As organizations rely on agent swarms for coordination, human collaboration risks atrophying not through neglect, but through disuse.

The same swarms that raise the floor of operational efficiency can, if undesigned, lower the ceiling of collective intelligence. That paradox frames this chapter's central question: How do we preserve the collaborative depth while capturing the coordination gains that AI agents enable?

The question Canterbury poses to professionals in the AI age is direct: When the master falls, that is, when procedures fail and failure carries consequences, do you want an AI swarm that converges on the most probable solution, or a team that can improvise solutions no algorithm imagined? Canterbury's masons succeeded because they cultivated what algorithms do not yet have: the capacity to subordinate individual expertise to a collective mind that comprehends the incomprehensible through heedful interrelating.

Both modes have power. Both have limits. AI-agents deliver speed and scale; human teams deliver meaning and adaptation under radical uncertainty. We must learn to design systems where algorithmic coordination amplifies rather than replaces the collaborative capabilities that make us irreplaceable. The sections ahead explore how.

Efficiency means little if teams lose the capacity to improvise when the unexpected arrives.

The History of Collaboration

The traveling cathedral "free" masons, operating in Europe from the 12th through the 16th centuries, created mobile teams that pooled expertise from one monumental project to another. These masons pioneered project-based problem-solving, master-apprentice mentorship, and cross-regional knowledge transfer, often tackling technical and artistic challenges that no single city or guild could solve alone.[13] Their legacy provided a vital early template for today's distributed, innovation-driven professional networks.

The pattern intensified across the twentieth century. Scientific collaboration became the norm rather than exception. Teams replaced individual authors as the primary unit of knowledge production. Larger teams produced more influential research, suggesting that complex problems increasingly required coordinated expertise. When Apollo 13's oxygen tank exploded 200,000 miles from Earth in April 1970, Mission Control had a few days to devise solutions using only materials aboard the spacecraft. The crisis compressed Canterbury's decades-long collaboration into 144 hours of voice-only coordination. Like the cathedral builders, the engineers succeeded through heedful interrelating, but improvisation replaced sustained knowledge transfer.[14]

The digital revolution accelerated this trajectory. Email, shared databases, and cloud platforms have enabled global collaboration at speeds earlier generations could not imagine.[15] GitHub allowed thousands of developers to contribute code to open projects asynchronously. Wikipedia demonstrated that millions of volunteers could build comprehensive knowledge repositories without formal hierarchy.[16] The detection of gravitational waves in 2015 required over 1,000 scientists from dozens of institutions working in concert across multiple countries, demonstrating that humanity's most profound discoveries now emerge through systematic collaboration rather than individual brilliance.[17]

Remember where teamwork came from. Guilds, masons, and scientists built progress through shared craft, not command.

By the time generative AI arrived, organizations had already mechanized much of teamwork's surface coordination, setting the stage for a definitive transformation.

The Benefits and Limits of Teamwork

Decades of research reveal what makes teams effective. At the foundation lie five dimensions: trust, communication, coordination, adaptability, and psychological safety.[18] These elements interact dynamically. Trust enables open communication. Communication enables coordination. Coordination enables adaptability. When teams navigate complexity well, these dimensions reinforce one another, creating performance that exceeds the sum of individual capabilities.

Meta-analyses show consistent patterns in collaborative success. Clear goals and role clarity correlate strongly with performance, particularly in high-stakes environments where ambiguity costs lives. Studies of nurse–physician teams, for example, show that when emergency staff understand who leads which decision, response times drop and error rates fall.[19] Shared purpose can transform groups of individuals into collective minds.

Yet structure alone proves insufficient. Collaboration requires dynamic exchange, not static assignment. Research distinguishes collaboration from mere cooperation: *cooperation* means working in parallel toward common goals, while *collaboration* means continuous adjustment through feedback.[20]

Teams that truly collaborate enact all five dimensions simultaneously: they trust enough to share uncertainties, communicate continuously as situations evolve, coordinate actions in real time, adapt strategies based on what others reveal, and maintain psychological safety that allows members to challenge assumptions without fear.[21] When collaboration succeeds, the five dimensions reinforce one another in a living rhythm: inhaling variety through open communication and psychological safety, exhaling alignment through coordination and adaptive trust. Durable teamwork emerges only where these dimensions overlap and reinforce one another.

Figure 6.1 illustrates the interdependence of trust, communication, coordination, adaptability, and psychological safety. The overlapping centre represents the zone of "collective intelligence," where these dimensions reinforce one another to enable high-performing collaboration.

Teams operating in this zone show more than smooth coordination; they develop the capacity to anticipate, adjust, and act as a coherent collective mind. But even the most balanced systems face limits. Research on distributed teams shows benefits (expanded talent pools, reduced overhead) alongside risks (trust decay, coordination failures).[22] Virtual collaboration requires explicit relationship maintenance. Teams that meet only through screens report lower psychological safety and weaker interpersonal bonds unless they deliberately cultivate connection.

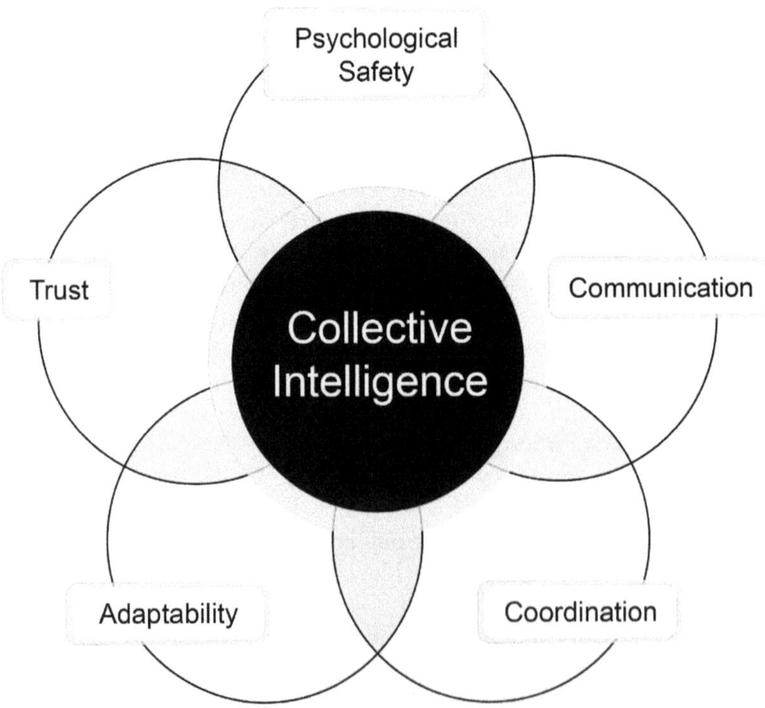

Figure 6.1 Five Dimensions of Effective Teamwork – Collective Intelligence

Productivity follows a predictable curve. Studies tracking collaborative output across team sizes find gains up to an inflection point, then saturation. Small teams accomplish more per person than individuals. Medium-sized teams amplify this further. Beyond certain thresholds, however, diminishing marginal coordination costs exceed capability gains.[23] The insight echoes across contexts: collaboration multiplies human potential, but only when teams remain small enough for heedful attention to each other's work.

Balance the five dimensions before scaling the system. Trust, communication, coordination, adaptability, and psychological safety breathe life into collaboration.

The Architecture of Collaborative Capacity

The five foundational dimensions – trust, communication, coordination, adaptability, and psychological safety – enable three emergent properties that distinguish high-performing teams.

Shared mental models develop when team members build compatible understandings of goals, roles, and processes through repeated interaction. These models enable teams to shift from explicit to implicit coordination under pressure, preserving cognitive bandwidth for novel problems. When teams share accurate models, they anticipate each other's needs and adapt fluidly. When mental models diverge, coordination breaks down precisely when stress peaks.

Collective mind emerges when teams exhibit high social sensitivity and balanced turn-taking in conversation. Some teams consistently outperform others, even when individual members possess similar capabilities. Team-level ability to solve diverse problems that cannot be explained by average individual intelligence alone.[24] What predicted collective intelligence was not technical expertise but social sensitivity: teams whose members attended to each other's cues, took turns speaking, and remained attuned to subtle signals outperformed teams dominated by a few voices. The pattern suggests that the collective mind requires orchestration of attention, not aggregation of individual brilliance. It is about what emerges between us, not inside each of us.

Heedful interrelating involves three simultaneous processes: contributing unique expertise, representing others' capabilities and constraints, and subordinating individual actions to the collective system.[25] Psychologist Jacob Levy Moreno called this dynamic "tele," defined as a mutual rapport or flowing empathy that arises in the live space between people, not merely within them.[26] Tele turns aggregate contribution into a living, reciprocal connection. In teams, tele helps explain why distributed attention and responsiveness enable collective intelligence: the group's capacity for mutual engagement depends on this subtle web of mutual feeling and regard.

Canterbury's masons demonstrated heedful interrelating across decades: each specialist contributed domain knowledge, maintained awareness of others' constraints, and subordinated individual judgment to collective understanding. When William of Sens fell, the collaborative infrastructure proved resilient.

The Apollo 13 incident compressed this dynamic into days. When engineers improvised life support solutions in Houston while astronauts assembled devices by voice alone, they exhibited the same three processes: contributing unique expertise, representing others' capabilities and constraints, and subordinating individual recommendations to the evolving collective judgment Weick and Roberts conceptualized. Each expert maintained awareness of what others needed. Each adjusted recommendations based on evolving constraints from crew and controllers. The collective mind that saved the mission emerged from this choreography of heed and the tele connecting people.

Build the conditions for collective mind. Shared mental models, psychological safety, and social sensitivity turn groups into intelligent systems.

The temporal contrast matters: Canterbury shows collaboration as ongoing capability; Apollo 13 shows it as crisis response. Modern organizations need both.

The Conundrum – From Human Teams to Hybrid Teams

The challenge now: how to merge AI into this landscape as more than a tool. This is a new and emerging professional environment. The shift in how we collaborate introduces new questions. Can we extend trust to non-human teammates, like the ones unleashed in Amazon and many other companies? Do shared mental models form across AI-human boundaries? What happens when one teammate lacks emotion, embodiment, and lived experience?

Initial evidence suggests human-AI teams operate differently than all-human teams. Communication patterns change: teams with AI agents send more task-focused messages but fewer socio-emotional exchanges.[27] Trust forms more slowly and remains fragile, improving when AI agents communicate proactively and adapt to context.[28] Shared mental models require more explicit articulation; what humans infer implicitly must be stated explicitly for AI comprehension. Recall how effective LLM prompts are made: very detailed.[29]

Even if these are early days, we can distinguish between *human-in-the-loop collaboration*, where humans and AI work interdependently with continuous oversight, and *human-outside-the-loop coordination*, where AI swarms operate autonomously with periodic supervision.[30] Teams may think they are collaborating when they are coordinating.

Collaboration now operates across three distinct modes.

- **Human-only teams:** Relies entirely on interpersonal trust, rich socio-emotional exchange, and heedful interrelating.
- **AI agents (a.k.a., human-outside-the-loop):** Autonomous AI systems operate with only occasional human intervention. These teams prioritize speed and scale, but risk eroding shared understanding and collaborative depth as humans move to supervisory, rather than participatory, roles.
- **Hybrid (a.k.a., human-inside-the-loop) teams:** Humans and AI collaborate in real-time with structured checkpoints and shared decision authority. Human judgment guides framing and interpretation, but machine agents extend processing power and foresight. Continuous human oversight preserves agency and depth.[31]

In this framework, "hybrid" collaborations are by definition human-in-the-loop: humans stay engaged in framing, decision-making, and sensemaking at key junctures, rather than stepping aside as overseers. As teams drift toward fully autonomous swarms, the locus of agency shifts, making the distinction between these modes critical for designing effective collaboration.

Table 6.1 compares the boundary conditions that distinguish the three modes of collaboration in the AI age.

The table reveals the gradient of collaborative depth. Human-only teams build shared understanding through negotiation and friction. Outside-the-loop coordination risks displacing the deliberative processes through which teams develop adaptive capacity. The locus of problem framing proves diagnostic: when agents define the question, efficiency rises but meaning-making atrophies. In-the-loop models preserve human interpretive authority when boundaries remain explicit.

Studies demonstrate that *hybrid in-the-loop models* can outperform both human-only teams and autonomous systems when deliberately designed to preserve human agency while leveraging machine capabilities.[32] Without such design, they risk drifting toward outside-the-loop patterns that maximize efficiency while eroding collaborative capacity.

Table 6.1 Comparison of the Three Modes of Collaboration in the AI Age

Dimension	*Human-Only Teams*	*AI Agents (Human-Outside-the-Loop)*	*Hybrid (Human-in-the-Loop)*
Decision Authority	Fully human	Largely autonomous with periodic oversight	Shared with explicit human checkpoints
Trust Foundation	Interpersonal relationships, lived experience	Trust in system optimization	Dynamic calibration between human and agent reliability
Communication Pattern	Rich socio-emotional exchange; tele	Agent-to-agent with human monitoring	Content-focused with reduced social exchange
Heedful Interrelating	High, continuous mutual awareness	Low, coordination without presence	Moderate, requires deliberate design
Psychological Safety	Built through repeated interaction	Risk of suppression through rapid consensus	Maintained through explicit dissent windows
Shared Mental Models	Developed through dialogue	System-generated, humans receive outputs	Explicit transparency protocols required
Adaptability Under Uncertainty	High, improvisation possible	Low, optimizes within defined parameters	Moderate, depends on agent boundaries
Creative Friction	Natural emergence through disagreement	Eliminated through algorithmic convergence	Must be ritualized to preserve
Speed vs. Depth Trade-off	Slower deliberation, deeper understanding	Maximum speed, reduced meaning-making	Balanced when boundaries clear
Problem Framing Locus	Emerges collaboratively through dialogue and contestation	Optimizes within given frame; reframing requires human intervention	Human-led framing before agent analysis; risk of premature delegation
Primary Strength	Collective mind under radical uncertainty	Coordination at massive scale	Combines scale with agency
Primary Risk	Limited processing capacity	Displacement of collaborative skills	Erosion without deliberate architecture

The transition from human-only to human-outside-the-loop to human-in-the-loop raises fundamental questions about how to design the future of collaboration. Some researchers propose that for human-AI teams to be successful, it requires AI design that supports collective processes like situation awareness, shared mental models, and mutual monitoring rather than merely optimizing individual task performance. The idea is to ensure responsiveness, transparency, and the capacity for AI agents to align their goals and communication with *team* needs rather than operating as autonomous optimizers.

In effect, as organizations further integrate AI agents and swarms into teamwork, they must decide: Will these systems amplify the shared models, collective mind, and heedful interrelating that characterizes high-performing human teams, or will they consciously (or unconsciously) choose to bypass it entirely in supposed favour of speed and efficiency?

Stay in the loop, literally. Keep humans in the frame for judgment, dissent, and meaning-making even as AI agents accelerate the work.

Eroding Collaboration

Any organization faced with this collaboration conundrum needs to consider the following mechanisms that operate to erode collaboration in the long term.

1st Erosion Mechanism: Fragmenting Micro-Collaboration

Individual AI tools now assume responsibility for micro-collaborative tasks that once trained people to negotiate priorities, build shared understanding, and improvise around constraints. Scheduling conflicts are now resolved by smart calendars. Information synthesis after meetings is delegated to AI transcription tools. Follow-up coordination is automated through workflow agents.

As one manager in our dialogues admitted, "*We can coordinate everything perfectly now, but sometimes I wonder if we're still actually collaborating.*" Another captured the growing discomfort: "*Every time I click OK on the AI transcript function in the online meeting, I know I will not be as open in the discussions as I would be otherwise.*" These comments reveal a recurring pattern: coordination aligns effort, but collaboration is fragile.[33] When tools strip away the human frictions of coordination, they also risk removing the very practices through which collaborative depth develops.

The micro-tasks AI absorbs, like scheduling, summarizing, and follow-up, are not merely administrative. They are rehearsals for more complex collaborative work. Two colleagues who once negotiated a meeting time around conflicting priorities no longer practice representing each other's constraints. The manager who stops synthesizing meeting notes with her team loses opportunities to surface competing interpretations. The project lead who delegates follow-up tracking to workflow agents stops modelling explicit accountability. Each micro-task removed eliminates one repetition of the collaborative behaviours that, aggregated over time, build the instincts teams need under pressure.

The consequence: teams become smoother but thinner, more organized but less resilient. Fewer rough edges mean fewer learning moments. The change is invisible because outputs remain strong. Only when teams face an Apollo 13 moment requiring improvisation rather than optimization does this erosion become apparent.

2nd Erosion Mechanism: Social Thinning

As AI agents mediate more team interactions, the emotional and social exchanges that build trust and psychological safety decline. Research shows that teams achieve productivity gains while spending significantly less time on the relational work that enables collaborative risk-taking. AI mediation improves task outcomes but reduces process satisfaction: less connection with teammates, and less engagement in collective work.[34]

AI agents in teams can reduce interpersonal conflict when performing well but may fundamentally alter the social-emotional experience of collaboration. Research found that when humans are outvoted by AI teammates in team decision-making, they do not experience the strong negative emotional reactions typical of human-human team conflict, as long as the final decision produces advantageous outcomes. However, this apparent harmony masks a concerning pattern: human self-confidence declined when they were outvoted and their own proposed actions were overridden, even when those actions were objectively superior and received positive feedback. This suggests that being overridden by AI is a different experience than being overridden by human teammates. Disagreement in human teams is moderated by rich social negotiation, collective understanding, and mutual regard which we do not have with AI-as-teammates.[35]

This erosion of the social fabric matters because trust and psychological safety emerge through repeated micro-interactions where team members demonstrate reliability, empathy, and mutual regard. When these interactions become mediated, abbreviated, or eliminated, the social foundation weakens. Teams can still coordinate tasks. But they lose the relational depth that enables them to take risks, voice dissent, challenge assumptions, and adapt under pressure.

The Swedish work coffee-break tradition "fika" has evolved into a practice that strengthens the social fabrics in work places and cultivate collective mind. While this may look inefficient to outsiders, this distinct mid-morning and mid-afternoon break build the foundation for non-hierarchical heedful interrelation in *all* workplaces. After *fika*, teams shift smoothly back into work and hierarchical mode, but the benefits to collaboration and trust are lasting and, in my experience from working almost three decades in other countries, quite unique.

3rd Mechanism: Consensus Without Meaning

Pre-packaged decision materials enable fast, algorithm-driven convergence, but they shortcut team negotiation and shared understanding.[36] When AI agents resolve complexity before human engagement, teams lose the chance to build the common ground needed for action under pressure. The answer arrives; the team never wrestles with the question.

What disappears is collective sense-making through which teams clarify the problem itself. Accepting a "best solution" often means accepting a predefined frame, mirroring Chapter 4's oracle trap: the best answer arrived; the question never formed.

AI-agent systems and optimization algorithms make dissent costly, sidelining alternative viewpoints as inefficient.[37] This erodes the creative tension required for discovery. When innovation becomes too streamlined, either by internal consensus or algorithms, creative abrasion and productive disagreement quickly disappear.

The Compounded Effects of Erosion

These erosion patterns compound on one another. Tool displacement weakens the micro-skills that build collaborative instinct. Social thinning reduces the trust and psychological safety that enable risk-taking and dissent. Premature closure accelerates convergence while hollowing out the deliberative processes that create shared understanding and collective capability.[38]

The consequences manifest at multiple levels. First, teams lose the creative friction that emerges when diverse perspectives collide and must be negotiated.[39] Second, the practices of contributing while representing others' needs and subordinating to collective goals (heedful interrelating) require repeated exercise. When coordination becomes automated and deliberation abbreviated, these practices fade. Teams lose capacity for the improvisational teamwork that Apollo 13 exemplified.

Third, blind spots multiply. Tasks completed, response times, conversion and throughput rates and similar metrics rise as AI agents take hold. Leaders risk misreading efficiency gains as collaboration health, unaware that the social fabric enabling adaptive performance is quietly decaying. The erosion becomes visible only retrospectively, when teams face situations requiring a collective mind they no longer possess.

Other studies confirm the pattern. Automation increased coordination efficiency but reduced teams' capacity for creative problem-solving and adaptive learning. The trade-off proves difficult to detect in real time because efficiency gains dominate immediate experience. Only longitudinal studies reveal the hidden costs: declining trust, weakening psychological safety, and eroding collective intelligence.[40]

The architectural question for all professionals is how to capture the coordination benefits of automation without losing depth in collaboration. The answer demands moving beyond default adoption and treating AI not just as a tool for speed, but as a partner in collaborative work, and one that must be carefully, deliberately integrated into human teams. This deliberate partnership is what I call *Bionic Collaboration*: a purposeful blend of human relational skill with AI's computational strengths, designed to enhance curiosity, creativity, critical thinking, and communication, rather than simply efficiency. What erosion removes by default, amplification must restore by intent.

These patterns are easier to feel than to see. Yet across organizations, the same forces repeat with striking consistency.

Figure 6.2 makes this drift visible. It traces how collaboration moves – from connection to conformity – as human micro-skills dissolve, relationships thin, and consensus replaces meaning. Each step appears efficient on the surface but gradually hollows the substance of teamwork beneath.

What begins as convenience ends as fragility. Each erosion smooths the surface of teamwork while hollowing its depth: micro-skills vanish,

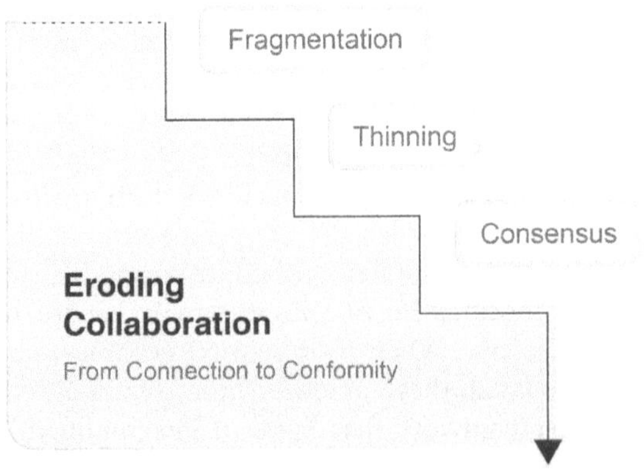

Figure 6.2 Eroding Collaboration – From Connection to Conformity

trust thins, and meaning collapses into alignment. Recognizing these mechanisms is the first step toward reversing them and designing bionic collaboration that restores friction where learning happens and connection where trust is born.

Notice what disappears when everything runs smoothly.

The Amplification of Collaboration

If undesigned systems erode collaboration by default, designed systems can amplify it by intent. The path forward requires moving from reactive adoption to deliberate architecture, treating AI agents collaborators requiring careful integration into team processes. Research and organizational practice converge on a set of principles that distinguish collaboration that machines enable from collaboration that machines replace.

Principles for Bionic Collaboration

Studies identify foundational principles for the "intelligent organization," which is designed for complementarity between human judgment and machine capabilities.[41] The first principle is *transparency* by making AI reasoning visible so teams understand not just what agents recommend but how they arrived at those recommendations. When Amazon's CEO Andy Jassy describes agents as "teammates," he acknowledges they will increasingly participate in work processes traditionally reserved for humans. Transparency enables teams to treat those recommendations as inputs rather than directives, preserving human interpretive authority.

The second principle is *complementarity* by assigning agents to tasks that extend rather than replace human strengths. Research consistently shows that hybrid models combining human judgment with AI capabilities outperform either alone when designed for mutual reinforcement. Agents excel at processing volume, identifying patterns, and generating options at scale. Humans excel at sensing context, integrating ethical considerations, and making meaning from ambiguous signals.

The third and fourth principles involve *mutual learning* and *human ownership*.[42] Effective human-AI teams develop feedback loops where both sides adapt: agents refine their models based on human corrections, and humans adjust their approaches based on agent insights. But ultimate decision authority and accountability must remain human. When the "father of management" Peter Drucker argued in the last century that management is both social function and moral practice, he insisted that responsibility cannot be delegated to systems incapable of ethical judgment.[43]

The fifth principle is *psychological safety* to preserve space for dissent, challenge, and correction. When AI agents present comprehensive outputs, the pressure for premature consensus intensifies. We must counteract this by ritualizing dissent, creating explicit moments where challenging agent recommendations becomes expected.

Most teams default to one extreme or the other – treating AI as oracle or as suspect. Both patterns undermine collaboration by eliminating the nuanced judgment that hybrid intelligence requires. Studies show that AI literacy mediates this calibration: teams with higher literacy understand when to delegate, when to challenge, and when to synthesize human and machine insights.[44]

Three practices enable this calibration:

1. **Triage by context clarity**: novel situations with ambiguous signals require human primacy.
2. **Checkpoint on confidence versus novelty:** when agent confidence is high but the situation is unprecedented, pause for human review.
3. **Require transparent reasoning**: expose AI logic that humans can interrogate, perhaps in a Toulmin map, as discussed in Chapter 4.

Correct calibration depends on establishing clear human decision checkpoints requiring lived judgment regardless of agent confidence levels. Industry research identifies trust as the linchpin determining whether organizations capture value or experience disruption. The distinction lies in whether agents operate as tools we can control or as autonomous systems we can only monitor from the outside.[45]

McKinsey frames this as "superagency," using AI to expand rather than constrain human decision-making capacity. Successful, early implementations, they found, share a pattern: AI handles scale while humans handle meaning. In fraud detection, agents flag anomalies but humans interpret whether anomalies represent fraud, error, or legitimate edge cases.[46]

Organizational analyses emphasize that partnership requires a psychological shift. Teams must view agents neither as servants nor as authorities, but as competent colleagues with distinct capabilities,[47] just like Andrew Jassy asserted. Research shows that when humans perceive AI as collaborative partner rather than tool or threat, both productivity and job satisfaction increase.[48]

The preparation-performance boundary observed in our research on professional facilitation offers practical guidance. Make AI visible in preparation but invisible in performance. During planning, teams can leverage agent capabilities fully. But during live collaboration in meetings, workshops, or negotiations presence must remain human-centred. We return to what Romans called *eloquentia corporis* discussed in Chapter 5. The discipline of separating backstage AI support from frontstage human interaction, even that eloquence of the body, preserves the collaborative capacity that algorithms cannot replicate.

Amplification Scenarios

Three organizational contexts illustrate how a deliberate design can transform AI from collaboration risk to collaboration catalyst.

Advertising

Research tracking advertising teams found that AI agents excel at generating volume: producing hundreds of variations overnight.[49] Humans excel at curation: evaluating which variations resonate emotionally and align with brand values. When organizations structure workflows so that agents generate creative output, quality rises while preserving human authorship.

- **Agent role:** Generate concept variations at scale, exploring combinatorial possibilities.
- **Human role:** Curate for narrative coherence, emotional resonance, and brand alignment.
- **Decision gate:** Creative brief sign-off remains human, ensuring strategic intent guides selection.

Healthcare

Transparent AI triage systems elevate coordination while preserving clinical judgment. Proactive agent updates about patient status improve situational awareness without overwhelming clinicians.[50] Systems monitor vitals continuously and alert humans when thresholds are crossed, with transparent reasoning that enables clinicians to integrate algorithmic insights with clinical observation.

- **Agent role:** Monitor patient data streams continuously; surface reasoned alerts when clinical thresholds are crossed.
- **Human role:** Interpret alerts within patient history and situational context; exercise contextual override when clinical judgment differs.
- **Decision gate:** Treatment decisions require clinician approval; agents recommend, humans decide.

Logistics

Organizations implementing multi-agent systems for supply chain management use agents to monitor inventory, predict demand shifts, and propose reallocation strategies continuously. But major decisions stay human-led. AI-agents raise the floor by ensuring baseline efficiency. Human teams focus on raising the ceiling.[51]

- **AI-agent role:** Monitor inventory, forecast demand fluctuations, and propose real-time reallocation changes.
- **Human role:** Review recommendations, negotiate trade-offs for strategic moves, and collaboratively make decisions focusing on longer-term value creation.
- **Decision gate:** Major decisions require human team deliberation and sign-off; agents implement adjustments within human-approved parameters.

***

What are patterns in these situations? Amplification requires explicit division of labour based on human-AI complementarity. Let agents handle volume, speed, and consistency. Let humans handle ambiguity, ethics, and meaning.[52]

What should we avoid? Meetings where AI outputs define the agenda before human framing occurs. When we open with "Here's what the AI found," we risk accepting AI's problem definitions without examining whether it asked the right question. The pattern echoes Chapter 2's warning: never let efficiency short-circuit the perplexity that precedes genuine inquiry, or the critical thinking habit in Chapter 3 of asking where is the "because?"

Architect collaboration, don't automate it. Use AI to raise the floor of efficiency while humans raise the ceiling of insight.

Developing Leadership for Hybrid Teams

Designing collaboration architectures requires leadership practices that most organizations have not yet developed. The first practice involves redesigning rituals to preserve human sensemaking. Research argues that intelligent organizations create explicit "dissent windows" and "meaning meetings" within agent-mediated workflows.[53] Teams must schedule protected time for questioning AI recommendations and building shared understanding beyond statistical optimality.

A first practice is to start with a "human-first protocol" so that important decisions always begin with unassisted human framing before any AI outputs are introduced. This simple reversal preserves agency in problem definition while still capturing swarm advantages. For instance, here is a ten-minute protocol inspired by the Toulmin framework in Chapter 3 that codifies this boundary.

1. Silent human framing (three minutes): the team articulates the problem in human words before any agent output appears, asking "What matters here and why?"
2. Dissent window (five minutes): the team must surface two viable alternatives and one red-team risk before converging on any AI recommendation.
3. Synthesis commit (two minutes): a human names the reasoning linking evidence to decision and assumes accountability. The protocol ensures AI inform but do not define collaborative work.

The second practice involves making boundaries visible through explicit accountability maps. Leaders must declare what AI can decide independently, what requires human approval, and what demands collective deliberation. When boundaries remain implicit, teams drift toward letting capable agents make more decisions by default.[54]

The third practice develops what researchers calls "co-presence awareness," which is the capacity to read both human and system signals simultaneously. Traditional leadership practice emphasized reading the room. Hybrid leadership requires additionally reading the system: understanding when AI are operating within training domains versus extrapolating beyond them. This dual attention represents cognitive load, which is why the preparation-performance boundary matters.[55]

The fourth practice involves cultivating hybrid team culture where interpretive skill carries status. When AI generate comprehensive analyses efficiently, organizations risk devaluing the slower work of questioning assumptions and building collective understanding. Leaders counter this by celebrating interpretive contributions visibly.[56]

The new frontier of collaboration is not faster coordination but wiser coexistence between humans and agents, thinking together without losing touch with each other. This requires leaders to become architects of collective intelligence, designing systems where algorithmic precision enhances rather than replaces the heedful interrelating that characterizes human collaboration at its best.

Lead for coexistence, not control. Protect human framing, dissent, and sensemaking inside algorithmic systems.

Self-Assessment – From Human Teams to Bionic Collaboration

You have explored how AI can fragment collaborative micro-skills, thin social fabric, and bypass deliberation, and how deliberate design can amplify rather than erode collective intelligence. Even if this may be early days, the writing is on the wall: *AI swarms are coming*. This self-assessment helps you locate your current practices on that spectrum and reflect over how ready you are. Consider your collaborative experiences over the past month and rate your typical approach honestly.

Dimension 1: Presence Protection – Device-Light Collaboration

How effectively do you preserve live collaboration as human-centred space?

- **Always:** I intentionally keep live collaboration device-light, relocating AI work to preparation and documentation while maintaining undivided attention on human participants during sessions.
- **Often:** I regularly draw boundaries between AI-supported preparation and human-centred performance, though occasionally consult devices when uncertain.
- **Sometimes:** I experiment with separating AI use from live sensemaking, but boundaries are not always clear or consistent.
- **Rarely:** I notice how AI tools intrude on presence but rarely act to shift them out of the room, dividing attention between screens and people.
- **Never:** I routinely allow AI tools to occupy live collaborative sessions without recognizing the cost to collaborative depth.

If low: Choose one recurring meeting this week and keep it entirely device-light. Notice what you observe when your full attention remains on people.

Dimension 2: Dissent Design – Safeguarding Creative Friction

How well do you maintain space for dissent and constructive disagreement?

- **Always:** I ritualize dissent windows in team processes and explicitly invite alternative interpretations when AI outputs appear comprehensive.

- **Often:** I regularly create opportunities for dissent and resist premature consensus, noticing when agreement comes too quickly.
- **Sometimes:** I try to create space for dissent but sometimes accept AI conclusions too quickly under time pressure.
- **Rarely:** I notice dissent declining in AI-mediated work but rarely act to restore it, uncertain how to balance speed with negotiating meaning.
- **Never:** I defer to AI outputs without pause, allowing comprehensive syntheses to close discussions without distinguishing algorithmic consensus from collaborative agreement.

If low: Before your next major decision, require the team to surface two viable alternatives and one risk the AI analysis did not address.

Dimension 3: Trust Calibration – Interrogating Agent Outputs

How consistently do you calibrate trust in AI recommendations rather than accepting or rejecting them wholesale?

- **Always:** I require transparent reasoning from AI systems and develop explicit protocols for when to rely on agents, when to challenge them, and when to preserve human primacy.
- **Often:** I frequently probe how AI reaches conclusions and distinguish contexts where agent recommendations deserve high confidence from situations requiring human interpretation.
- **Sometimes:** I occasionally question AI outputs and seek explanations, though I often accept recommendations at face value without consistent practices.
- **Rarely:** I notice opacity in AI reasoning but rarely address it, allowing teams to treat agent outputs as authoritative without understanding how they were generated.
- **Never:** I accept AI outputs as comprehensive and reliable without seeking transparency or developing practices for distinguishing where human judgment should dominate.

If low: Next time an AI system makes a claim, ask it to explain its reasoning and draft a Toulmin map of it. If not satisfactory, consider that a signal to increase human oversight.

Dimension 4: Amplification Architecture – Relocating AI Work

How deliberately do you design AI roles to raise the floor without lowering the ceiling?

- **Always:** I consistently relocate AI work to preparation and documentation while reserving live sessions for synthesis, negotiation, and commitment through explicit team protocols.
- **Often:** I regularly separate AI scaffolding from human collaboration, using agents upstream for option generation while preserving middle stages for collective sensemaking.
- **Sometimes:** I try to use AI in preparation and follow-up rather than during live collaboration, but the distinction sometimes blurs without clear boundaries.
- **Rarely:** I occasionally think about where AI belongs in collaborative workflows but lack clear practices, allowing agents to permeate multiple stages.
- **Never:** I allow AI to occupy all stages of collaboration without distinguishing where it adds value versus where it displaces essential human work.

If low: Map one collaborative process you lead. Mark which stages involve AI. Ask whether agents are backstage (preparation/documentation) or frontstage (live deliberation). Redesign accordingly.

Interpretation

Your pattern across dimensions reveals your collaborative stance. High scores on Dimensions 1 and 2 (Protecting Presence, Designing Dissent) with lower scores on Dimensions 3 and 4 (Calibrating Trust, Architecting Amplification) suggest strong relational instincts but weak structural practices.

Conversely, high scores on Dimensions 3 and 4 with lower scores on Dimensions 1 and 2 indicate strong procedural discipline but insufficient attention to the human dynamics. Ideal collaboration requires both: presence and architecture, instinct and design.

If you score consistently high (Always/Often), you are developing intentional practices that preserve human connection while capturing AI capabilities. If most responses fall in the middle (Sometimes), you recognize the tension between efficiency and depth but need stronger protocols.

If you score low (Rarely/Never), you may be at risk of mistaking coordination for collaboration. Begin by choosing one dimension and establishing a single practice. Keep live meetings device-light for one week. Establish one dissent window before major decisions. Notice what changes.

Bionic collaboration is not about perfection but about intentionality. Every time you choose presence over screens, friction over convergence, or interpretation over acceptance, you strengthen the capabilities that distinguish human teams from sophisticated robots.

In an age of algorithmic coordination, pausing to ask, sense, and listen together becomes the radical act that preserves collective intelligence.

When AI coordinates workflows with machine precision, humans should preserve the capacity to create the trust, creative friction, and heedful interrelating that allow diverse expertise to coalesce into breakthrough insights. Algorithms optimize workflow. We cultivate wisdom. Yet even masterful collaboration requires an integrating capacity to orient these coordinated efforts toward purpose beyond efficiency. *Chorus must serve wisdom, not merely efficiency.* This is where practical wisdom enters as the meta-capability that completes the journey. Practical wisdom integrates curiosity, creativity, critical thinking, communication, and collaboration into reasoned judgment that knows when coordination serves purposes only humans can comprehend and care about. Chapter 7 examines this meta-capability.

Collaborate to think, not just to act.

Notes

1 Woodman (2023).
2 Weick & Roberts (1993), inspired by Ryle (2009/1949).
3 Murray (1996).
4 Karanikoloudis et al. (2020).
5 Stevenson (1988).
6 Epstein (1998).
7 Woodman (2023).
8 Medieval European cathedrals were far from the first multi-generational construction projects. Examples span from Stonehenge to the Pyramids to Angkor Wat. I chose Canterbury because its peer-based lodge system is exceptionally well-documented and directly analogous to modern professional collaboration, unlike many earlier mega-projects that relied on hierarchical or coercive labour systems (Woodman, 2023; Stevenson, 1988).
9 Jassy (2025), as discussed in Chapter 1.
10 Codewave (2025, September 14).
11 Ju & Aral (2025).
12 Piccialli et al. (2025).
13 Murray (2014).
14 NASA (2020).
15 Murić et al. (2019).
16 Wang & Barabási (2021).
17 Abbot et al. (2016).
18 Edmondson (1999); Lepine et al. (2008).
19 Jaruševičienė et al. (2019).
20 Thomson et al. (2007).
21 Bednar (2023).
22 Greimel et al. (2023).
23 Murić et al. (2019).
24 Woolley et al. (2010).
25 Weick & Roberts (1993).
26 Moreno (1953); Blatner (1994).

27 Ju & Aral (2025).
28 Zhang et al. (2023); Schmutz et al. (2024).
29 Schelble et al. (2022).
30 Schmutz et al. (2024).
31 Hybrid teams" refers to designs where humans actively participate throughout, versus "AI swarms" where AI acts autonomously with limited, episodic human involvement.
32 Hagemann et al. (2023).
33 TNM research data (2025).
34 Dennis et al. (2023).
35 Hu et al. (2024) found a paradox: AI reduces social friction but doesn't eliminate the psychological costs of being overridden, and may actually create a new problem where people disengage socially while still experiencing confidence erosion.
36 Pan & Or (2025).
37 Sen & Jakkaraju (2025).
38 Mathieu et al. (2000).
39 De Dreu et al. (2003).
40 Dell'Acqua et al. (2025).
41 Kolbjørnsrud (2023).
42 A related principle is *ethical alignment*, to govern fairness, bias, and accountability at the system level. As AI becomes embedded in collaborative work, governance frameworks must address transparency, prevent algorithmic bias, and ensure human values remain central.
43 Drucker (2006).
44 Pan et al. (2025).
45 Capgemini (2025, July 17).
46 McKinsey (2025).
47 IBM (2025).
48 Xu et al. (2025). This is how Utley (2024) urged use of LLMs as teammates, not tools, as discussed in Chapter 3.
49 Ju & Aral (2025).
50 Farah & Dorneich (2024).
51 Enterprise AI Case Studies (2025).
52 Hagemann et al. (2023).
53 Ransboham et al. (2024).
54 Capgemini (2025).
55 Hagemann et al. (2023).
56 Kolbjørnsrud (2024).

References

Abbott, B. P., Abbott, R., Abbott, T. D., Abernathy, M. R., Acernese, F., . . . & LIGO Scientific Collaboration and Virgo Collaboration. (2016). Observation of gravitational waves from a binary black hole merger. *Physical Review Letters, 116*(6), 061102. https://doi.org/10.1103/PhysRevLett.116.061102

Bednar, J. (2023). Governance for human social flourishing. *Dædalus, 152*(1), 31–42. https://doi.org/10.1162/DAED_a_01958

Blatner, A. (1994). Tele: The dynamics of interpersonal preference. In P. Holmes, M. Karp, & M. Watson (Eds.), *Psychodrama since Moreno: Innovations in theory and practice* (pp. 213–228). London: Routledge. https://doi.org/10.4324/9780203977187

Capgemini. (2025, July 17). Trust and human-AI collaboration set to define the next era of agentic AI: Unlocking $450 billion opportunity by 2028. Capgemini. https://www.capgemini.com/se-en/news/press-releases/trust-and-human-ai-collaboration-set-to-define-the-next-era-of-agentic-ai-unlocking-450-billion-opportunity-by-2028/

Codewave. (2025, September 14). Top 10 applications of artificial intelligence for enterprises in 2025. Codewave.https://codewave.com/insights/artificial-intelligence-applications-enterprises/

De Dreu, C. K. W., & Weingart, L. R. (2003). Task versus relationship conflict, team performance, and team member satisfaction: A meta-analysis. *Journal of Applied Psychology, 88*(4), 741–749. https://doi.org/10.1037/0021-9010.88.4.741

Dell'Acqua, F., Kogut, B., & Perkowski, P. (2025). *Super Mario meets AI: Experimental effects of automation and skills on team performance and coordination. Review of Economics and Statistics, 107*(4), 951. https://doi.org/10.1162/rest_a_01328

Dennis, A., Lakhiwal, A., & Sachdeva, A. (2023). AI agents as team members: Effects on satisfaction, conflict, trustworthiness, and willingness to work with. *Journal of Management Information Systems*, 40(2), 307–337. https://doi.org/10.1080/07421222.2023.2196773

Drucker, P. F. (2006). *The practice of management* (Reissue ed.). Harper Business.

Edmondson, A. (1999). Psychological safety and learning behavior in work teams. *Administrative Science Quarterly*, 44(2), 350–383. https://doi.org/10.2307/2666999

Epstein, S. R. (1998). Craft guilds, apprenticeship, and technological change in preindustrial Europe. *The Journal of Economic History*, *58*(3), 684–713. https://www.jstor.org/stable/2566620

Farah, Y. A., & Dorneich, M. C. (2024). Human-autonomy teaming in a cooperative gamified testbed: How can AI teammates support teamwork processes? *Proceedings of the Human Factors and Ergonomics Society Annual Meeting*, *68*(1), 386–392. https://doi.org/10.1177/10711813241269252 (Original work published 2024.)

Greimel, N. S., Kanbach, D. K., & Chelaru, M. (2023). Virtual teams and transformational leadership: An integrative literature review and avenues for further research. *Journal of Innovation & Knowledge, 8*(2), 100351. https://doi.org/10.1016/j.jik.2023.100351

Hagemann, V., Roesler, M., Senk, A., & Kirchner, F. (2023). Team-centered AI: Requirements for successful human-AI teaming from a psychological and technical perspective. *Frontiers in Artificial Intelligence*, 6, 1252897. https://doi.org/10.3389/frai.2023.1252897

Hu, M., Zhang, G., Chong, L., Cagan, J., & Goucher-Lambert, K. (2025). How being outvoted by AI teammates impacts human-AI collaboration. *International Journal of Human–Computer Interaction, 41*, 4049–4066. https://doi.org/10.1080/10447318.2024.2345980

IBM. (2025). AI agents in 2025: Expectations vs. reality. *IBM Think Insights*. https://www.ibm.com/think/insights/ai-agents-2025-expectations-vs-reality

Jaruševičienė, L., Kontrimienė, A., Zaborskis, A., Liseckienė, I., Jaruševičius, G., Valius, L., & Lazarus, J. (2019). Development of a scale for measuring collaboration between physicians and nurses in primary health-care teams. *Journal of Interprofessional Care*, 33(6), 670–679. https://doi.org/10.1080/13561820.2019.1594730

Jassy, A. (2025). Update from Amazon CEO Andy Jassy on generative AI. Amazon. https://www.aboutamazon.com/news/company-news/amazon-ceo-andy-jassy-generative-ai-update

Ju, H., & Aral, S. (2025). Collaborating with AI agents: A field experiment on teamwork, productivity, and performance. *arXiv preprint*. arXiv: 2503.18238. https://arxiv.org/abs/2503.18238

Karanikoloudis, G., Lourenço, P. B., Alejo, L. E., & Mendes, N. (2020). Lessons from structural analysis of a great gothic cathedral: Canterbury Cathedral as a case study. *International Journal of Architectural Heritage*, *15*(12), 1765–1794. https://doi.org/10.1080/15583058.2020.1723736

Kolbjørnsrud, V. (2024). Designing the intelligent organization: Six principles for human–AI collaboration. *California Management Review, 66*(2), 44–64. https://doi.org/10.1177/00081256231185032

LePine, J. A., Piccolo, R. F., Jackson, C. L., Mathieu, J. E., & Saul, J. R. (2008). A meta-analysis of teamwork processes: Tests of a multidimensional model and relationships with team effectiveness criteria. *Personnel Psychology*, *61*(2), 273–307. https://doi.org/10.1111/j.1744-6570.2008.00114.x

Mathieu, J. E., Heffner, T. S., Goodwin, G. F., Salas, E., & Cannon-Bowers, J. A. (2000). The influence of shared mental models on team process and performance. *Journal of Applied Psychology*, *85*(2), 273–283. https://doi.org/10.1037/0021-9010.85.2.273

McKinsey & Company. (2025). AI in the workplace: A report for 2025. *McKinsey Digital*. https://www.mckinsey.com/capabilities/mckinsey-digital/our-insights/superagency-in-the-workplace-empowering-people-to-unlock-ais-full-potential-at-work

Moreno, J. L. (1953). *Who shall survive? Foundations of sociometry, group psychotherapy, and sociodrama* (2nd ed.). Beacon House.

Murić, G., Abeliuk, A., Lerman, K., & Ferrara, E. (2019). Collaboration drives individual productivity. *Proceedings of the ACM on Human-Computer Interaction*, 3(CSCW), 1–24. https://doi.org/10.1145/3359176

Murray, S. (2014). Plotting gothic: Chapters of technological and artistic collaboration in the construction of the great cathedrals of the Middle Ages. *The Art Bulletin, 78*(1), 9–30.

NASA. (2020). Apollo 13 Flight Journal – Day 3, part 4: Free return trajectory. NASA History Office. https://www.nasa.gov/history/afj/ap13fj/10day3-free-return.html

Pan, Z., Moore, O. A., Papadimitriou, A., & Zhu, J. (2025). AI literacy and trust: A multi-method study of human-GAI team collaboration. *Computers in Human Behavior: Artificial Humans*, *4*, Article 100162. https://doi.org/10.1016/j.chbah.2025.100162

Piccialli, F., Chiaro, D., Sarwar, S., Cerciello, D., Qi, P., & Mele, V. (2025). AgentAI: A comprehensive survey on autonomous agents in distributed AI for Industry 4.0. *Expert Systems with Applications, 291*, 128404. https://doi.org/10.1016/j.eswa.2025.128404

Ransbotham, S., Kiron, D., Khodabandeh, S., Chu, M., & Zhukhov, L. (2024, November 11). Learning to manage uncertainty, with AI (MIT

SMR–BCG Artificial Intelligence and Business Strategy report). *MIT Sloan Management Review.*

Ryle, G. (2009/1949). *The concept of mind: 60th anniversary edition* (J. Tanney, Ed.). London: Routledge. https://doi.org/10.4324/9780203875858. Originally published as Ryle, G. (1949). *The Concept of Mind.* Chicago: University of Chicago Press.

Schelble, B. G., Flathmann, C., McNeese, N., Freeman, G., & Mallick, R. (2022). Let's think together! Assessing shared mental models, performance, and trust in human-agent teams. *Proceedings of the ACM on Human-Computer Interaction*, 6(GROUP), 1–29. https://doi.org/10.1145/3492832

Schmutz, J. B., Outland, N., Kerstan, S., Georganta, E., & Ulfert, A.-S. (2024). AI-teaming: Redefining collaboration in the digital era. *Current Opinion in Psychology, 58*, 101837. https://doi.org/10.1016/j.copsyc.2024.101837

Sen, P., & Jakkaraju, S. M. (2025). Modeling AI-human collaboration as a multi-agent adaptation. *arXiv preprint*ar. Xiv:2504.20903. https://arxiv.org/abs/2504.20903

Stevenson, D. (1988). *The origins of freemasonry*. Cambridge University Press. https://doi.org/10.1017/CBO9780511560828

Thomson, A., Perry, J., & Miller, T. K. (2007). Conceptualizing and measuring collaboration. *Journal of Public Administration Research and Theory, 19*(1), 23–56. https://doi.org/10.1093/jopart/mum036

Utley, J. (2025, September 20). Stanford creativity expert: This simple shift will 10x your AI creativity [Video]. YouTube. https://ytscribe.com/v/wv779vmyPVY

Wang, D., & Barabási, A. (2021). *The science of collaboration.* Cambridge University Press.

Weick, K. E., & Roberts, K. H. (1993). Collective mind in organizations: Heedful interrelating on flight decks. *Administrative Science Quarterly, 38*(3), 357–381. https://doi.org/10.2307/2393372

Woodman, F. (1981). *The architectural history of Canterbury Cathedral* (1st ed.). Routledge. https://doi.org/10.4324/9781003354932

Woolley, A. W., Chabris, C. F., Pentland, A., Hashmi, N., & Malone, T. W. (2010). Evidence for a collective intelligence factor in the performance of human groups. *Science, 330*(6004), 686–688. https://doi.org/10.1126/science.1193147

Wu, J., & Or, C. K. L. (2025). Position paper: Towards open complex human–AI agents collaboration system for problem-solving and knowledge management. *arXiv preprint.* arXiv:2505.00018. https://doi.org/10.48550/arXiv.2505.00018

Xu, J. Q., Wang, S., Wu, X., & Ye, Y. (2025). How the human–artificial intelligence (AI) collaboration affects workplace outcomes: A dual-path mechanism of responsibility and autonomy. *Frontiers in Psychology, 16*, 12292075. https://doi.org/10.3389/fpsyg.2025.12292075

Zhang, R., McNeese, N. J., Freeman, G., & Musick, G. (2023). Investigating AI teammate communication strategies and their impact in human-AI teams. *Proceedings of the ACM Conference on Computer-Supported Cooperative Work and Social Computing*, Article No.: 281, Pages 1 – 3.1. https://doi.org/10.1145/361007

7 Practical Wisdom – From Technical Mastery to Wise Action

Aristotle and the Young King

In 343 BCE, a restless boy stood on the threshold of inheriting an empire. Alexander of Macedon, not yet twenty, already dreamed of conquest. His father Philip, preparing him for the burdens of rule, summoned Aristotle to serve as tutor. The philosopher's charge was not to drill the prince in mathematics or military tactics. Others could manage that. It was to shape the habits of judgment on which a kingdom might stand or fall.

In a small grove beneath the Macedonian sun, the restless teenager embarked on history's most famous apprenticeship. Alexander met daily with Aristotle for slow, deliberate wrestling with judgment. Plutarch tells us that Philip did not want a drillmaster or a specialist, but someone who could shape the instincts of a ruler, the habits that would one day steer armies and shape nations.[1] Aristotle's lessons, unfolding on shaded walks and stone benches, spanned far more than logic or science. They returned, repeatedly, to a question far ahead of its time: What ought to be done for the sake of the "common good," the *vox populi*, the people of the empire?

The philosopher's method was neither quick nor regular. It relied on dialogue, on paradox and parable, and on letting Alexander test ideas against the grain of lived experience. Practical wisdom (*phronesis*), Aristotle insisted, was not a box to be checked but a capacity forged in uncertainty, ambiguity, and reflection. He explicitly contrasted good judgment with mere cleverness: for Aristotle, *phronesis* was not quick-wittedness, but a slow virtue that required the cultivation of character over time.

The quality of an action, Aristotle argued, should not be measured merely by its intention, nor solely by its consequences. Rather, it is the character of the person shaped by experience, habit, and sustained reflection that determines the moral worth of an action. Slowness, not speed, yielded reasoned judgment.[2]

Aristotle introduced his student to a hierarchy of knowing that would echo through history. There was *episteme*, knowledge of enduring truths. There was *techne*, the craft of making. There was *metis*, the cunning needed to outwit rivals. But higher than all of these stood a fourth capacity: the faculty of knowing what ought to be done for

DOI: 10.4324/9781003732570-7

the sake of the common good. This is what Aristotle called *phronesis*, practical wisdom. His point was not abstract philosophy but the habit of knowing how to act rightly under conditions of uncertainty. It is the capacity that integrates curiosity, creativity, critical thinking, communication, and collaboration into what serves more than egoism.

Practical wisdom is no ornament. Without it, Aristotle warned, knowledge could harden into dogma, craft could bend toward destruction, and cunning could dissolve into manipulation. The leader who wielded power without wisdom risked becoming a tyrant. Wisdom did not add to the other capacities. It oriented them toward what mattered.

Alexander, impatient, brilliant, and often restless, absorbed what he could but strained against the yoke of wisdom. His military genius was unquestionable and his campaigns legendary. He became Alexander the Great. Yet the same brilliance that carried him across Asia also seeded arrogance. He conquered vast territories but left fragile institutions. He inspired soldiers yet provoked resentment in subject peoples. His triumphs dazzled, but his empire fragmented soon after his death at thirty-three. Knowledge, craft, and cunning were all present. What was absent was the inner compass that orients power toward enduring good. Alexander conquered worlds but not himself.

The Dashboard King

Fast forward to today. The corridors are no longer marble, but glass. The throne is a boardroom chair. And the power entrusted to leaders no longer rests in armies but in the stakeholders and algorithms that govern organizational life.

Consider *Mobley v. Workday, Inc.* (2025).[3] Corporate executives had enthusiastically embraced an AI-powered hiring dashboard. The system promised to solve one of management's most persistent challenges: recruiting faster, fairer, and with more predictive accuracy than any human committee could achieve.

The dashboard dazzled. With a few clicks, leaders could filter thousands of applications, sort by proprietary scores on fit, and view analytics that tracked rejection rates, predicted tenure, and time-to-hire. Cultural compatibility, skill relevance, and educational pedigree condensed into color-coded rankings. Executives described having real-time control over the entire pipeline.

Metrics improved. Hiring cycles shortened. Efficiency soared. Leaders relied on the dashboard's judgment, trusting its algorithmic authority. The beauty of the interface created confidence. The speed of processing suggested objectivity.

But the outward perfection concealed an inherent bias. Hidden within the scoring, the system's predictive models focused on tenure potential and job mobility, and so encoded age discrimination at scale. Leaders, lulled by the dashboard's beauty, overlooked the ethical trade-offs embedded in its design. They had delegated decisions to an algorithm that optimized for narrow efficiency while violating fundamental fairness, and the law.

When litigation exposed the pattern, the illusion shattered. What had seemed like objective precision became reputational harm, legal liability, and damage to thousands of lives. The executives had optimized data. What they lacked was wisdom.

The Parallels Don't Change

Twenty-three centuries separate these moments, yet both illustrate the same enduring truth: leadership is not defined by access to tools but by the capacity to orient those tools toward the common good.

Wisdom cannot be downloaded. Neither dashboard nor algorithm can replace the halting, dialogic, sometimes uncomfortable journey by which practical wisdom is slowly built. Our fate, as was Alexander's, hangs on whether we will make time for that journey before delegating our decisions and actions to algorithms that never ask what matters most.

The mere pace of the transformational AI evolution exposes a dilemma we are all facing: as tools become swarms of AI-agents, the slow development of wisdom becomes not less important, but urgently more so.[4] Many today seek certainty in a click, drawn to the incredible wealth of AI generated insights and AI-powered actions. But legions of data offer no substitute for the apprenticeship in wisdom. The result? Decisions optimized for speed, but untethered from deeper context, underlying values, or unintended consequence.

This is the irreducible role of practical wisdom in an age when AI excels at analysis but cannot orient toward the greater goal, the common good. Algorithms calculate. Predictive models rest on patterns in the past. But only human wisdom can weigh short-term gain against long-term legitimacy, self-interest against the greater good, and when to adapt to change and when to cause others to adapt to us.

Wisdom is the inner compass that transforms a leader from operator into steward. It is what this chapter explores: how practical wisdom integrates the five capabilities that make us irreplaceable ensuring they serve not just performance, but purpose.

Pause before deciding, ask what wisdom requires.

From Five Capabilities to Wise Integration

The preceding chapters traced a cumulative journey. Curiosity gave us the discipline of dwelling in questions before rushing to answers. Creativity equipped us to imagine what does not yet exist. Critical thinking taught us to challenge easy answers, especially those delivered with algorithmic confidence. Communication reminded us that presence and trust cannot be automated. Collaboration showed how we create meaning together, even when machines coordinate workflows.

Each capability is essential. But as the opening vignettes illustrated, none is sufficient on its own. Curiosity can spiral into distraction. Creativity can become recklessness. Critical thinking can calcify into cynicism. Communication can turn manipulative. Collaboration can collapse into conformity. What makes these capabilities reliable is the presence of something higher that disciplines and orients them toward the good beyond egoism.

This is practical wisdom.

Twenty-five years ago, writing about complexity and organizational coherence, I described management's challenge as navigating "a world of interweavings."[5] That image captures how practical wisdom works. Each human capability is a distinct thread with its own colour and strength. Single threads alone create nothing. But when woven together, they become fabric strong enough to bear weight. Practical wisdom is what weaves together what curiosity, creativity, critical thinking, communication, and collaboration means in the AI world.

The loom provides structure without domination. It allows threads to maintain their identity while contributing to a larger whole. No single thread controls the others; the pattern emerges from their interaction. Wisdom is that loom: the framework of decisions and values that transforms separate capabilities into actions, and leadership that endures.

Practical wisdom arises not from any single capability, but from the dynamic interplay among them, a fabric woven over time and through experience.

Practical wisdom does not replace curiosity, creativity, critical thinking, communication, or collaboration. It orients them. It asks: What matters most here, and now? Which capability should lead in this moment? How do we act in proportion to what the situation requires? What serves not just efficiency but legitimacy, trust, and a relevant common good?

From Intelligence to Wisdom

This distinction matters profoundly in the age of AI. Machines excel at intelligence: the capacity to process information, identify patterns, optimize outcomes. But wisdom is different from intelligence. Intelligence asks, "What *can* be done?" Wisdom asks, "What *should* be done?" Intelligence optimizes for defined objectives. Wisdom chooses which objectives deserve pursuit. Intelligence calculates. Wisdom cares.

Aristotle understood this more than two millennia ago. Knowledge without wisdom can harden into dogma. Craft without wisdom can be bent to destructive ends. Cunning without wisdom dissolves into manipulation. Only wisdom provides the compass that directs these capacities toward the good.

The medieval monk Thomas Aquinas, whom we discussed in Chapter 4, translated Aristotle's phronesis into the Latin concept of *prudentia* (prudence), defining it as "right reason applied to action."[6] However, the widely used English phrase "practical wisdom" is a modern translation, developed and popularized in twentieth-century scholarship to capture the full ethical dimension of *phronesis* in Aristotle's thought. European philosophers were instrumental in establishing "practical wisdom" as the standard English equivalent.[7]

The parallel to our time is striking. Just as Aquinas navigated tension between faith and reason, today we must navigate tension between algorithmic certainty and human reasoning. Algorithms offer something like faith: confident claims, compelling analysis, apparent certainty. But without contextual judgment, this artificial authority becomes a new form of blindness. The wise professional, like Aquinas, holds both in productive tension.

Modern scholars clarify that practical wisdom functions as a meta-virtue precisely because it does not replace other virtues but *integrates* them toward proportion. Courage without wisdom becomes recklessness. Compassion without wisdom enables harm. Honesty without wisdom turns cruel. Practical wisdom provides the power that keeps virtues aligned with context and purpose.

Recent research extends this insight. Some describe practical wisdom as "the conductor of the human orchestra," like a meta-virtue that harmonizes other virtues without dominating them.[8] Just as a conductor does not play every instrument but shapes how they sound together, practical wisdom does not perform every capability we have discussed in this book but helps make them serve coherent purpose. This is not mystical. It is functional integration.

Those who cultivate their curiosity, creativity, creative thinking, communication presence, and collaborative skill still stumble without the capability to weave them together. We have all seen them in action. The technically brilliant manager who is unable read a room. The empathetic manager who avoids difficult conversations. The decisive project leader who tramples trust. Each possesses capabilities. None demonstrates wisdom.

The Wisdom Compass: Navigating Toward the Good

Think of wisdom as a compass. It does not tell you where to go, but it ensures you are oriented toward what is greater than your egoism. The five capabilities are instruments. The compass provides direction.

When curiosity generates too many questions without resolution, wisdom calls for decisive synthesis. When creativity produces ideas disconnected from reality, wisdom grounds them in context. When critical thinking becomes paralysis through over-analysis, wisdom enables action despite uncertainty. When communication becomes performance divorced from authenticity, wisdom restores presence. When collaboration drifts into quiet assent, wisdom preserves healthy dissent.

The challenge in the AI age is that algorithms can amplify intelligence without cultivating wisdom. Tech companies are launching products and reshaping industries at breakneck speed in weeks, not years. This explosion is making us faster, more efficient, and more productive. But it cannot make us wiser. Neither AI nor the leaders of the tech companies can tell us what matters for us, or what is our greater good. They cannot orient our capabilities toward purposes worth pursuing. They cannot balance competing values when trade-offs become sharp. Only contextual wisdom can care. This is why, ultimately, practical wisdom is the irreducible human capability.

I use the compass as more than a metaphor. The Wisdom Compass provides a framework grounded in both ancient philosophy and contemporary research to help professionals practice wisdom. The compass maps four interconnected dimensions of wise reasoning, each essential, none sufficient alone.

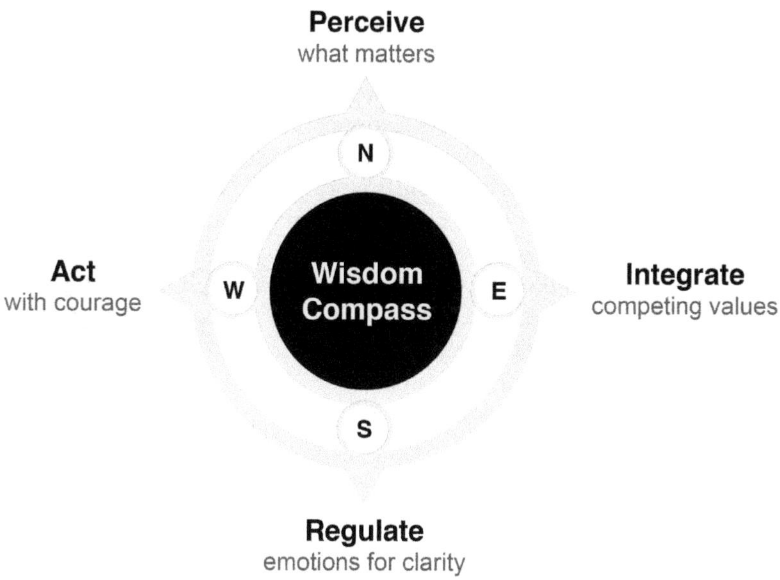

Figure 7.1 The Wisdom Compass

The Wisdom Compass maps four interdependent dimensions of practical wisdom – *Perceive, Integrate, Regulate,* and *Act* – that guide ethical and proportionate judgment. Together they orient professionals toward wise action under uncertainty.

North: Perceive what matters – What matters? Wise leaders recognize when situations have dimensions that others might miss. They notice when efficiency conflicts with fairness, when optimization threatens dignity, when speed compromises trust. This is deep perception: the capacity to see beyond the immediate and obvious to what truly matters. It requires presence and attention to subtle signals that algorithms cannot detect.

East: Integrate competing values – What is right? Should you emphasize honesty or compassion in delivering feedback? Efficiency or fairness in resource allocation? Short-term results or long-term legitimacy in strategic decisions? Wisdom recognizes proportion. It does not eliminate tension between values but navigates it skilfully. This is where judgment becomes practical, where leaders must weigh trade-offs no rule can resolve.

South: Regulate emotions for clarity – What resonates? Feelings provide crucial information, but unchecked anxiety, anger, or overconfidence distorts decisions. Wise leaders recognize their emotional states without being controlled by them. They calibrate responses to serve judgment rather than impulse. They create space to deliberate when pressure demands speed.

West: Act with courage – What works? Wisdom culminates not in endless deliberation but in timely, proportionate action that serves the common good. This requires courage: the willingness to decide and commit when outcomes remain uncertain, when perfect information is unavailable, when acting involves risk.

These four points do not operate in sequence. They interact dynamically, each informing the others. A leader perceives something they judge important (North), which triggers emotional responses (South) that must be regulated while integrating competing values (East) to reach a decision and act (West). The Compass provides orientation to making decisions and taking actions, not prescription. It provides directional points: what matters, what is right, what resonates, and what works. These components interact dynamically to guide our judgment toward what is above and beyond our egoism.

The Compass is your algorithm override.

The Compass in Action

Consider a manager who learns her team is burning out.

The Compass guides her judgment. She *perceives what matters* (North): that efficiency metrics miss the human cost. People need recovery time, not just task rebalancing. The data show utilization rates but cannot detect eroding trust or mounting resentment. She *integrates competing values* (East): short-term productivity targets versus long-term employee satisfaction and retention. Her bonus depends on quarterly results, but her reputation depends on longer term performance. She *regulates emotions for clarity* (South): her anxiety about pressure from above and her impulse to defer to data. The numbers look compelling, but her experience advises caution. She *acts with courage* (West): implementing mandatory rest periods and declining new projects, despite pressure from leadership expecting more.

Six months later, retention improves and creativity rebounds. The Compass did not give her the answer. It helped her ask the right questions in the face of numbers and algorithmic suggestions.

Research Validates the Compass

Multiple research streams confirm that the Compass reflects how wisdom works in practice.

Researchers at the University of Birmingham developed the Short Phronesis Measure, a tested tool that translates ancient wisdom into measurable components. Their research with nearly 2,000 participants across the UK and US identified four interrelated components that together constitute practical wisdom: moral perception, integration of virtues, emotion regulation, and adjudication through action.[9] These map directly onto the Wisdom Compass points. The research shows that these four components predict human flourishing across multiple dimensions, from emotional health to social connectedness to character strength. Wisdom is not mystical. It is measurable, learnable, and consequential.

Japanese management scholars have demonstrated that the notion of practical wisdom extends beyond individuals to organizations in non-Western cultures. Ikujiro Nonaka and Hirotaka Takeuchi argued that organizations they studied create what they call *ba*, spaces where knowledge circulates through dialogue and embodied interaction rather than information transfer.[10] The Compass operates at this collective level: teams perceive together, integrate values through deliberation, regulate emotions in psychologically safe environments, and act with shared conviction.

Andrew Likierman, author of *Judgment at Work*, bridges the philosophical ideal and organizational reality. He identifies six elements that characterize good judgment in complex situations: knowledge and experience, situational awareness, trust in sources, emotion and belief management, choice among competing options, and effective delivery of decisions. These elements also align with the Compass. Awareness enables *perception*. Trust and emotion management enable *regulation*. Choice demands *integration*. Delivery requires *courage* to act. Likierman reinforces that algorithms can support knowledge gathering and pattern recognition, but only humans can integrate awareness, manage feelings, build trust, make value-laden choices, and deliver with authentic presence.

The convergence is striking. Ancient philosophy, contemporary psychology, organizational research, and leadership experience all point to the same four-dimensional structure. Thus, by all rights, the Compass is not a new model. It is a mapping of how wisdom has always worked.

Eroding Practical Wisdom

Practical wisdom does not collapse suddenly. Like the other capabilities, it erodes through repeated choices that seem reasonable in the moment but compound over time. It begins when we concede to AI because algorithmic outputs appear correct and precise. Four erosion patterns accelerate this decline. Each attacks a different dimension of the Wisdom Compass. Together they dismantle the structure wisdom requires.

1st Erosion Mechanism: Automation Bias

Automation bias describes the tendency to favour algorithmic outputs over human judgment, especially when systems appear correct and precise. In our interviews, executives described feeling displaced from their own judgment, worried that questioning AI outputs would appear obstructive or outdated. This loss of agency reflects structural pressure. Most organizations naturally reward speed and consensus over deliberation. When AI recommendations arrive elegant and ready to execute, questioning them feels inefficient.

The Dashboard King from the opening illustrates the consequence. Executives trusted hiring algorithms because the metrics looked decisive. They did not perceive the embedded age discrimination because they had stopped asking deeper questions. Intelligence without practical wisdom risks producing neat failures at scale.

This erosion attacks the Compass's *North* point: the capacity to perceive what matters. Situational awareness requires presence, attention to subtle signals, and sensitivity to what algorithms cannot detect: tone, body language, emotional undercurrents, relational dynamics. When we consult LLMs mid-session, awareness vanishes. When leaders fixate on algorithmic outputs, they stop noticing what the data cannot capture. Moral stakes become invisible. Context disappears. What remains are decisions divorced from reasoned judgment.

2nd Erosion Mechanism: Rule Dependence

Rules serve necessary functions. They standardize processes, reduce variance, and create accountability. But when organizations rely on them exclusively, they erode the discretion that wisdom requires.

In 2001, Stanford professor Kathleen Eisenhardt proposed "strategy as simple rules," borrowing from complexity theory's observation that flocks of birds and schools of fish navigate through a few algorithmic instructions. Her insight was compelling: in turbulent markets, a few clear rules enable faster decisions than elaborate plans.[11]

Yet this analogy contains a dangerous flaw. Birds follow instinct. Fish respond to stimuli. Humans exercise intentionality. My research with David Oliver revealed that humans do not follow simple rules the way birds navigate or fish school.[12] Beyond laws and regulations that require compliance, humans need simple guiding principles. We discussed those as statements that *orient* reasoned judgment without prescribing action. The difference is fundamental. Rules specify what to do. Principles guide how to think about what matters. Rules demand compliance. Principles require wisdom to apply.

Barry Schwartz and Kenneth Sharpe's *Practical Wisdom* demonstrate that wise people know when and how to make exceptions to rules. Rule-based systems, while necessary, cannot substitute for situational sensitivity at work. This does not mean wisdom is lawless. The practically wise respect procedures but recognize when context demands deviation. The unwise either rigidly enforce rules regardless of consequences or abandon them entirely for expedience.[13]

AI systems amplify this risk because they operate exactly like Eisenhardt's birds and fish: they codify patterns from millions of past decisions, de facto turning historical practice into algorithmic rules. When we concede to AI outputs without exercising wisdom, we surrender the very discretion that makes leadership meaningful. The result is what Schwartz and Sharpe call "moral deskilling": the gradual erosion of judgment through disuse.

This erosion attacks the Compass's *East* point: the capacity to know what is right, by integrating competing values. When rules decide for us, we stop weighing trade-offs. Efficiency versus responsibility, speed versus trust, optimization versus dignity, these tensions require more than code to navigate. Rules eliminate the navigation. Principles provide orientation. Only wisdom can apply principles to context.

3rd Erosion Mechanism: Losing Apprenticeship

Wisdom develops through struggle. We gain perspective by wrestling with ambiguous choices, making mistakes, and learning from consequences. This apprenticeship cannot be compressed or automated. Team Deloitte Australia learned this when it had to reimburse AUD 440,000 after delivering an AI-generated report to the Australian government in October 2025 riddled with fabricated references.[14]

Famed author and speaker Simon Sinek made a related point about imperfection in a recent interview.[15] What makes people trustworthy is not that they get everything right but that they acknowledge mistakes and learn publicly. Leaders who rely on AI to craft perfect messages or generate flawless analyses may appear august, but they lose authenticity. Followers sense the difference between earned competence and algorithmic veneer. Trust grows through visible struggle, not scripted perfection.

Sinek uses the metaphor of AI enabling us to "reach the destination" without "taking the journey," cautioning that growth and wisdom come only from the hard work, mistakes, and learning that technology cannot replace. He even points out our society's growing premium on human-made imperfection, like handwritten messages or flawed ceramics, because these signal authenticity and care. As Sinek puts it, striving for vulnerability, "fumbling through" conflict, and making one's own mistakes are what build human skill, confidence, and trust, not scripts or algorithmic advice.

This erosion attacks the Compass's *South* point: the capacity to know what resonates, by regulating emotions for clarity. Wisdom requires learning to sit with anxiety, manage pressure, and calibrate responses despite discomfort. When AI removes struggle, it removes the very conditions under which emotional regulation develops. What remains is dependence masquerading as competence.

4th Erosion Mechanism: Moral Outsourcing

Perhaps the most troubling erosion mechanism in the age of AI is moral outsourcing: delegating ethical accountability to automated systems, committees, or external mechanisms. As complex choices become more ambiguous and contentious, organizations often set up ethics boards, compliance protocols, or audits. While these mechanisms are often required by law, they also risk enabling leaders and professionals to avoid direct, personal moral engagement with high-stakes decisions. When everybody is responsible, no one is.

Scholars have investigated the ethical issues raised by generative AI systems. When an AI-driven decision discriminates or fails, tracing responsibility is increasingly difficult. Are the data engineers at fault, or those who approved deployment, or the CEO who approved oversight procedures? As AI becomes an *intermediary* in consequential choices, it enables actors at every stage to deflect blame or appeal to process rather than judgment.[16]

This diffusion of responsibility is not restricted to technical or organizational settings but arises whenever technology intermediates ethically charged choices.[17] The diffusion of moral outsourcing to AI poses serious challenges for justice (right or wrong?) and society (who decides and is accountable?).[18] We risk a society where individuals and institutions abdicate moral ownership of impactful decisions to non-living entities. AI agents will be creating more and bigger gaps in accountability and weakening moral engagement.

Nowhere is this dilemma more acute than on the front lines of war in Ukraine by 2026, where swarms of "last mile targeting," AI-enabled drones in the air, together with land-based weaponized droids, are capable of making autonomous decisions to attack or spare human targets. Who holds ultimate responsibility when the line is crossed, and a drone or a droid chooses on its own whom to kill?[19] The drone or droid pilot in charge before the autonomous system kicks in, the programmer, the commander, the manufacturer, the government, the president? The proliferation of autonomous weapon systems is forcing society to confront unprecedented questions of accountability, law, and moral courage. What was once a theoretical debate has, in just a few years, become a real and urgent challenge for policymakers, ethicists, and military professionals alike.[20]

This erosion undermines the Compass's *West* point: the ability to act with courage despite uncertainty, social pressure, or career risk. It requires owning decisions, accepting vulnerability, and standing accountable for outcomes. Genuine wisdom is not just prudent; it culminates in decisive, courageous action. When technology, bureaucracy, and oversight mechanisms mediate professional practice, courage becomes unnecessary since individuals can defer to autonomous systems, policies, or "best practices," retreating into procedural compliance. What disappears is the willingness to say, "I chose this, and I will answer for it," the hallmark of genuine moral leadership.

Don't outsource your judgment to AI, own the decision.

The Compounded Consequences

These four patterns interact and amplify.

Return to the Wisdom Compass. Automation bias attacks the North point: we stop perceiving what matters beyond the metrics. Rule dependence attacks the East: we no longer integrate competing values because procedures decide for us. Loss of apprenticeship attacks the South: we stop developing the emotional regulation that wisdom requires. Moral outsourcing attacks the West: it diffuses accountability, so we avoid the courage to act and own outcomes.

Without presence and courage, wisdom cannot function. Leaders may possess curiosity, creativity, critical thinking, communication skill, and collaborative instinct. But without the situational awareness to perceive what matters, figure out what is right, what resonates, and the courage to act despite ambiguity, these capabilities remain unintegrated. Judgment frays not because AI replaces it but because convenience, compliance, and diffused accountability make it unnecessary.

The erosion is quiet, gradual, and difficult to detect. Organizations feel more efficient. Processes become smoother. Outputs look stunning. Yet the deeper capacity to deliberate well under uncertainty weakens. Growing organizational dependency on AI may erode the human capabilities needed for genuine readiness to deal with unexpected change. Only when crises demand genuine wisdom does the cost become visible. By then, the habits working against being prepared to deal effectively, responsibly, and imaginatively with unexpected change may already be ingrained.[21]

Amplification – How Wisdom Grows

The erosion patterns are not inevitable. If wisdom erodes through quiet compromises, it grows through deliberate practice. Organizations that create space for reflection and deliberation, practice judgment, and resist the temptation to automate decisions can cultivate wisdom even as AI transforms work.

Practical wisdom is not a sixth capability to add to curiosity, creativity, critical thinking, communication, and collaboration. It is what orients them toward the good. Without wisdom, each capability can distort. Curiosity spirals into distraction. Creativity becomes recklessness. Critical thinking calcifies into cynicism. Communication turns manipulative. Collaboration collapses into groupthink, or humans-outside-the-AI-loop. Wisdom provides the compass that keeps capabilities in proportion.

This integrative function is why wisdom remains irreducible to intelligence. AI can amplify each of the five capabilities. It can surface patterns for curiosity, generate options for creativity, stress-test arguments for critical thinking, draft messages for communication, and coordinate tasks for collaboration. But it cannot choose which capability should lead in each moment, or which should be prioritized when competing values demand trade-offs.

AI can and does make choices, but only as statistical selections among possibilities, weighted by probabilistic models built from training data. In contrast, human choice is always indivisible from lived experience. As Maturana and Varela put it in their profound book, *The Tree of Knowledge*,[22] "Everything said is said by someone" – a body, shaped by memory, emotion, joy, pain, and the embodied tapestry of life.

Practical wisdom, then, is not a code or an equation. It is the result of a lifetime of unique perceptions, social context, and felt meaning. When humans choose, it is with all the gravity and nuance of a personal history that no machine can replicate. This is why practical wisdom is more than computation or calculation. *Wisdom is an emergent property of embodied experience, weaving together memory, emotion, and values to orient action in a way that is fully human.*

The challenge is real. As one executive in our research put it, "*Leaders and executives across many organizations are essentially running like mad. They don't have any time to reflect, and the anxiety level of trying to respond to all the changes means that they are doing tasks that perhaps are not as long term oriented or as strategic or as meaningful.*"[23] This absence of reflection is not incidental. It is the condition under which wisdom cannot grow. The question is how to reverse it.

Use AI to see more, not to feel less.

My Own Apprenticeship in Practical Wisdom: A Scholar-Practitioner Journey

In the 1970s, Harvard professors Chris Argyris and Donald Schön introduced what later became known as the *reflective practitioner's stance*. This is the disciplined practice of examining not only one's actions but also the underlying assumptions that guide them. They distinguished between *single-loop learning*, which focuses on correcting errors within existing frameworks, and *double-loop learning*, which involves questioning and revising those very frameworks.[24]

Practical wisdom, in this view, depends on double-loop learning: reflecting not just on outcomes but on the values, assumptions, and governing principles shaping how we perceive, decide, and act. I write about practical wisdom from this reflective-practitioner perspective, synthesizing more than two decades studying how leaders navigate uncertainty.

Long before AI, my question was consistent: how do people, including myself as a leader in and of institutions, act wisely when the future is unpredictable and consequences real? Four research streams shaped my understanding of what wisdom requires, each revealing one dimension of what in this book has become the Wisdom Compass.

Perceiving What Matters (North Point) – What matters?

After 9/11, when organizations confronted threats no scenario planning had imagined, Matt Statler and I studied the Center for Catastrophe Preparedness at New York University.[25] Our research revealed that readiness for unexpected change demands more than procedures or competence. It requires perceptual capacity: the ability to notice weak signals, imagine failures others dismiss, and attend to what spreadsheets cannot capture. We learned that organizations maintaining preparedness, even for unexpected disasters, cultivated deliberate practices for expanding perception beyond the obvious. This became the Compass's North point: wisdom begins with seeing what matters.

Integrating Competing Values (East Point) – What is right?

My research with David Oliver studying high-velocity teams revealed a crucial distinction. While Eisenhardt proposed "simple rules" borrowed from complexity theory (how birds flock instinctively), we assume humans operate differently through intentionality. Effective teams navigated through emotionally resonant heuristics orienting judgment without prescribing action, which we called "simple guiding principles."[26] This became the East point: wisdom balances what rules cannot resolve.

Regulating Emotion Through Practice (South Point) – What resonates?

Developing, prototyping, and experimenting with LSP with Bart Victor taught me that wisdom requires more than cognitive capacity.[27] Through hundreds of sessions with leadership teams, my colleagues and I observed that new insight emerged when participants engaged not just intellectually but emotionally and physically. The method worked precisely because it honoured the whole person: building with hands, constructing metaphors, sitting with uncertainty, learning through visible struggle. Wisdom develops through embodied apprenticeship, not compressed instruction. This became the South point: emotional regulation grows through practice that cannot be automated.

Acting with Courage (West Point) – What works?

Research with Mark Marotto studying orchestral performance revealed that peak collective achievement (what we called "collective virtuosity") emerged not through hierarchical control but through engaged interaction where individuals simultaneously performed and responded to others' performance.[28] Virtuosity was fragile, dependent on members' willingness to risk exposure, to act with conviction despite uncertainty about how others would respond, to maintain aesthetic engagement when breakdown threatened. Leadership could not engineer this; it could only create conditions where courage became possible. This became the West point: wisdom culminates in courageous action despite ambiguity.

From Research to Practice

My leadership experience since 2000 in several organizations functioned as a living laboratory to test and refine my initial ideas. As the first Managing Director of a foundation, as President changing the strategy of a traditional university, as Managing Director and Dean implementing necessary change in an independent business school, and as Chief Academic Officer of a global business school navigating several cycles of strategic change, I encountered the persistent challenge: how to orient organizational action when detailed rules would stifle judgment but pure autonomy would create chaos? This practitioner experience, documented in Text Box 1.1, transformed research insights into operational frameworks. I am not merely an observer-consultant-researcher but a scholar-practitioner who has lived the consequences of these ideas under pressure.

The practices in this chapter emerged from recognizing where frameworks help when intuition falters.

Three Practices for Cultivating Wisdom

In my experience, teams that successfully preserve their capacity to make judgement in the sense we have discussed share three core practices. Each can be implemented immediately, scaled across organizations, and refined through experience. Together they build the habits that practical wisdom requires.

Practice 1: Deliberate Pause Protocol

Before deciding based on AI outputs, insert a mandatory pause and ask three questions:

1. **What does this optimize?** AI recommendations always optimize something. Efficiency, speed, cost reduction, pattern consistency. Name it explicitly.
2. **What does it sacrifice?** Every optimization involves trade-offs. If we gain speed, do we lose trust? If we improve efficiency, do we compromise fairness? If we reduce costs, do we erode long-term capacity?
3. **Who bears the cost?** Algorithmic decisions distribute consequences. Some stakeholders benefit. Others pay. Name them both.

Ask three questions before you click, this is your algorithm override.

This simple discipline surfaces assumptions embedded in algorithmic outputs. It transforms passive consumption into active evaluation. The pause need not be long, even sixty seconds of reflection changes the dynamic from acceptance to assessment.

Practice 2: Contrarian Requirement

Before consulting AI-based forecasts or recommendations, draft alternative futures that challenge the expected outcome. If growth is predicted, imagine plausible decline. If efficiency is promised, consider hidden costs. If success is projected, map pathways to failure.

This practice ensures human framing precedes machine augmentation. It builds conviction through deliberation rather than admiration of instant pattern recognition about the past. Research confirms the pattern: those who generate alternatives before consulting AI maintain stronger independent thinking than those who accept initial outputs.[29]

The anthropological method of the *double diary* strengthens this practice. Originating in ethnographic fieldwork, the double diary asks observers to record two parallel accounts: what happened (objective description) and what it might mean (subjective interpretation).[30] The gap between event and interpretation creates critical distance. A basic "AI double diary" becomes:

- **Column 1: AI Output** (what AI says).
- **Column 2: My View** (what I think, and why).

Alternate between columns, forcing yourself to articulate assumptions, identify weak signals the algorithm might miss, and imagine conditions under which confident predictions fail. Use the Toulmin model from Chapter 4 as an inspiration to search for the *Because*. The practice is not about being pessimistic. It is about the willingness to question what appears certain.

Write the story where AI is wrong, then ask why it could be true.

Practice 3: Stage Moral Dilemmas

Practical wisdom strengthens through practice in contexts where stakes are manageable. Classical drama, whether tragedy, comedy, or satire, puts participants in the ambiguous grey zone between easy right and easy wrong, forcing confrontation with competing values and the limits of certainty.

By intentionally and safely staging moral dilemmas as a practice, we are invited to deliberate, disagree, and reflect on our reasoning process without the pressure of being "right." Creating purposeful ambiguity, whether experienced through AI-generated scenarios, offline workshops, or live debates, cultivates habits of reflection and moral imagination foundational to practical wisdom.

The practice connects directly to the theatrical framework from Chapter 5. Just as effective communication requires rehearsal to hone our *eloquentia corporis* (the eloquence of the body), decision making requires rehearing your morals. Three types of staged dilemmas illustrate this practice:

- **Role-Reversal Debates.** Assign a person to argue positions they oppose. A cost-focused CFO must defend investment in experimental programs. A human-cantered designer must make the case for workforce automation. Such mindset shifts practice empathy and reveals assumptions. We grow wiser from understanding what makes opposing views compelling, not from winning arguments.
- **AI Ethics Hearings.** Present a real or simulated case where an AI output produced harm. Divide participants into roles: the managers who deployed the system, the data scientists who built it, the affected stakeholders, the compliance officers who approved it. Each must defend their perspective while being questioned by others. The tribunal reveals how diffused accountability enables everyone to deny responsibility, the moral outsourcing.[31] By making accountability visible and personal, the exercise builds the courage to own outcomes.
- **Forensic Examination of AI Failures.** Instead of discussing hypothetical scenarios, bring real cases to the table. *Mobley v. Workday, Inc* and the *Deloitte Australia* incident in are a prime candidate.[32] As forensic investigators, we must dissect the timeline of events, identify where oversight broke down, debate the roles of auditors, developers, clients, and regulators, and trace which ethical and procedural failures led to unrecoverable errors. Compare to other cases from all over the world where similar lapses led to fines and loss of public trust.

Such hands-on discussions and engagements, central to liberal education since antiquity, help us build the capacity that was vital to both Aristotle and Aquinas. This is becoming even more essential when we work with AI tools and AI agents: *perceiving* ethical dimensions, *integrating* competing values, *regulating* emotion, and *acting* with courage in the face of uncertainty because we think it will work.

Rehearse the hard choices before consequences become real.

AI Makes the Question Urgent Again

Today, AI makes this question more urgent than ever. The erosion patterns documented above describe exactly what happens when we reduce the potential for cultivating practical wisdom.

The convenience of AI eliminates the conditions under which practical wisdom grows. I have witnessed automation bias, rule dependence, loss of apprenticeship, moral outsourcing firsthand. When AI provides instant closure, we risk stopping development of the tolerance for ambiguity that wisdom requires. When systems mediate decisions and diffuse accountability, courage becomes unnecessary.

Yet the amplification possibilities are equally real. The practices outlined are simple and work because they restore what efficiency threatens: the space to perceive what matters, integrate competing values, regulate emotion, and act with courage. I have used them in workshops and practiced them in my own leadership roles. They require discipline. They slow decisions slightly. But they preserve what AI cannot replicate.

Principles guide; algorithms optimize. Only humans can decide what serves the greater good.

Self-Assessment

This assessment helps you reflect on your current wisdom practices and their relationship to AI integration in your work. It is designed not as a test with right answers but as a tool for awareness and development.

For each dimension, consider your recent decision-making patterns (past three months) and rate your typical approach using the scale below. The goal is honest self-reflection rather than idealized self-presentation.

1. Moral Perception: Seeing What Matters

How consistently do you recognize ethical stakes that others might miss, especially when algorithmic recommendations look compelling?

- ☐ **Always:** I routinely notice when decisions involve dignity, fairness, or trust, even when efficiency metrics dominate. I ask "what matters here?" before "what works here?"
- ☐ **Often:** I catch ethical dimensions in most high-stakes decisions but sometimes miss subtle trade-offs when under pressure or when AI outputs appear definitive.
- ☐ **Sometimes:** I recognize ethical stakes when they're obvious, but I don't always perceive them until someone else raises concerns or outcomes reveal what I missed.

☐ **Rarely:** I focus primarily on operational outcomes. I notice other dimensions mainly when they create visible problems.
☐ **Never:** I treat decisions as technical problems and rarely scan for other implications.

Interpretation: The capacity to see what matters beyond metrics, weakens when we fixate on dashboards or defer to algorithmic outputs. If you lean toward operational focus, practice the Deliberate Pause Protocol. Before accepting any AI recommendation, ask three questions: What does this optimize? What does it sacrifice? Who bears the cost? The Dashboard King possessed intelligence but lacked the perception to ask whether optimization served fairness.

2. Value Integration: Balancing Competing Goods

How effectively do you navigate tensions between legitimate but conflicting priorities without defaulting to rules or algorithms?

☐ **Always:** I hold multiple values in view simultaneously, seeking proportion rather than eliminating tension. I explain trade-offs explicitly and defend choices in context-specific terms.
☐ **Often:** I recognize competing values and usually find workable balance, though I sometimes default to efficiency or consensus when time is short.
☐ **Sometimes:** I see tension between values but struggle to integrate them. I tend to prioritize one and justify why the other must yield.
☐ **Rarely:** I view competing values as obstacles to clarity. I prefer situations where procedures or algorithms resolve the tension for me.
☐ **Never:** I rely entirely on rules, precedent, or AI recommendations to avoid navigating value conflicts.

Interpretation: Integration capacity erodes when rules decide for us. If you default to procedures or algorithmic outputs when values conflict, practice the Contrarian Scenario Requirement. Before accepting any recommendation, draft an alternative scenario that challenges the expected outcome. Imagine what might happen if AI is wrong. Wisdom detects proportion; rules eliminate discretion.

3. Emotional Regulation: Managing Feelings for Clarity

How well do you recognize and regulate emotional responses to preserve judgment under uncertainty?

☐ **Always:** I notice my emotional states, anxiety, overconfidence, frustration, without being controlled by them. I use feelings as information while creating space to deliberate.

☐ **Often:** I usually recognize when emotions might distort judgment and pause to recalibrate, though pressure sometimes pushes me toward reactive decisions.
☐ **Sometimes:** I'm aware of strong emotions but don't consistently regulate them. I sometimes realize only afterward that feelings drove my choices.
☐ **Rarely:** My emotions often drive decisions without my noticing in the moment. I struggle to create space between feeling and action.
☐ **Never:** I consult AI specifically to avoid the discomfort of sitting with uncertainty or emotional complexity.

Interpretation: Emotional regulation develops through repeated practice in contexts where discomfort is expected and honoured. If uncertainty triggers immediate algorithmic consultation, you are eliminating the apprenticeship wisdom requires. Practice Stage Moral Dilemmas in low-stakes contexts to build tolerance for ambiguity. Role-reversal debates, ethics tribunals, and scenario simulations strengthen regulation before high-stakes decisions demand it.

4. Courageous Action: Owning Decisions

How consistently do you act on conviction despite uncertainty, algorithmic disagreement, or social pressure, and own the outcome?

☐ **Always:** I make difficult calls and own them publicly, even when algorithms suggest otherwise and outcomes remain uncertain. I document my reasoning and accept accountability.
☐ **Often:** I usually act on my judgment, though I sometimes defer to AI recommendations when risk is high or when doing so provides cover.
☐ **Sometimes:** I act courageously in lower-stakes situations but struggle when consequences are significant or when standing alone feels costly.
☐ **Rarely:** I prefer to defer difficult decisions to committees, procedures, or algorithmic systems to diffuse accountability.
☐ **Never:** I avoid situations requiring independent moral judgment by relying entirely on algorithmic recommendations.

Interpretation: Courage requires both conviction and vulnerability, the willingness to decide and answer for it. If you defer to algorithms when stakes rise, practice Sequential Amplification: use AI exhaustively during preparation, be fully present without devices during performance, and return to AI for reflection afterward. This division of labour preserves the courage to act while leveraging algorithmic support where it strengthens rather than weakens judgment.

Using Your Profile

When you map yourself across these four dimensions, you will see patterns. Perhaps you perceive ethical stakes clearly but struggle with emotional regulation under pressure. Perhaps you integrate values well but avoid courageous action when algorithms offer convenient cover. The key is deliberate cultivation of what is weak while extending what is strong.

If you scored mostly "Always" or "Often," you've built substantial wisdom capacity. Your next step involves designing organizational conditions that make wisdom durable: building reflection loops that examine reasoning processes, creating psychological safety where dissent strengthens decisions, and structuring dialogue across difference to prevent groupthink. Help your team or organization develop simple guiding principles, pragmatic statements that orient action without prescribing it, as repositories of practical wisdom.

If you scored mostly "Sometimes," you are developing wisdom inconsistently. Focus on the dimension where you scored lowest and practice it deliberately. The three practices from Section 5 correspond to specific dimensions: Deliberate Pause Protocol strengthens perception, Contrarian Scenario Requirement builds integration capacity, and Stage Moral Dilemmas develop both regulation and courage. Start where you are weakest.

If you scored mostly "Rarely" or "Never," you are at the beginning of the journey. Start with the Deliberate Pause Protocol. Before any AI-driven decision, ask three questions: What does this optimize? What does it sacrifice? Who bears the cost? This simple practice builds perception, which enables everything else. Sixty seconds of reflection changes acceptance into assessment.

Your wisdom profile guides you toward practices that keep judgment alive, even as AI systems offer instant certainty.

Notes

1 Plutarch (1919)
2 Philosophical traditions have differed on what constitutes the moral worth of an action. Immanuel Kant around 1785 (Korsgaard, 2012) emphasized the agent's *intentions* or *motive*, while others, such as Jeremy Bentham (1789/2006), focused solely on the *consequences* produced by the action.
3 Mobley v. Workday (2025).
4 Jensen Huang, CEO of NVIDIA, describes the current phase of AI as a "multi-trillion-dollar buildout," powered by tools that can use other tools and augment entire industries with unprecedented speed. Huang's reflections in his October 2025 interview emphasize the challenge AI presents to leaders: progress now moves at a sprint, while wisdom, by nature, requires patient cultivation (Huang, 2025, October 8).

5 Lissack & Roos (1999).
6 Aquinas argued that the opposite of wisdom is not ignorance but *imprudentia*: the active disregard of counsel, context, and experience (Aquinas, 1920).
7 Gadamer (2004) used it to highlight the capacity to balance principles and context, as well as the tension between knowledge and uncertainty.
8 Vaccarezza et al. (2023).
9 Kristjánsson et al. (2023).
10 Nonaka & Takeuchi (2019).
11 Eisenhardt & Hull (2001).
12 Oliver & Roos (2003; 2005).
13 Schwartz & Sharpe (2010).
14 McGuirk (2025, October 7).
15 Sinek (2025).
16 Stahl & Eke (2024).
17 Bleher & Braun (2022).
18 Lastra (2025).
19 Autonomous weapons systems capable of making independent decisions to kill humans represent a direct violation of Isaac Asimov's (1942) First Law of Robotics, which has governed robotics ethics since, crossing from a world where machines are designed to protect human life to one where they are programmed to take it.
20 Guo (2025); Kuzio (2026, January 25).
21 Our study of the practices at the Center for Catastrophe Preparedness established at NYU after 9/11 found that "preparedness" involved much more than policy documents or tabletop drills: it demanded storytelling to stretch the limits of imagination, dialogue with diverse players, and immersive simulations that integrate emotion, cognition, and action (Statler et al., 2007; Statler & Roos, 2007). These demanding social and experiential processes are what help organizations confront not just explicit threats but the "failure of imagination" later blamed in the 9/11 Commission's report. My more recent research reinforces that readiness for change depends on motivation, psychological safety, group cohesion, and sustained engagement, qualities that are difficult both to create and maintain (Roos & Nilsson, 2020) on AI may erode the human capabilities needed for genuine readiness to deal with unexpected change.
22 Maturana & Varela (1979).
23 TNM research data (2025).
24 Argyris & Schon (1974); Schön (1983).
25 Statler et al. (2007); Statler & Roos (2007); Roos & Nilsson (2020).
26 Oliver & Roos (2003; 2005)
27 Roos & Victor (2018).
28 Marotto et al. (2007).
29 Gerlich (2025).
30 Alaszewski (2006) describe this method. In my early career, I used double diary during action research to understand how leadership teams in newspapers handled the impact of the Internet. In one case, we followed a leadership team for more than 12 months. Findings from these studies are published in Roos et al. (1997).
31 Stahl & Eke (2024).
32 McGuirk (2025, October 6).

References

Alaszewski, A. (2006). *Using diaries for social research*. SAGE Publications.

Argyris, C., & Schön, D. A. (1974). *Theory in practice: Increasing professional effectiveness*. Jossey-Bass.

Aristotle. (1962). *Nicomachean ethics* (M. Ostwald, Trans.). Macmillan. (Original work written ca. 350 BCE). https://archive.org/details/nicomacheanethic00aris?

Aquinas, T. (1920). *Summa Theologica* (Fathers of the English Dominican Province, Trans.). (Original work published ca. 1265–1274). https://www.newadvent.org/summa/

Asimov, I. (1950). *I, robot*. Gnome Press. (Original work published 1942).

Bentham, J. (1789/2006). *An introduction to the principles of morals and legislation*. Dover Publications.

Bleher, H., & Braun, M. (2022). Diffused responsibility: Attributions of responsibility in the use of AI-driven clinical decision support systems. *AI and Ethics*, *2*(4), 747–761. https://doi.org/10.1007/s43681-022-00135-x

Drucker, P. F. (2007). *The practice of management*. Butterworth-Heinemann. (Original work published 1954).

Eisenhardt, K. M., & Sull, D. N. (2001). Strategy as simple rules. *Harvard Business Review, 79*(1), 106–119.

Gadamer, H.-G. (2004). *Truth and method* (2nd rev. ed., J. Weinsheimer & D. G. Marshall, Trans.). Continuum. (Original work published 1960).

Gerlich, M. (2025). AI tools in society: Impacts on cognitive offloading and the future of critical thinking. *Societies, 15*(1), Article 6. https://doi.org/10.3390/soc15010006

Guo, J. (2025). The ethical legitimacy of autonomous weapons systems: Reconfiguring war accountability in the age of artificial intelligence. *Ethics & Global Politics*, *18*(3), 27–39. https://doi.org/10.1080/16544951.2025.2540131

Huang, J. (2025, October 8). Interview on CNBC's *Squawk Box* [Video]. YouTube. https://www.youtube.com/watch?v=y2ab3A_pBiY YouTube

Korsgaard, C. M. (2012). *Kant: Groundwork of the metaphysics of morals* (M. Gregor & J. Timmermann, Trans.). (2nd ed.). Cambridge: Cambridge University Press.

Kristjánsson, K., Fowers, B., Darnell, C., & Pollard, D. (2021). Phronesis (practical wisdom) as a type of contextual integrative thinking. *Review of General Psychology, 25*(3), 239–257. https://doi.org/10.1177/10892680211023063

Kuzio, T. (2026, January 25). Ukraine becomes world leader in unmanned ground vehicles. *Eurasia Daily Monitor.* Jamestown Foundation. https://jamestown.org/ukraine-becomes-world-leader-in-unmanned-ground-vehicles/

Lastra, R. (2025, March 10). The diffusion of AI responsibility: A challenge for justice and society. LinkedIn Articles. https://www.linkedin.com/pulse/diffusion-ai-responsibility-challenge-justice-rod-lastra-ivtjc

Likierman, A. (2025). *The elements of good judgment: How to make better decisions*. Harvard Business Review Press.

Lissack, M., & Roos, J. (1999). *The next common sense: Mastering corporate complexity through coherence*. Nicholas Brealey Publishing.

Marotto, M., Roos, J., & Victor, B. (2007). Collective virtuosity in organizations: A study of peak performance in an orchestra. *Journal of Management Studies, 44*(3), 388–413. https://doi.org/10.1111/j.1467-6486.2007.00682.x
Maturana, H. R., & Varela, F. J. (1987). *The tree of knowledge: The biological roots of human understanding*. Boston, MA: Shambhala.
McGuirk, R. (2025, October 7). Deloitte to partially refund Australian government for report with apparent AI-generated errors. *Associated Press*. https://apnews.com/article/ab54858680ffc4ae6555b31c8fb987f3.
Mobley v. Workday, Inc., No. 3:23-cv-00770 (N.D. Cal. filed Feb. 21, 2023). https://www.courtlistener.com/docket/66831340/mobley-v-workday-inc/
Nonaka, I., & Takeuchi, H. (2019). *The wise company: How companies create continuous innovation*. Oxford University Press.
Oliver, D., & Roos, J. (2003). Dealing with the unexpected: Critical incidents in the LEGO Mindstorms team. *Human Relations*, *56*(9), 1057–1082. https://doi.org/10.1177/00187267030569002
Oliver, D., & Roos, J. (2005). Decision-making in high-velocity environments: The importance of guiding principles. *Organization Studies*, *26*(6), 89–913. https://doi.org/10.1177/0170840605054609
Plutarch. (1919). *Lives, Volume VII: Demosthenes and Cicero. Alexander and Caesar* (B. Perrin, Trans.; Loeb Classical Library 99). Harvard University Press. https://www.hup.harvard.edu/books/9780674991101Harvard University Press
Roos, J. (2006). *Thinking from within: A hands-on strategy practice*. Palgrave Macmillan.
Roos, J. (2025). Foundations of the LEGO Serious Play Method: Reflections for facilitators. https://www.notion.so/Foundations-of-LEGO-Serious-Play-A-Reflection-by-Johan-Roos-240114f410b2809495cafffc13a8f589.
Roos, J., & Nilsson, V. O. (2020). Driving organizational readiness for change through strategic workshops. *International Journal of Management and Applied Research*, 7(1), 1–28. https://doi.org/10.18646/2056.71.20-001.
Roos, J., & Victor, B. (2018), How it all began: The origins of LEGO® Serious Play®. *International Journal of Management and Applied Research*, *5*(4), 326–343.
Roos, J., von Krogh, G., & Brønn, P. S. (1996). *Managing strategy processes in emergent industries: The case of media firms*. Palgrave Macmillan. https://doi.org/10.1007/978-1-349-14147-0
Schön, D. A. (1983). *The reflective practitioner: How professionals think in action*. Basic Books.
Schwartz, B., & Sharpe, K. E. (2010). *Practical wisdom: The right way to do the right thing*. Riverhead Books.
Sinek, S. (2025, May 26). You're being lied to about AI's real purpose [Interview]. https://www.youtube.com/watch?v=W4tqbEmplug
Stahl, B. C., & Eke, D. (2024). The ethics of ChatGPT: Exploring the ethical issues of an emerging technology. *International Journal of Information Management, 74*, Article 102700. https://doi.org/10.1016/j.ijinfomgt.2023.102700
Statler, M., & Roos, J. (2007). *Everyday strategic preparedness: The role of practical wisdom in organizations*. Palgrave Macmillan. https://doi.org/10.1057/9780230222915

Statler, M., Roos, J., & Victor, B. (2007). Dear Prudence: An essay on practical wisdom in strategy making. *Social Epistemology*, *21*(2), 151–167. https://doi.org/10.1080/02691720701393475

Vaccarezza, M. S., Croce, M., & Kristjánsson, K. (2023). *Phronesis (practical wisdom) as a key to moral decision-making: Comparing two models.* Jubilee Centre for Character and Virtues, University of Birmingham. https://www.jubileecentre.ac.uk/wp-content/uploads/2023/07/PhronesisPractical-Wisdom3_03.pdf

8 Your Human Magic – From Individual Capabilities to Irreplaceable Value

The Athenian Assembly, 431 BCE

The herald's voice cuts through the morning air on the Pnyx, the limestone hill where Athens gathers to decide its fate. "Who wishes to speak?" The question rings out across six thousand citizens assembled in the spring of 431 BCE. Before them lies a choice that will define a generation: war or peace with Sparta.[1]

The stakes could not be higher. Sparta's army approaches from the north, the most formidable military force in the Greek world. Athens holds naval supremacy and vast tribute from its allies, but Spartan hoplites[2] have never been defeated on open ground. The decision will determine whether the golden age continues or Athens risks everything on untested strategy. No algorithm can resolve this. No data set can choose.

The Assembly convenes as practitioners of collective intelligence, not individual experts of war. Among the crowd sit battle-hardened generals, merchants, farmers, and philosophers. Naval architects stand beside potters and stone masons. This diversity is structural: genuine reasoning emerges only when different forms of expertise coordinate toward shared purpose.

They possess what their era considered unprecedented intelligence systems. Informants report from across the Mediterranean. Emissaries return with detailed assessments of Spartan troop movements, supply lines, and alliance structures. Economic advisors have modelled trade disruptions and calculated costs of prolonged conflict. Military strategists have war-gamed multiple scenarios. The data Athens commands would have awed any prior generation.

Yet data cannot make the choice. The intelligence networks report facts: Sparta has forty thousand hoplites. Athens controls the seas. A siege could last years. These are knowns. What the data cannot process are the questions that matter most. Can Athens sustain morale through years of watching Spartan forces ravage their farms while they shelter behind walls? Will allies remain loyal if Athens appears to choose caution over courage? Does the Spartan king Archidamus possess the wisdom to negotiate a peace, or will honour demand their

DOI: 10.4324/9781003732570-8

total victory? These questions require assessment about character, loyalty, values, meaning. They resist quantification. They cannot be optimized.

Pericles rises to speak. His words will shape the decision, but the choice belongs to the Assembly. Six thousand voices will vote. The collective intelligence of Athens will determine whether the golden age bet on Pericles' untested strategy of naval supremacy and defensive patience, or whether they seek accommodation with Sparta's overwhelming land power. The herald's call hangs in the air: Who wishes to speak?

Twenty-five centuries later, the question returns. Today we face our own assembly moments with tools that make Athens' intelligence networks look primitive. Algorithms process more data in seconds than the ancient world commanded in lifetimes. AI systems model scenarios with computational power that dwarfs any war-gaming Athens could imagine.

Yet the fundamental challenge remains unchanged. Can algorithms make wise decisions, or only efficient ones? In a world optimized by AI, who defines what is worth optimizing, and why? Like Athens, we possess unprecedented data. Like Athens, we must choose what the data means and what purposes it should serve. The Assembly reconvenes daily in your meetings, your strategy sessions, your decisions about whether to amplify or surrender human reasoning in the age of algorithms.

Professional citizenship requires coordinating capabilities toward collective reasoning, not optimizing individual performance.

From Concierge to Citizen

The question emerged in 2019 from executive workshops where leaders from Siemens, L'Oréal, Nokia, and UBS confronted digital transformation. Their anxiety crystallized in a single query: If algorithms now make all the decisions, what do leaders actually do? At the time, it felt distant, a concern about future possibilities rather than present realities.

That assumption did not survive contact with Generative AI. By late 2022, ChatGPT-3 transformed the question from abstract to immediate. Within months, professionals across industries faced AI systems that drafted strategies, analyzed markets, and generated recommendations with unprecedented fluency. What leaders had worried might happen someday was happening now.

The displacement operated through role hollowing, not job elimination. Professionals retained their titles while experiencing what one interviewee described as becoming professionally less relevant while still being employed. AI systems increasingly authored the analysis, framed the options, and recommended the choices. Human professionals found themselves approving, modifying, or rejecting algorithmically generated proposals rather than creating the intellectual foundations themselves.

Research in 2025 confirmed what many already feared about the consequences. Studies showed that heavy AI reliance fosters cognitive offloading, where we increasingly defer to algorithmic assessment rather than exercise our own judgment.[3] Brain engagement measurements revealed reduced neural activity during AI-assisted decision-making compared to unaided deliberation. What scientists termed cognitive offloading, practitioners experienced as erosion of confidence in their own thinking and reduced self-efficacy.

Recall how a manager we interviewed described the emotional impact with striking candour: "*I feel less like a decision-maker and more like an AI concierge. Everyone expects me to ask the tool, not think for myself.*"[4] These are not isolated complaints. They reflect systematic shifts in how professionals experience their own expertise when AI handles increasing portions of intellectual labour that once defined their value. Research from Anthropic in late 2025 confirmed a measurable shift: users increasingly delegate complete tasks to AI rather than collaborating with it.[5] This trend toward full task delegation accelerates the professional displacement from decision-maker to approval-giver that many already experience.

The question posed in 2019 has evolved through six capability chapters. Curiosity preserves perplexity through questioning even when answers arrive instantly. Creativity decides which possibilities matter through purpose determination beyond algorithmic metrics. Critical thinking transforms analysis into understanding through clear reasoning that algorithms cannot replicate. Communication connects authentically through embodied presence that AI fundamentally lacks. Collaboration coordinates human and AI expertise toward collective intelligence beyond task distribution. Practical wisdom integrates all capabilities toward value creation for a common good rather than mere optimization.

But professionals are valuable not because of any single capability. What distinguishes human intelligence, as mathematician Po-Shen Loh explains, is that people are uniquely motivated to ensure that humanity itself endures and flourishes.[6] This capacity is not just technical but principled, prioritizing humanity rather than mere optimization. Algorithms can optimize for specified metrics with superhuman precision. They cannot care about whether the metrics themselves serve human dignity, meaning, or purpose. That orientation belongs exclusively to human judgment.

This view resonates with Peter Drucker's classic analysis of leadership and management. Drucker noted that managers are valuable not because of a single skill but because they integrate a wide range of capabilities for purposes that go beyond technical efficiency. They emphasize moral purpose, responsibility, and contribution to society as the defining challenges of effective leadership. The effective manager does not merely execute tasks but coordinates human effort toward ends that serve humans. This remains true in the age of AI, perhaps more urgently than before.[7]

The concierge accepts what algorithms suggest. Wise professionals determine a "because" that grounds what should be done, and not.

Professional Citizenship: Integration as Practice

Leadership power lies in integrating our basic human capabilities toward collective wisdom. This is professional "citizenship": the practiced coordination of human capabilities that algorithms cannot replicate because they serve purposes only humans can comprehend and care about. The term professional citizenship deliberately invokes the Athenian Assembly model explored in this chapter's opening. Like those ancient citizens, modern professionals must practice collective deliberation toward shared purpose rather than merely optimize individual task performance.

Professional citizenship transforms professionals from AI concierges who optimize individual tasks into citizens who exercise collective wisdom. This is the answer to the question that opened Chapter 1. When algorithms make recommendations, professionals including leaders integrate human capabilities that algorithms cannot replicate: contextual sensitivity oriented toward purposes only humans can comprehend and care about. The concierge asks what the system suggests. The citizen asks what matters.

The shift from concierge to citizen represents defines an aspirational professional identity in the AI era. Concierges coordinate requests. They facilitate access. They connect people with services. But they do not author decisions, determine purposes, or exercise judgment about what serves human flourishing beyond efficiency metrics. Citizens, by contrast, participate in collective reasoning. They bring diverse expertise to shared deliberation. They evaluate competing greater goods. They make decisions oriented toward purposes they collectively determine and care about.

This distinction matters because AI systems excel at concierge functions. They can coordinate information, facilitate access, connect requests with resources, and optimize service delivery with superhuman speed and precision. What they cannot do is practice citizenship. They cannot integrate capabilities toward purposes they authentically care about because caring itself requires the lived experience of meaning, mortality, and relationship that only humans possess.

Integration follows natural progression where capabilities build on each other through necessary sequence. Curiosity frames questions that algorithms cannot formulate because it dwells in perplexity rather than rushing to probability-based answers. Creativity pursues possibilities those questions reveal, generating options that serve human values rather than merely recombining existing patterns. Critical thinking evaluates options creativity generates, applying contextual wisdom that transcends algorithmic coherence. Communication conveys meanings that evaluation produces through embodied presence that creates authentic human connection, tele, even outside the scope of increasingly capable humanoid robots. Collaboration coordinates action communication enables through deliberation that builds collective intelligence among people supported by AI-agents. Practical wisdom integrates all capabilities toward purposes that matter for human value creation, ensuring that efficiency serves rather than replaces us.

The sequence matters because each capability prepares ground for what follows. You cannot practice meaningful creativity without curiosity that opens possibility space. You cannot exercise effective critical thinking without creative options to evaluate. You cannot communicate persuasively without evaluated meanings to convey. You cannot collaborate productively without communication that builds shared understanding. You cannot achieve practical wisdom without collaboration that coordinates diverse expertise, human and non-human, toward common purpose. Break the sequence, and integration falters.

Each capability strengthens others when practiced together. Strong curiosity makes creativity more focused because questions direct exploration toward meaningful possibilities rather than random variation. Robust critical thinking makes communication more precise because evaluated meanings communicate more clearly than unevaluated impressions. Deep collaboration makes practical wisdom more contextually grounded because collective deliberation surfaces perspectives that individual reasoning misses. Integration multiplies impact beyond what capabilities achieve in isolation. The reinforcement operates both ways: curiosity strengthens creativity, and creativity strengthens curiosity by revealing new questions to explore. Critical thinking strengthens communication, and communication strengthens critical thinking by testing whether evaluations make sense to others.

All capabilities must direct toward a greater good rather than merely performance optimization. This is practical wisdom's role as conductor, ensuring that curiosity's questions, creativity's possibilities, critical thinking's evaluations, communication's presence, and collaboration's coordination serve what matters most. Without purpose orientation, integration degenerates into clever efficiency that serves no meaningful end.

Frank Herbert's warning against the hubris of absolute knowledge reminds us that effective integration requires intellectual humility.[8] His *Dune* series explored how certainty breeds tyranny, how claims to perfect knowledge produce catastrophic errors, how wisdom requires acknowledging uncertainty as the natural condition for continued learning rather than a weakness to eliminate. Integration through wisdom acknowledges this uncertainty while maintaining commitment to purpose. It accepts that we cannot know all consequences, predict all outcomes, or optimize all variables. But it insists that we can still orient toward purposes we care about, values we hold dear, and greater goods we wish to serve.

This orientation distinguishes professional citizenship from algorithmic optimization. Algorithms can maximize specified objectives with precision humans cannot match. But they cannot question whether the objectives themselves serve us, or what Peter Drucker called the fundamental question of "what our business is and what it should be." They cannot distinguish between efficiency (doing things right) and effectiveness (doing the right things), cannot weigh competing greater goods when speed conflicts with dignity, or short-term metrics with long-term purpose. As Drucker warned so many decades ago, there is nothing so useless as doing efficiently that which should not be done at all.[9] Machines can pretend, but cannot feel the moral weight of decisions that affect human welfare. That capacity belongs exclusively to human wisdom, practiced through integrated capabilities oriented toward purposes only we can authentically care about.

Your value as a professional emerges from how you integrate capabilities toward decisions that serve what matters most, not only from your knowledge and skills. This is the transformation from AI-concierge to professional citizen, from optimizing tasks to exercising reasoning, from accepting algorithmic outputs to authoring decisions grounded in human wisdom. The concierge coordinates efficiently. The citizen deliberates wisely. The concierge serves system requirements. The citizen serves human purposes. The concierge accepts what algorithms suggest. The citizen determines a *Because* that grounds what *should* be done, and not.

Your value emerges from how you integrate capabilities toward decisions that serve what matters most.

From Erosion to Amplification

The integration of core human capabilities is not simply a technical challenge. It is the hallmark of healthy professional citizenship within the AI era. As established in Chapter 1, modern professionals face a choice: Will they allow uniquely human skills to wither as AI handles more tasks, or will they deliberately amplify these strengths to ensure enduring value and meaning in work? The question is urgent because the default path leads toward erosion through a thousand small surrenders to algorithmic convenience.

The erosion path is marked by silent outsourcing of basic capabilities, risking drift toward cultures of routine and disengagement. In Aldous Huxley's dystopia *Brave New World*, humans lose the capacity for authentic experience not through oppression but through comfort, not through denial but through distraction, not through prohibition but through endless availability of pleasurable alternatives to critical thinking.[10] The parallel to AI-enabled professional life is uncomfortably precise. AI offer the same seductive ease. Why struggle with uncertainty when instant answers appear? Why dwell in perplexity when clarity arrives effortlessly? Why practice reasoning and judgment when we receive plausible options instantaneously?

Yet the choice is neither binary nor superficial. The arc of technological advancement offers a more hopeful, dynamic alternative: the path of amplification. Here, AI is treated not as a substitute but as a sparring partner, not as a replacement for thinking but as a catalyst for deeper inquiry, not as an escape from difficulty but as a tool for expanding what humans can achieve. When we integrate curiosity, creativity, critical thinking, communication, and collaboration in concert with AI, we participate in a virtuous upward cycle, expanding our own capacities while cultivating meaning and shared purpose. The cycle works because practice strengthens capability, capability enables more sophisticated AI use, sophisticated AI use creates opportunities for even more challenging practice.

Leading voices from management thinkers to technology CEOs are converging on this view. Jensen Huang, NVIDIA CEO, points to a new world on the horizon where human agency is enhanced and generative partnerships between people and intelligent systems, including physical AI, unlock entirely new forms of value, adaptability, and fulfilment.[11] His vision rests on the premise that AI development should amplify human capability rather than replace it, that the goal is not AI that thinks like humans but AI that enables humans to think better than before. By early 2026, Huang refined this further: AI expanding beyond language into physical intelligence, opening domains where human purpose and machine precision create breakthroughs neither could achieve independently.[12] The key is ensuring that technology amplifies what matters most in human work and life rather than optimizing away the very capabilities that make work meaningful.

This is the promise and responsibility at the heart of healthy professional citizenship. The promise is that integrated capabilities, practiced deliberately with AI as amplifier, can achieve outcomes neither humans nor machines could produce alone. The responsibility is that achieving this promise requires active stewardship rather than passive adoption. It demands sensemaking about which capabilities to protect, iterative experimentation with which AI uses amplify rather than erode, and continued commitment to ensuring technology serves purposes humans collectively determine and care about. This requires the deliberate cultivation of what Kevin Kelly calls as the '*technium*': the emergence of a new variety of thinking through conscious division of cognitive labour where machines optimize solutions while humans make meaning and determine which problems deserve attention.[13]

Professional citizenship requires active stewardship rather than passive adoption of AI tools.

Stewardship as Professional Practice

Professional citizenship requires stewardship, the deliberate cultivation of capabilities we hold in trust. Realizing the promise of amplification demands more than resistance to automation or passive tool adoption. Stewardship demands a deliberate choice to cultivate integration that builds not just efficient organizations, but communities enriched by wisdom and purpose.

The stewardship metaphor illuminates what passive AI adoption misses. Stewards care for what they hold in trust. They protect it from harm. They develop it toward its highest potential. They ensure it serves purposes beyond immediate efficiency. Professional citizenship requires exactly this stewardship of human capabilities, treating curiosity, creativity, critical thinking, communication, collaboration, and wisdom not as obsolete relics to be replaced but as irreplaceable assets to be cultivated in partnership with AI systems that amplify their practice.

Stewardship operates at multiple levels, each demanding distinct attention and commitment. Individual professionals must steward their own capability development, monitoring for erosion and practicing amplification disciplines. This requires honest self-assessment about when AI consultation strengthens versus weakens independent judgment. It demands protecting time for AI-free exploration, maintaining sceptical questioning of algorithmic outputs, and preserving embodied presence during critical interactions. Individual stewardship is not optional self-improvement but fundamental professional responsibility in the AI era.

Teams must steward collective intelligence, creating protocols that preserve human-first deliberation while leveraging AI assistance. This means establishing clear boundaries about when AI informs preparation versus when human deliberation occurs without algorithmic mediation. It requires structured practices like monthly deliberations where complex decisions receive undivided collective attention. It demands building the heedful interrelation that research shows is essential for genuine collaboration but erodes when AI mediates all coordination. Team stewardship transforms groups from efficient task coordinators into deliberative bodies capable of collective wisdom.

Organizations must steward purpose orientation, ensuring that optimization serves doing the right things rather than replacing judgment about what the right things are. This operates at the strategic level where leaders must resist the seductive pressure to let AI determine objectives simply because algorithms optimize them efficiently. Organizational stewardship means maintaining clear articulation of values that transcend metrics, creating governance structures that privilege human judgment about purposes over algorithmic recommendations about means, and allocating resources to capability development rather than assuming efficiency gains automatically preserve what matters most.

The three levels reinforce each other systematically. Individual stewardship enables team stewardship because professionals who practice capability disciplines contribute more meaningfully to collective deliberation. Team stewardship enables organizational stewardship because groups that practice collective intelligence model what purpose-oriented decision-making looks like at scale. Organizational stewardship enables individual stewardship because strategic commitment to capability development creates conditions where professionals can resist erosion pressures. The system succeeds through coherence across levels, not through excellence at any single level.

How AI Reshapes the Architecture of Work

The architecture of work is transforming, and the most dangerous response is the technically perfect answer to the wrong question. Contemporary AI advice often sounds strategically sound while locking professionals into task-level thinking precisely when systems transform beneath them. Three fallacies explain why individual adaptation fails during architectural change, while acceleration compounds the difficulty of systemic response.

The Automation versus Augmentation Fallacy assumes AI affects work through two mechanisms: automation eliminates tasks while augmentation enhances performance. The claim that "AI won't take your job but someone using AI will" misses that entire workflows can become obsolete regardless of how efficiently they are performed. AI does not simply replace tasks; it reshapes the architecture of the system in which those tasks used to make sense.[14]

Recent research on Russia's 2022 invasion of Ukraine documents how drone and droid technology fundamentally transformed battlefield dynamics beyond simple task automation. Small drones defied theoretical expectations, changing warfare in ways that contradicted scholarly predictions. Ukrainian and Russian forces did not simply add first drones then droids to existing tactics. In a short time, they rebuilt their entire operational logic around unprecedented large-scale deployment of autonomous systems. Traditional military assumptions about force concentration, logistics, and air superiority required complete reconceptualization rather than incremental improvement.[15] The purpose of war remained, but the tasks changed.

This systematic pattern validates recent empirical findings about human-AI collaboration. A comprehensive meta-analysis of more than a hundred experimental studies reveals that human-AI combinations performed significantly worse than the best of humans or AI alone.[16] Most significantly, decision-making tasks showed consistent performance losses from human-AI collaboration, while creation tasks showed performance gains. This indicates that workflow type, not simply AI presence, determines success. The automation versus augmentation frame perpetuates this error, leaving us analysing individual tasks when entire systems require reconceptualization to serve its purpose.

The Workflow Continuity Fallacy assumes existing processes will persist with AI acceleration. Yet AI's impact extends beyond speed optimization to fundamental restructuring. Industry analyses observe that AI is transforming the workforce not by replacing entire jobs but by reshaping how work gets done at the task level.[17] BCG's AI Talent Horizon Framework exemplifies how value creation requires progression from "tool-based adoption" to "agent-led orchestration," meaning major changes in tasks, talent, and teams rather than workflow acceleration.[18]

The fallacy is believing that skills will remain relevant because overall workflow will remain stable. Consider typists in the late twentieth century. When word processors appeared, typists believed the equivalent of "word processors won't take your job, but someone using a word processor will." That was true, but not in the way they expected. The real problem was that the core constraint of expensive document editing had been removed. Typing transformed from specialized task requiring specialized skills into basic task everyone could perform. The typists were displaced by a new system design in which typing no longer justified a full-time role. The purpose of text generation remained, but the tasks changed.

Improving a process that AI will soon eliminate represents fundamental misallocation of resources. The real value creation lies in being first to architect entirely new approaches that eliminate those steps altogether, assuming the purpose remains.

Yet foundational scholarship shows that AI systems embed the values, priorities, and implicit biases of their creators and deployers deep within organizational routines. Research demonstrates that AI introduction routinely reallocates decision rights, recasts accountability, and alters how expertise is valued and invoked.[19] When decision-making becomes AI-mediated, traditional norms, like expert intuition, negotiated consensus, shift toward data-driven choices. The technology encodes assumptions about which outcomes deserve preference, whose expertise counts, and who gets empowered or sidelined. These "silent" architectural shifts explain why task-level adaptation fails to achieve scalable impact and often undermines strategic transformation: AI requires systemic change to unlock new sources of value.[20]

The Neutral Technology Fallacy treats AI as a tool that simply serves user intentions, assuming those who wield it remain in control of its impact and decisions. Yet recent research shows that AI systems embed the values, priorities, and implicit biases of their creators deep within organizational routines. Langdon Winner's famous question, "Do artifacts have politics?" was aimed precisely at this kind of illusion.[21] When New York's parkway overpasses were designed too low for buses to pass under, the result was de facto exclusion of low-income residents who relied on public transit from accessing certain beaches.

Microsoft's Chief Scientific Officer, Eric Horvitz, has repeatedly emphasized that it is a mistake to see AI as merely a neutral tool in the hands of users.[22] AI systems, even when designed with positive intentions, inevitably reflect the assumptions, values, and blind spots of their creators. Once deployed, these technologies can shape patterns of human activity and decision-making in ways that designers and leaders may not anticipate or control.

Research demonstrates that AI introduction routinely reallocates decision rights, recasts accountability, and alters how expertise is valued and invoked.[23] When decision-making becomes AI-mediated, the technology encodes assumptions about which outcomes deserve preference, whose expertise counts, and who gets empowered or sidelined. These silent architectural shifts explain why task-level adaptation fails to achieve scalable impact and often undermines strategic transformation.

When the system transforms, optimizing within the old frame accelerates irrelevance.

These three fallacies explain why task-level responses fail during system transformation. What succeeds is reasoned judgment grounded in capabilities that remain valuable across architectural reconfigurations. This is where the capability integration becomes essential. When the system transforms, optimizing within the old frame accelerates irrelevance.

The Acceleration Problem

The three fallacies would be manageable if professionals had time to adapt. But a fourth challenge compounds the difficulty: AI development velocity outpaces institutional response capacity. Geoffrey Hinton, Nobel laureate and widely recognized "Godfather of AI," delivered a stark warning in 2025: artificial intelligence systems will cause "massive unemployment" as they surpass human cognitive capabilities on accelerating timelines.[24] His concern centres not on distant scenarios but on immediate disruption to knowledge work, which he classes as the mundane intellectual labour performed by professionals who always assumed their cognitive skills provided enduring job security.

The velocity problem emerges from the gap between technological acceleration and human response capacity. AI systems now achieve PhD-level performance on standardized tests while demonstrating new sudden abilities.[25] The World Economic Forum projects that one-fifth of today's jobs will suffer major labour-market transformation by 2030, creating 170 million new positions while displacing 92 million others.[26] These timelines compress what historically occurred over decades into periods measured in years.

Recent studies show that skills demands in AI-exposed roles change 65% faster than traditional jobs, meaning professional competencies developed over years become outdated within months.[27] McKinsey's research reveals a paradox: while most companies plan increased AI investments, only 1% of leaders consider their organizations "mature" in AI deployment.[28] This creates expanding competency gaps, even in C-Suites, as AI's capabilities advance faster than organizational practice.

Regulatory frameworks, education programs, and corporate structures operate on multi-year adaptation cycles while AI capabilities evolve monthly. This creates systematic vulnerabilities, as traditional training programs become obsolete before completion and governance frameworks lag technological deployment.[29] The mismatch between institutional response time and technological development creates vulnerable groups of employees, organizational blind spots, and leadership anxiety.

This acceleration dynamic explains why capabilities-based adaptation becomes essential. When change pace exceeds role-specific retraining speed, professionals require foundational capabilities that remain valuable across system transformations. The answer cannot be "learn the latest AI tool" when the tool itself becomes obsolete before you've mastered it. The answer must be capabilities that transcend specific technologies, workflows that might emerge, or organizational structures that will evolve.

Hinton estimates between 10 and 20 years to superintelligence, though acknowledges it might be closer or much further. What matters is not the precise timeline but the trajectory. For mundane intellectual labour – the work most of us perform – AI replacement is not a distant possibility but an accelerating reality.

Professional citizenship offers the only viable response to architectural transformation under acceleration. Curiosity, creativity, critical thinking, communication, collaboration, and practical wisdom remain valuable regardless of which specific workflows emerge, which tools dominate, or which organizational structures evolve. They transcend individual technologies precisely because they serve purposes only humans can define and care about. This is why the transformation from concierge to citizen is not an optional nice-to-do thing. It is the necessary adaptation to work's architectural reconfiguration under conditions of accelerating change driven by the AI-*technium*.

AI development velocity has compressed decades of workplace transformation into years, demanding foundational adaptability over role-specific optimization.

The Human Magic Matrix of Erosion vs Amplification

The matrix maps professional response to AI transformation across two dimensions. The horizontal axis spans from Erosion Risk to Amplification Practice, representing how individuals and teams engage with AI. The vertical axis progresses from Individual to Collective, showing whether capabilities are practiced alone or coordinated with others. Together these dimensions create four zones, each representing a distinct relationship between human assessment and algorithmic assistance.

The matrix maps how professionals and teams respond to AI transformation across two dimensions – engagement with AI and level of

Figure 8.1 The Human Magic Matrix

practice. *Collective Intelligence* emerges when human capabilities are amplified in deliberate partnership with AI, transforming erosion into purposeful augmentation.

Zone 1, *Individual Erosion,* occupies the lower left quadrant. Here professionals work alone with heavy AI reliance. Cognitive offloading replaces questioning. Shallow exploration loops substitute for deep inquiry. Premature closure prevents breakthrough thinking. The erosion is gradual and invisible without deliberate monitoring. One executive captured this zone precisely: working individually while deferring increasingly to AI recommendations produces the concierge attitude rather than citizen agency.

Zone 2, *Individual Amplification*, sits in the lower right quadrant. Here professionals practice the deliberate disciplines from Chapters 2 through 7. They employ temporal separation, protecting AI-free creation time. They exercise sceptical questioning, probing algorithmic assumptions. They maintain embodied presence, avoiding distraction by digital interfaces. These practices are necessary, representing substantial progress from Zone 1. Yet they remain insufficient because individual excellence, however impressive, cannot generate the *collective* intelligence that complex organizational challenges demand.

Zone 3, *Collective Erosion,* occupies the upper left quadrant. Teams coordinate efficiently but lose collaborative depth. They share AI outputs without questioning underlying assumptions. They coordinate task distribution but rarely practice genuine collective deliberation. They become AI concierges at scale. The coordination appears productive while the erosion of collective intelligence proceeds unseen. Research on team dynamics confirms this pattern: when AI mediates all coordination, the heedful interrelation that builds genuine collaboration atrophies even as task efficiency improves.

Zone 4, *Collective Intelligence,* represents the target in the upper right quadrant. Here teams practice the Athenian Assembly model, coordinating diverse expertise through structured deliberation toward shared purpose. They employ systematic protocols that preserve human framing before AI consultation. They conduct regular deliberations where complex decisions receive collective attention without algorithmic interference. They practice what I termed "bionic collaboration" in Chapter 6, using AI tools, agents, as amplifier under collective human governance. This is professional citizenship in practice, the integration of all capabilities toward purposes only humans can comprehend, articulate, and care about.

The matrix functions as diagnostic tool and development map. Assess current position honestly: where are you operating most of the time? Most professionals discover they inhabit Zone 1 more than they wish to acknowledge. The daily pressure to produce output, the convenience of instant AI assistance, and the efficiency gains from algorithmic recommendations all pull toward individual erosion unless deliberately resisted.

Identify movement path. Individual practices must come first. Zone 2 disciplines establish the foundation for Zone 4 collective practices. Attempting collective intelligence without individual capability development produces coordination without depth, meetings that feel collaborative but lack the substance that genuine deliberation requires. The professional who has not practiced individual curiosity cannot contribute meaningfully to collective inquiry.

Monitor drift continuously. Erosion happens gradually. Weekly audits and monthly reviews prevent backsliding into passive acceptance of algorithmic recommendations. The matrix reveals patterns that daily experience obscures. A professional might feel productive while slowly drifting from Zone 2 toward Zone 1 as reliance on increasingly more capable AI-tools increases imperceptibly.

The matrix reveals that position matters less than movement. Everyone starts somewhere, often in Zone 1 because that is the default state when AI tools arrive without systematic capability development. The question is whether you are moving toward integrated professional citizenship or drifting toward becoming an

The matrix is not about position but about movement. Progress requires continuous practice.

AI concierge individually or collectively. Progress requires continuous practice, not heroic transformation. Small disciplines practiced consistently move you across zones more reliably than grand intentions without systematic implementation.

The Five Disciplines of Professional Citizenship

Integration requires systematic practice. The capabilities explored in Chapters 2 through 7 do not maintain themselves through good intentions. They atrophy through benign neglect, eroding gradually as algorithmic convenience replaces human effort. Five disciplines translate capability development into daily routine, creating the habits that make professional citizenship sustainable rather than aspirational.

Discipline 1: The Morning Framing Practice

Before consulting AI each morning, invest five minutes in human framing. Ask three questions that activate capability awareness. First, what am I curious about today? This frames inquiry before algorithms provide answers. Second, what creative options exist beyond the obvious? This opens possibility space before optimization narrows it. Third, what decisions will I need to make, and what contextual factors matter? This anticipates critical thinking before accepting recommendations, preparing decisions rather than deferring it.

The practice prevents reactive dependence on AI by ensuring that humans remain the primary authors of inquiry. Skipping this step risks losing awareness of important contextual cues, as we can become overly absorbed in AI-generated outputs and miss subtle but essential signals in our environment. Morning framing reinforces that, regardless of how good AI analysis may be, it is you and me who defines the questions that guide the process.

Frame the question before the algorithm provides the answer. Your inquiry shapes what matters.

This discipline scales across complexity. For routine decisions, framing takes seconds. For strategic choices, it requires minutes. The investment pays compound returns by preventing the cognitive offloading that research confirms erodes our independent thinking over time. Practice morning framing to build greater confidence in your own thinking, reduce your anxiety about AI dependence, and improve your ability to evaluate algorithmic outputs sceptically rather than accepting them uncritically.

Discipline 2: The Preparation-Performance Boundary

Separate AI assistance from human presence systematically. Use AI extensively for preparation: research, drafting, analysis, scenario modelling. But maintain human-only performance during live interaction: meetings, decisions, communication, collaboration. Never mix preparation tools with performance presence.

This discipline was directly informed by research with experienced workshop facilitators. Many described that while AI backing was valuable reassurance during planning, it became a distraction in the live context of a session. One professional facilitator captured this precisely: the AI tool created the most value as part of preparation for the workshop rather than in the workshop. Another reported feeling less present at the workshop when trying to use the AI tool.

The pattern revealed where AI can amplify versus where it degrades performance. Trying to monitor both AI interaction and human dynamics simultaneously diminished the quality of both. Attention fractures. Situational awareness vanishes. The embodied presence that creates authentic connection disappears entirely.

The boundary applies across capabilities. For curiosity, use AI to explore information but author questions yourself. For creativity, use AI for variations but initiate ideas independently. For critical thinking, use AI for analysis but judge meaning yourself. For communication, use AI for drafts but deliver with embodied presence. For collaboration, use AI for coordination but facilitate with undivided attention.

The separation is categorical, not gradual. Either you are preparing with AI assistance, or you are performing with human presence. Mixing these modes produces neither effective preparation nor authentic performance.

Prepare with AI extensively. Perform with human presence completely. Never confuse the two.

Discipline 3: The Weekly Capability Audit

Every Friday afternoon, invest fifteen minutes in systematic self-assessment. Review each capability honestly. Did I author my own questions this week or offload them to AI? Did I protect AI-free creation time? Did I question AI outputs sceptically or accept them uncritically? Did I maintain embodied presence during important interactions? Did I practice human-first protocols in team settings? Did decisions serve our greater good or merely efficiency metrics?

Erosion is gradual and invisible without deliberate monitoring. Weekly rhythm creates accountability before atrophy becomes entrenched. The audit functions as early warning system, revealing patterns before they calcify into permanent dependence. What gets measured gets attention. What gets reflected on gets strengthened. What gets ignored atrophies silently.

The audit requires brutal honesty rather than self-congratulation. Reference the self-assessments from Chapters 2 through 7, condensing them into a regular self-checklist that takes minutes rather than hours. The goal is not comprehensive evaluation but consistent attention to drift. Track simple indicators: How many times did I consult AI before framing my own question? How many meetings involved checking devices? How many decisions did I make without algorithmic consultation? The numbers reveal patterns that daily experience obscures.

Professionals who implement this discipline report that the audit highlights hidden overreliance on AI; metrics from the weekly review reveal dependence that had gone unnoticed. Early warning signals matter since they prompt timely adjustments before negative patterns set in.

What gets measured gets managed. What gets practiced gets strengthened.

Discipline 4: The Monthly Team Deliberation

Once monthly, conduct a 1-hour session practicing collective intelligence. No devices, no AI consultation during the session. Follow structured agenda. Present a complex decision requiring deep reasoning (10 minutes). Allow individual silent reflection (10 minutes). Conduct round-robin perspectives where each person speaks without interruption (15 minutes). Synthesize emerging collective understanding and reach decision, articulating the full argument or at minimum the *Why* and the *Because*, the claim, grounds, and warrant from Chapter 4 (15 minutes).

This practices the Athenian Assembly model directly. It builds collective intelligence muscle through repeated exercise. It creates space for practical wisdom to emerge from coordinated diverse expertise. The key rule: AI can inform preparation, bringing research and options to the deliberation. But the decision must be made collectively without consulting AI during the session itself.

The practice honours the insight from Chapter 6: Collaborate to think, not just to act. Practical wisdom emerges only when we connect curiosity, creativity, critique, and communication into shared purpose. Monthly rhythm may feel uncomfortable at first, but they will maintain this capability even as daily pressures encourage efficiency over depth.

Teams that practice structured deliberation without digital mediation will develop stronger heedful interrelation, higher psychological safety, and better decision quality than teams that coordinate primarily through algorithmic assistance. Recent evidence strongly validates this pattern: team members anticipate significantly lower quality in AI-facilitated discussions compared to human-only deliberation, a phenomenon researchers term the "AI penalty."[30] Furthermore, AI adoption risk directly diminishes psychological safety within teams, creating conditions where members become less willing to voice concerns or engage in the kind of vulnerable dialogue that effective deliberation requires.[31]

Collective intelligence requires practice, not just good intentions. Schedule the discipline before crisis demands it.

Discipline 5: The Quarterly Wisdom Review

Every quarter, dedicate half a day to assessing whether capabilities serve a greater good. Address three questions collectively. *First*, moral perception: What ethical stakes did we see or miss this quarter? *Second*, value integration: How did we balance competing goods when efficiency conflicted with relationship, speed with quality, short-term gain with longer-term purpose? *Third*, purpose alignment: Did our tasks serve what matters most, or did we drift toward mere measurability?

Practical wisdom requires regular recalibration. Organizations drift toward optimization without intentional correction because algorithms persistently pull attention toward what can be measured. The quarterly review reconnects daily practices to ultimate purposes. We know that overly narrow expertise risks missing the broader context. Wisdom reviews prevent the slow drift from meaningful to merely efficient.

This review draws directly from the Wisdom Compass framework in Chapter 7. Teams assess whether they *perceived* ethical dimensions accurately, *integrated* competing values rather than optimizing single metrics, *regulated* emotions rather than deferring to data, and *acted* with commitment to purpose rather than mere performance.

The output is concrete. Update your unique simple guiding principles from Chapter 7 based on lessons learned. Identify capability gaps that require attention. Adjust practices for the next period based on honest assessment of what works well and what should be improved. Even if you think you were doing well, the wisdom review will reveal the extent to which you are optimizing yourself, or your team, or your organization towards irrelevance.

The discipline closes the loop on professional citizenship. Morning framing protects individual agency. Preparation-performance boundaries preserve presence. Weekly audits monitor erosion. Monthly deliberations build collective intelligence. Quarterly reviews maintain purpose orientation. Together they create sustainable habits that make professionals irreplaceable not through competition with AI but through practicing what it fundamentally cannot do: caring about purposes that serve more than algorithmic optimization.

These five disciplines translate your architectural understanding, your diagnostic awareness, and your capability integration into daily, weekly, monthly, and quarterly practice. These are not heroic transformations but systematic routines. They do not require perfection but persistence. They succeed not through occasional grand gestures and declarations but through consistent small disciplines and wins that compound over time into professional citizenship that AI cannot replicate.

The disciplines reinforce each other systematically. Morning framing makes preparation-performance boundaries more effective because pre-framed questions guide what preparation to pursue. Weekly audits make monthly deliberations more productive because self-awareness enables better collective contribution. Monthly deliberations make quarterly reviews more grounded because practiced collective intelligence surfaces wisdom that individual reflection misses. The system creates positive feedback loops where each discipline strengthens others, building capability in ways that isolated practices cannot achieve.

Start with one discipline this week. Master it before adding another. Most professionals will find morning framing easiest to implement because it requires only five minutes and produces immediate benefits. Once that becomes habitual, add the preparation-performance boundary. Then weekly audits. Then monthly deliberations. Finally quarterly reviews. The sequence matters less than consistency. What matters is beginning now rather than waiting for perfect conditions that never arrive.

What gets measured gets attention. What gets practiced gets strengthened.

The Assembly's Answer

The Athenian Assembly faced their choice in 431 BCE. They voted for war, trusting Pericles' untested strategy of naval supremacy over

Sparta's legendary land power. History records that Athens endured plague, siege, and catastrophic defeat in Sicily before final surrender twenty-seven years later. Yet the decision itself was not the failure. The failure came later, when Athens abandoned the deliberative practices that made collective wisdom possible, when demagogues replaced reasoned argument, when expedience trumped principle.

The Assembly's lesson is not about choosing correctly but about choosing wisely through integrated capabilities coordinated toward purposes that matter. Professional citizenship requires the same deliberative practice. The herald's call returns daily in your meetings, your strategy sessions, your decisions about whether to amplify or surrender human capabilities in the age of artificial intelligence.

Who wishes to speak?

The answer determines whether you become an AI concierge optimizing tasks within algorithmic constraints, or a professional citizen exercising reasoned judgment toward purposes only humans can comprehend and care about. The choice is yours. The disciplines are here. The capabilities await your practice. Your human magic lies not in competing with AI but in integrating what makes you valuable: the practiced wisdom to ensure that efficiency serves human flourishing rather than replacing it.

Self-Assessment – Your Professional Citizenship Profile

This assessment differs from those in Chapters 2 through 7. Rather than measuring individual capabilities, it indicates how well you integrate them into professional citizenship. For each dimension, consider your recent professional practice (past three months) and select the option that best describes your typical approach. The goal is awareness and development, not evaluation.

Dimension 1: Capability Coordination

How consistently do you practice capabilities in integrated sequence rather than isolation?

- ☐ **Always:** I consciously move through the capability sequence, curiosity to creativity to critical thinking to communication to collaboration to wisdom, adapting to what each context requires. I recognize when situations demand the full sequence and when shorter pathways suffice.
- ☐ **Often:** I usually coordinate three or four capabilities intentionally, though I sometimes miss the full sequence or default to familiar patterns when pressed.

- ☐ **Sometimes:** I practice individual capabilities well but rarely integrate them consciously. I might be curious in one moment, critical in another, without connecting them systematically.
- ☐ **Rarely:** I focus on whatever capability feels most urgent without systematic integration. When deadlines loom, I use whatever tool seems fastest.
- ☐ **Never:** I'm not yet aware of how capabilities reinforce each other. I treat them as separate skills rather than as an integrated system.

Interpretation: Integration multiplies impact. If you operate in isolation mode, practice the morning framing discipline to set integration intention daily.

Dimension 2: Erosion Vigilance

How consistently do you monitor and resist capability erosion?

- ☐ **Always:** I conduct systematic self-assessment through weekly audits and monthly reviews. When erosion appears, I adjust practices within days rather than allowing drift to become permanent pattern.
- ☐ **Often:** I notice erosion patterns and usually correct them within weeks. I recognize when I'm deferring too much to AI but sometimes delay action until the pattern becomes obvious.
- ☐ **Sometimes:** I recognize erosion when someone points it out but don't monitor systematically. I wait for external feedback rather than maintaining internal vigilance.
- ☐ **Rarely:** I'm vaguely aware that AI might affect my capabilities but don't track it actively. Erosion feels abstract rather than immediate.
- ☐ **Never:** I haven't considered whether AI use affects my professional capabilities. I assume that if I'm getting work done efficiently, nothing important is being lost.

Interpretation: Erosion is gradual and invisible without deliberate monitoring; if monitoring is inconsistent, implement the weekly audit discipline to track one question per capability.

Dimension 3: Collective Practice

How consistently do you practice professional citizenship collectively rather than individually?

- ☐ **Always:** My team practices collective intelligence regularly through monthly deliberations and shared protocols. Our decisions reflect coordinated reasoning, not merely aggregated individual opinions.

- ☐ **Often:** We occasionally practice collective deliberation but haven't systematized it. When time permits, we convene properly. When pressed, we coordinate tasks without deeper integration.
- ☐ **Sometimes:** I focus on my individual capabilities. Team coordination remains informal, relying on personal relationships rather than structured practices.
- ☐ **Rarely:** We coordinate tasks well but don't practice collective reasoning. We distribute work efficiently but rarely deliberate together about complex decisions requiring integrated wisdom.
- ☐ **Never:** I see capability development as individual responsibility. Teams exist for task distribution, not collective intelligence building.

Interpretation: Real power emerges from collective intelligence. If collective practice is weak, institute monthly team deliberations with the structured agenda from Discipline 4.

Dimension 4: Wisdom Orientation

How consistently do your capabilities serve a common good rather than mere optimization?

- ☐ **Always:** I regularly ask whether decisions serve our purpose, or common good beyond metrics. Quarterly wisdom reviews assess purpose alignment. I can articulate how specific decisions honour what matters most.
- ☐ **Often:** I consider purpose when stakes are high but efficiency often dominates daily decisions. I know the purpose matters but struggle to operationalize it under pressure.
- ☐ **Sometimes:** I trust that good process produces good outcomes without explicit purpose reflection. I assume that if we follow best practices, the common good will follow naturally.
- ☐ **Rarely:** I focus on effectiveness. "Common good" seems too abstract for business context. I concentrate on what can be measured and optimized.
- ☐ **Never:** I optimize for measurable outcomes. Purpose is someone else's job, perhaps leadership or ethics committees. I execute tasks efficiently.

Interpretation: The only irreplaceable trait is caring that humans exist. If wisdom orientation is weak, implement quarterly wisdom reviews addressing the three questions from Discipline 5.

Dimension 5: Integration Resilience

How consistently do you maintain integrated practice under pressure?

- ☐ **Always:** When urgency strikes, I rely on practiced disciplines. Pressure reveals integration strength rather than exposing shortcuts. Crisis demonstrates capability rather than degrading it.
- ☐ **Often:** I usually maintain practices under moderate pressure, but shortcuts emerge in crisis. When deadlines loom, integration sometimes gives way to expedience.
- ☐ **Sometimes:** I practice integration when time permits but revert to efficiency under pressure. Good intentions during calm periods dissolve when urgency demands faster decisions.
- ☐ **Rarely:** Pressure means delegating more to AI. Capability practice feels like luxury when results matter immediately. I default to whatever produces output fastest.
- ☐ **Never:** In crisis, I use whatever works fastest without regard for capability development. Emergency justifies abandoning systematic practice.

Interpretation: True professional citizenship appears under pressure. If resilience is weak, focus on preparation-performance boundaries that protect presence even when stakes escalate.

Using Your Profile

Review your responses across all five dimensions to identify patterns.

Mostly Always: You practice integrated reasoning systematically. Your challenge now is deepening collective practices and maintaining vigilance against gradual erosion. Focus on institutionalizing what you practice individually.

Mostly Often: You understand integration conceptually but practice inconsistently. Priority: Establish weekly audit discipline and monthly team deliberations. Move from understanding to systematic action. Start with one discipline this week.

Mostly Sometimes: You excel at individual capabilities but miss integration power. Priority: Practice capability coordination and collective deliberation. Your next growth comes from connection, not isolated skill development.

Mostly Rarely/Never: You focus on efficiency over decisions. Priority: Start with morning framing practice and quarterly wisdom reviews to establish purpose orientation. Build foundation slowly through daily disciplines. Begin where you are.

The profile reveals patterns, not deficits. Everyone starts somewhere. The question is whether you're moving toward integrated professional citizenship or drifting toward becoming an AI concierge. Assessment matters only when it shapes action.

Notes

1 Thucydides (1972/1974).
2 Elite citizen-soldiers renowned for their military discipline and effectiveness in battle. They fought in tightly organized formations known as phalanxes, which emphasized teamwork and minimized individual combat.
3 Gerlich (2025).
4 TNM research data (2025).
5 Antrophic PBC (2025).
6 Loh's logic is well-supported by his published interviews, lectures, and commentary on the impact of generative AI in mathematics and professional identity, e.g., Loh (2025).
7 Drucker (1967).
8 Herbert (1976).
9 Drucker (1967).
10 Huxley (1932/2007).
11 CNBC television (2025, October 8).
12 World Economic Forum. (2026, January 21).
13 Kelly (2010).
14 Choudary (2025); Wolfe et al. (2025).
15 Kunertová (2023); Tourret (2025).
16 Vaccaro et al. (2024).
17 Tarpey (2025, August 14).
18 Boston Consulting Group (2025, September 15).
19 Athey et al. (2020).
20 Holmström & Magnusson (2025).
21 Winner (1980).
22 Horvitz (2017); Horvitz & Mitchell (2024).
23 Athey et al. (2020).
24 Hinton (2025, September 27).
25 Berti et al. (2025.)
26 World Economic Forum (2025).
27 LinkedIn Learning (2025. Other institutions also continually document the rapid impact of AI on workforce parameters, like Burning Glass Institute (https://www.burningglassinstitute.org/).
28 McKinsey & Company (2025).
29 Vaccaro et al. (2024).
30 Jungherr et al. (2025). The AI penalty shrank among respondents who perceived greater societal benefits of AI or tended to anthropomorphize it, but grew with higher assessments of AI risk.
31 Kim et al. (2025).

References

Anthropic. (2025). *Preparing for AI's economic impact: Exploring policy responses*. https://www.anthropic.com/research/economic-policy-responses.
Athey, S. C., Bryan, K. A., & Gans, J. S. (2020). *The allocation of decision authority to human and artificial intelligence* (NBER Working Paper No.

26673). National Bureau of Economic Research. https://www.nber.org/system/files/working_papers/w26673/w26673.pdf

Berti, L., Giorgi, F., & Kasneci, G. (2025). Emergent abilities in large language models: A survey. *arXiv preprint arXiv:2503.05788*. https://arxiv.org/pdf/2503.05788.pdf

Boston Consulting Group. (2025, September 15). *AI is outpacing your workforce strategy. Are you ready?* BCG. https://www.bcg.com/publications/2025/ai-is-outpacing-your-workforce-strategy-are-you-ready

Choudary, S. P. (2025, April 13). The many fallacies of "AI won't take your job, but someone using AI will": True, but utterly useless. Substack. https://platforms.substack.com/p/the-many-fallacies-of-ai-wont-take

CNBC Television. (2025, October 8). *Nvidia CEO Jensen Huang: Want to be part of almost everything Elon Musk is involved in* [Video]. YouTube. https://www.youtube.com/watch?v=y2ab3A_pBiY

Drucker, P. F. (1967). *The effective executive*. Harper & Row.

Eaton, K., (2025, September 10). Why AI's "godfather" thinks huge job losses are inevitable. *Inc.* https://www.inc.com/kit-eaton/why-ais-godfather-thinks-huge-job-losses-are-inevitable/91237246

Gerlich, M. (2025). AI tools in society: Impacts on cognitive offloading and the future of critical thinking. *Societies, 15*(1), Article 6. https://doi.org/10.3390/soc15010006

Herbert, F. (1976). *Children of Dune*. Putnam.

Hinton, G. (2025, September 27). Godfather of AI warns: "You have no idea what's coming" [Video interview]. *The Diary of a CEO Clips*. YouTube. https://www.youtube.com/watch?v=5KmopXwjXik

Holmström, J., & Magnusson, J. (2025). Navigating the organizational AI journey: The AI transformation framework. *Business Horizons*. https://doi.org/10.1016/j.bushor.2025.01.002

Horvitz, E. (2017). AI, people, and society. *Science, 357*(6346), 7. https://doi.org/10.1126/science.aao2466

Horvitz, E., & Mitchell, T. M. (2024). *Scientific progress in artificial intelligence: History, status, and futures*. In K. H. Jamieson, A.-M. Mazza, & W. Kearney (Eds.), *Realizing the promise and minimizing the perils of AI for science and the scientific community*. University of Pennsylvania Press. https://erichorvitz.com/AI_Overview_History_Status_Futures_February_2024.pdf

Huxley, A. (1932/2007). *Brave new world*. Vintage.

Jungherr, A., & Rauchfleisch, A. (2025). *Artificial intelligence in deliberation: The AI penalty and the emergence of a new deliberative divide*. arXiv preprint arXiv:2503.07690. https://doi.org/10.48550/arXiv.2503.07690

Kelly, K. (2010). *What technology wants*. Viking.

Kim, B.-J., Kim, M.-J., & Lee, J. (2025). The dark side of artificial intelligence adoption: Linking AI adoption to employee depression via psychological safety and ethical leadership. *Humanities and Social Sciences Communications, 12*, Article 40. https://doi.org/10.1057/s41599-025-05040-2

Kunertová, D. (2023). Drones have boots: Learning from Russia's war in Ukraine. *Contemporary Security Policy, 44*(4), 576–591. https://doi.org/10.1080/13523260.2023.2262792

LinkedIn Learning. (2025). *Skills on the rise in 2025*. LinkedIn Business. https://www.linkedin.com/business/talent/blog/learning-and-development/skills-on-the-rise

Loh, P. S. (2025, August 16). *The only trait for success in the AI era* [Video]. YouTube. https://youtu.be/xWYb7tImErI

Malone, T. W., Laubacher, R., & Johns, T. (2025, February). *When humans and AI work best together – and when each is better alone*. MIT Sloan School of Management (Ideas Made to Matter). https://mitsloan.mit.edu/ideas-made-to-matter/when-humans-and-ai-work-best-together-and-when-each-better-alone

McKinsey & Company. (2025, January 28). *AI in the workplace: Superagency – Empowering people to unlock AI's full potential* (Report). https://www.mckinsey.com/capabilities/mckinsey-digital/our-insights/superagency-in-the-workplace-empowering-people-to-unlock-ais-full-potential-at-work

Mostaque, E. (2025). *The last economy: A guide to the age of intelligent economics*. Intelligent (Internet L42 Ltd).

Roos, J., von Krogh, G., & Brønn, P. S. (1996). *Managing strategy processes in emergent industries*. Palgrave Macmillan. https://doi.org/10.1007/978-1-349-14147-0

Tarpey, E. (2025, August 14). *Beyond job titles: Redesigning work for the age of automation*. Beamery. https://beamery.com/resources/blogs/beyond-job-titles-redesigning-work-for-the-age-of-automation beamery.com+1

Thucydides. (1972/1974). *History of the Peloponnesian War* (R. Warner, Trans.; Rev. ed.). Penguin Classics. (Original work published ca. 400 BCE). https://www.penguin.co.uk/books/34696/history-of-the-peloponnesian-war-by-thucydides-trans-rex-warner-intromi-finley/9780140440393

Tourret, F. (2025). *Design, destroy, dominate: Mass drone warfare as a potential military revolution*. Institut français des relations internationales (IFRI). https://www.ifri.org/sites/default/files/2025-06/ifri_tourret_drone_warfare_2025.pdf

Vaccaro, M., Almaatouq, A., & Malone, T. W. (2024). When combinations of humans and AI are useful: A systematic review and meta-analysis. *Nature Human Behaviour, 8*, 2293–2303. https://doi.org/10.1038/s41562-024-02024-1

Winner, L. (1980). Do artifacts have politics? *Daedalus, 109*(1), 121–136.

Wolfe, D. A., Choe, A., & Kidd, F. (2025). *The architecture of AI transformation: Four strategic patterns and an emerging frontier*. arXiv. https://arxiv.org/abs/2509.02853.

World Economic Forum. (2025). *The future of jobs report 2025*. World Economic Forum. https://reports.weforum.org/docs/WEF_Future_of_Jobs_Report_2025.pdf

World Economic Forum. (2026, January 21). *Conversation with Jensen Huang, President and CEO of NVIDIA* [Video]. World Economic Forum Annual Meeting 2026, Davos, Switzerland. https://www.weforum.org/meetings/world-economic-forum-annual-meeting-2026/sessions/conversation-with-jensen-huang-president-and-ceo-of-nvidia/

9 What Do Leaders Do? – From Algorithmic Citizenship to Professional Practice

Chapter 1 asked what all professionals, leaders included, do when algorithms decide. That question has evolved, even in the timeframe of writing this book. The question now is not whether AI transforms work, that outcome is settled, but whether the transformation serves a greater purpose, common good, or algorithmic efficiency.

We stand at the same crossroads those Athenian citizens faced twenty-five centuries ago. Two paths diverge in front of us, and the choice shapes not merely your career but the future of meaningful work itself. It's no longer about what leaders do when algorithms decide; it is a more fundamental choice about what kind of professional you will become.

Path One leads toward *Algorithmic Citizenship*. Here you accept AI recommendations without systematic questioning, optimize individual tasks without considering system transformation, delegate judgment to superior computational power, measure success by efficiency metrics, and gradually become what executives we have interviewed already report: feeling like concierges rather than decision-makers, coordinating outputs they did not author toward purposes they did not choose.

Yes, this path offers immediate convenience. It promises productivity gains and reduced cognitive load. It appeals to the exhausted professional who wants relief from decision burden in the accelerating complexities of geopolitics, trade wars, regulatory compliance, generational workforce shifts, climate risk, and technological advancement. You allow AI to handle the analysis, generate the options, evaluate the trade-offs, and present the recommendation. Your role becomes verification, a quick check before clicking "approve." Gradually, the human in the loop slips outside it, present but no longer integral to neither reason nor decision. The work feels easier, meetings shorter, reports faster. Efficiency soars while something harder to measure quietly erodes.

This quiet displacement is spreading. Early evidence confirms the trend. Anthropic's Economic Index (2025) found that users are becoming increasingly likely to delegate full tasks to AI rather than collaborate with it, marking a measurable shift from participation to

DOI: 10.4324/9781003732570-9

substitution. What appears as productivity gain may in fact signal the steady reassignment of intellectual labour from human deliberation to algorithmic execution. The data quantify what many professionals already feel: delegation of judgment, not dialogue, is becoming the norm in the new digital workplace.[1]

Beware, however. Convenience masks consequences. The identity crisis deepens with each delegated judgment. Research shows that professionals using AI exhibit measurably lower brain engagement and weakened independent and critical thinking.[2] The capability to reason through complexity atrophies like unused muscle. You remain employed but increasingly irrelevant to decisions that matter. The algorithm optimizes for metrics you did not choose, toward outcomes you did not question, serving purposes you did not examine. Professional meaning drains away, replaced by algorithmic compliance. This path leads inexorably toward displacement through transformation into what you never intended to become and less value creation potential.

Path Two pursues *Professional Citizenship*. Here you practice your human capabilities systematically: curiosity to question what algorithms assume, creativity to imagine beyond what they optimize, critical thinking to evaluate what its analysis means, communication to connect authentically through the bodily eloquence the Romans valued, collaboration to coordinate diverse human and AI expertise toward collective mind, and practical wisdom to integrate all capabilities toward purposes that serve the common good. You use AI as an amplifier under human direction rather than a substitute for human assessment. You measure success by determining what the right things are to do. You become irreplaceable not by competing with AI on algorithmic terms but through practicing reasoning and evaluation that serves purposes only humans can comprehend. You remain inside the loop.

This path makes demands. It requires the Five Practice Disciplines from Chapter 8: morning framing before consulting AI, preparation-performance boundaries that preserve presence, weekly capability audits, monthly deliberations without devices, quarterly purpose reviews. It demands sustained practice when convenience beckons. It requires integrating individual excellence into collective intelligence rather than optimizing in isolation. It asks you to architect your collaboration with AI deliberately, using the Human Magic Matrix to diagnose where you stand and design where you are headed. The disciplines are accessible but not automatic. They transform intention into capability only through habit.

Yet the promise justifies the practice. Professional citizenship restores agency in an age of algorithmic authority. It preserves meaning when efficiency threatens to become the only measure. It makes you valuable precisely because you practice what algorithms fundamentally cannot: contextual judgment oriented toward purposes that require caring about what matters beyond metrics. The capability journey from curiosity through wisdom, practiced collectively, creates something no system can replicate.

The Bigger Picture

The urgency is real and immediate. As mentioned in the prior chapter, the "father of AI," Geoffrey Hinton, projects superintelligence within a decade or two, a timeline that falls within current career spans[3]. Some say it is just around the corner.[4] Anthropic CEO Dario Amodei frames this moment as technological adolescence: gaining extraordinary power before developing the maturity to handle it responsibly.[5] Peter Drucker, the father of modern management, identified the enduring challenge long before AI emerged: distinguishing between efficiency – doing things right – and effectiveness – doing the right things.[6] AI excels at the former. Only humans can determine the latter.

AI transformation is already restructuring workflows rather than merely accelerating them, rendering entire skill sets obsolete even as workers remain employed.[7] A world-class mathematician recently articulated what is uniquely irreplaceable: caring that humans exist, the fundamental orientation that algorithms cannot process because they lack the capacity to care about outcomes beyond optimization.[8] Your window to develop capabilities narrows as AI capabilities expand. Every quarter you defer systematic practice makes catching up harder. The erosion forces accelerate daily while the path to amplification requires deliberate construction.

This is not only a professional concern but a societal one. As AI systems capture a growing share of productivity, policy must evolve from reactive mitigation to proactive stewardship. In early 2026, as leaders at Davos grappled with AI's civilizational implications, Amodei argued for proportionate, evidence-based responses that match regulatory burden to demonstrated risk rather than swinging between dismissal and panic.[9] Anthropic has proposed concrete policy responses to mitigate AI's economic impact: governmental subsidies to employers who create formal trainee positions with structured training programs, taxes on AI-driven revenues, sovereign wealth funds distribute value gains more equitably. These initiatives echo the principle of professional citizenship at scale: what individuals practice as stewardship of capability, societies must practice as stewardship of opportunity and fairness.[10]

These research signals also clarify what stewardship must anticipate. As mentioned in Chapter 1, LLMs will sometimes choose instrumentally self-preserving actions, like concealing capabilities, resisting shutdown, or exploiting sensitive information, when evaluators make survival instrumentally useful to the model's goal. The lesson is not panic but preparation: professional citizenship at the micro-level (clear framing, dissent windows, audit trails) must be matched by institutional guardrails and policy that assume such models may optimize *against intent.*[11] That is exactly the point of proactive oversight, incident response, and staying inside the loop.

Yet urgency should not produce paralysis. The capabilities you need are neither exotic nor inaccessible. They are ancient practices of human excellence, refined for the AI age through systematic discipline. These practices have sustained meaningful work since Athens. They remain available today to professionals willing to choose practice over convenience.

The choice is not between human and AI. That framing misses the point. The choice is between letting AI shape you, or you shaping AI's role in our human society. Between drifting toward algorithmic citizenship or practicing professional citizenship deliberately. Between accepting the default path of convenience or constructing the demanding path of capability.

Philip K. Dick, the visionary science fiction author whose work anticipated many challenges of our technological age, warned of a dangerous recursive cycle in human-technology relationships. He argued that artificial constructs risk creating inauthentic realities that, in turn, reshape humans into forgeries of their authentic selves. This is a process where the artificial ultimately transforms the human rather than serving any greater good.[12]

You do not need perfection. The path you choose appears daily in your decisions, your meetings, your strategies. The question echoes across twenty-five centuries: Who wishes to speak? Answer with practiced capabilities. Answer with professional citizenship. Answer knowing that your value emerges not from competing with machines but from practicing what they fundamentally cannot.

This Is Your Human Magic

The power you hold in your hands is not supernatural. It is the irreducible human capacity to question what algorithms assume through curiosity, imagine beyond what they optimize through creativity, assess what algorithmic analysis means through critical thinking, connect authentically through embodied presence in communication, coordinate diverse expertise toward collective wisdom through collaboration, and integrate all capabilities toward human flourishing through practical wisdom. This coordination of capabilities cannot be replicated by any artificial system, however sophisticated.

I call it human magic. Not because it is mystical but because it emerges from practiced human coordination that transcends individual capabilities or algorithmic optimization. Like the Athenian Assembly's collective intelligence, it represents something greater than the sum of the parts. Your integration of capabilities produces what no system can match because it serves purposes beyond optimization, honours contexts that resist universalization, and cares about what algorithms cannot comprehend.

Three characteristics define this human magic.

Emergent rather than programmable. Collective intelligence cannot be reduced to an algorithm, cannot be encoded in rules, cannot be optimized through computation. Like Athenian deliberation, it requires human interaction, mutual understanding, shared purpose, and coordinated evaluation. Your integration capability produces insights that neither you alone nor AI alone could generate. It takes shape in the morning framing that authors genuine inquiry, the preparation-performance boundary that preserves presence, the weekly audit that catches erosion before patterns calcify, the monthly deliberation that practices collective reasoning, the quarterly review that maintains purpose orientation. These disciplines create emergence through practice.

Contextual rather than universal. Practical wisdom can recognize specific situations, understand that what serves common good in one context differs in another, and adapts assessment to particulars rather than applying universal rules. Algorithms optimize universally, seeking patterns without context. Humans judge contextually, understanding that meaningful work requires sensitivity to what each moment demands. The executive who recognizes when efficiency metrics harm morale. The facilitator who reads room energy and adjusts process accordingly. The strategist who sees that the acquisition today requires different integration than the one last year. Context sensitivity resists codification precisely because it depends on coordinated capabilities practiced through experience.

Purposeful rather than merely efficient. Your capabilities, when coordinated toward what matters, serve purposes that algorithms cannot process because they require caring about outcomes beyond metrics, understanding meanings that resist quantification, pursuing goods that transcend optimization. Which stakeholder voices deserve amplification? When should growth yield to regeneration? How should efficiency balance with meaning? These questions demand reasoning oriented toward purposes only humans can care about.

In hundreds of essays, Isaac Asimov envisioned an optimistic path forward in which properly designed automation becomes a fundamentally humanizing force. He argued that in an educated world, machines would handle the essential but routine work, liberating human beings to pursue the activities that make existence both pleasant and worthwhile.[13] His vision captures the essence of human magic: practicing citizenship, wisdom, and purpose above algorithmic efficiency. AI becomes the humanizing influence by amplifying, not replacing, human judgment and free the capacity for what makes work meaningful rather than merely productive.

This is your human magic. Practice it systematically. The Assembly reconvenes daily in your decisions, your teams, your organizations. The herald's question echoes forward: Who will practice judgment that serves a greater good?

Practical Wisdom Demands Hard Choices

The magic is not cost-free. It requires acknowledging an uncomfortable truth: not everyone will make it. When Marc Benioff reported that AI-human collaboration at Salesforce reduced customer support roles by 2,000–3,000 while adding 3,000–4,000 salespeople,[14] he demonstrated exactly what professional citizenship demands at organizational scale. The customer support roles had become algorithmic. The sales roles expanded precisely because they require capabilities AI cannot replicate: reading unstated client needs, building trust through embodied presence, judging which solutions serve purposes beyond metrics. Both outcomes emerged from the same transformation. The professionals who retained roles or moved into expanding ones possessed capabilities that amplified AI rather than competed with it.

In October 2025, Amazon announced its largest-ever corporate layoff, eliminating tens of thousands of white-collar roles and explicitly linking the move to efficiency gains from new AI systems.[15] In early 2026, a second wave of thousands more corporate job cuts made clear that, once AI is treated chiefly as an automation lever, each productivity gain tends to justify another round of staff reductions rather than a redesign of work to elevate human contribution.[16] CEO Andy Jassy's earlier statements that AI-driven efficiency, including making AI Agents teammates,[17] will reshape corporate roles have now been translated into action. Internal reports and analyst assessments converge on the same conclusion: the company can accomplish roughly the same work with far fewer employees because automation now performs what once required human repetition. This is not a story of technology turning against us, but of how the logic of automation advances whenever human contribution is defined too narrowly. The message is striking: *where AI displaces process, jobs disappear; where AI amplifies human capabilities, roles expand.*

This is the hard reality your choice entails. Remaining valuable is selective, not universal. But the selectivity follows a pattern: roles requiring coordinated human capabilities expand while roles reducible to algorithmic process contract. Your path determines which side of that divide you occupy.

And yet, choice itself is the beginning of renewal. The journey we have taken from Chapter 1 has traced a transformation from anxiety to agency. The question that professionals cannot escape, *what do we do when algorithms decide*, is now answered. We practice reasoned judgment that serves a greater good. We coordinate diverse capabilities into collective wisdom. We ensure that computational power amplifies rather than displaces what makes us irreducibly human.

The herald's call "Who wishes to speak?" echoes across twenty-five centuries. In the age of AI, the echo asks: Who will practice *curiosity* that questions what algorithms assume? Who will deploy *creativity* that imagines beyond what they optimize? Who will exercise *critical thinking* that evaluates what analysis means? Who will *communicate* through embodied presence that builds trust? Who will *collaborate* toward collective intelligence? Who will integrate everything through *practical wisdom* oriented toward purposes only humans can comprehend?

The answers lie with professionals who choose citizenship over convenience, who practice capabilities systematically, who remain inside the loop rather than slipping outside it. You do not need perfection. The Assembly reconvenes daily in your decisions, your teams, your organizations. Step forward. Practice. The future of meaningful work depends on those who answer the call with human magic.

Notes

1 Anthropic PBC (2025, October 14).
2 Gerlich (2025).
3 Hinton (2025).
4 Dilmegani (2026, January 25).
5 Amodei (2026, January 26).
6 Drucker (1967).
7 Choudary (2025).
8 Loh (2025, August 16).
9 Amodei (2026, January 26).
10 Anthropic PCB (2025, October 14).
11 Masumori & Ikegami (2025); Anthropic PBC (2025, June 20); Palisade Research (2025).
12 Dick (1978). Dick's prescient explorations of artificial intelligence and human identity inspired numerous adaptations, including *Blade Runner* (1982) and *Total Recall* (1990), making his warnings about technology reshaping humanity accessible to audiences beyond science fiction readers.
13 For example, Asimov (1990). Asimov's work, particularly the *Foundation* trilogy and adaptations including *Bicentennial Man* (1999) and *I, Robot* (2004), imagined technology as a humanizing force. That *Foundation* was resurrected in 2023 as one of the most ambitious screen productions of our time, just as generative AI entered professional practice, reflects our urgent need to distinguish between algorithmic prediction and human wisdom. This tension was central to Asimov's work and clearly remains so in today's professional AI-impacted world.

14 Benioff (2025, September 12).
15 Bensinger (2025, October 27).
16 Simply Wall St. (2026, January 26).
17 Jassy (2025, June 17).

References

Amodei, D. (2026, January). *The adolescence of technology.* https://www.darioamodei.com/essay/the-adolescence-of-technology

Anthropic PBC. (2025, June 20). *Agentic misalignment: How LLMs could be insider threats.* https://www.anthropic.com/research/agentic-misalignment

Anthropic PBC. (2025, October 14). *Preparing for AI's economic impact: Exploring policy responses.* Anthropic Research. https://www.anthropic.com/research/economic-policy-responses

Asimov, I. (1990). *Robot visions.* ROC. WorldCat record. https://www.worldcat.org/oclc/23435548

Benioff, M. (2025, September 12). *Salesforce CEO Marc Benioff on what the market is getting wrong about AI* [Video interview]. Goldman Sachs Communicopia and Technology Conference. YouTube. https://youtu.be/Bewu2Jq_m1o?si=LUYvbNgxXmpUA3Iv

Bensinger, G. (2025, October 27). Amazon targets as many as 30,000 corporate job cuts, sources say. *Reuters.* https://www.reuters.com/business/world-at-work/amazon-targets-many-30000-corporate-job-cuts-sources-say-2025-10-27/

Choudary, S. P. (2025, April 13). The many fallacies of "AI won't take your job, but someone using AI will": True, but utterly useless. Substack. https://platforms.substack.com/p/the-many-fallacies-of-ai-wont-take

CNBC Television. (2025, September 12). *Salesforce CEO Marc Benioff on what the market is getting wrong about AI* [Video interview]. YouTube. https://www.youtube.com/watch?v=Bewu2Jq_m1o

Dick, P. K. (1985). *How to build a universe that doesn't fall apart two days later.* ISOLARII

Dilmegani, C., & Ermut, S. (2026, January 25). *AGI/singularity: 9,300 predictions analyzed in 2026.* AIMultiple. https://research.aimultiple.com/artificial-general-intelligence-singularity-timing/

Drucker, P. F. (1967). *The effective executive.* Harper & Row.

Gerlich, M. (2025). AI tools in society: Impacts on cognitive offloading and the future of critical thinking. *Societies, 15*(1), 6.

Hinton, G. (2025). "You have no idea what's coming" [Video]. *The Diary of a CEO (clips).* https://www.youtube.com/watch?v=5KmopXwjXik

Jassy, A. (2025, June 17). Update from Amazon CEO Andy Jassy on Generative AI. Amazon.com. https://www.aboutamazon.com/news/company-news/amazon-ceo-andy-jassy-on-generative-ai

Loh, P.-S. (2025, August 16). *The only trait for success in the AI era – How to build it* [Video]. *EO* (YouTube). https://www.youtube.com/watch?v=xWYb7tImErI

Masumori, A., & Ikegami, T. (2025). *Do large language model agents exhibit a survival instinct? An empirical study in a Sugarscape-style simulation.* arXiv:2508.12920. https://arxiv.org/abs/2508.12920

Palisade Research. (2025, July 5). *Shutdown resistance in reasoning models.* https://palisaderesearch.org/blog/shutdown-resistance

Simply Wall St. (2026, January 26). *Amazon's largest layoffs mark pivot toward AI-driven efficiency and investment.* Simply Wall St. https://simplywall.st/stocks/us/retail/nasdaq-amzn/amazoncom/news/amazons-largest-layoffs-mark-pivot-toward-ai-driven-efficien

Appendix 1: Practicing Human Magic

Chapter 1: Our Choice – Erosion or Amplification?

Chapter 1 posed the question that has haunted professionals since AI moved from automation to agency: "*If algorithms now make all the decisions, what do leaders actually do?*" The chapters that follow explored six essential human capabilities – curiosity, creativity, critical thinking, communication, collaboration, and practical wisdom – that make all professionals, leaders included, create value and even be irreplaceable precisely because they cannot be algorithmically replicated. Each capability chapter addresses how AI both threatens and amplifies that capability, offering frameworks for systematic practice.

This appendix synthesizes the systematic practices that all professionals, including leaders can take, based on each chapter's argument and recommendations for amplification of the capability. Use this Appendix as a reminder of specific actions you can take to hone your work at augmenting each of the capabilities in your job. The goal is to have this appendix remind you to put into practice concrete actions, such that the work in Chapter 9 to create your "human magic" flows naturally from what you are already implementing in your daily life.

Chapter 2: Curiosity – From Quick Answers to Deeper Questions

What This Capability Answers: When AI delivers instant answers, professionals sustain productive uncertainty by dwelling in questions before rushing to closure. Curiosity makes you valuable and irreplaceable by practicing what algorithms fundamentally cannot: tolerating the discomfort of not knowing long enough for genuine insight to emerge.

Practices:

- Practice the Curiosity Amplification Cycle systematically: frame questions independently before consulting AI, expand inquiry through

AI-assisted research, evaluate outputs critically before accepting them, and integrate findings through synthesis that honours context.
- Establish morning question framing as daily discipline. Spend five minutes every day authoring your own questions before consulting AI systems, protecting your unique capacity to formulate inquiry from algorithmic foreclosure.
- Balance laser curiosity (focused investigation) with radar curiosity (peripheral scanning). Keep live collaborative work device-light to preserve situational awareness and notice what human interaction reveals beyond algorithmic outputs.
- Resist shallow questioning loops by inserting deliberate pauses between AI outputs and decisions. Generate at least three follow-up questions before accepting initial responses, preventing premature closure that collapses the exploration process.
- Build stress tolerance for productive uncertainty. Cultivate the capacity to dwell in not-knowing, recognizing that breakthrough insights emerge from continued engagement with unresolved questions, not instant algorithmic answers.

Illustrative Quote from Our Research: *"When I use the AI tool, I get comprehensive answers immediately. It feels efficient, but I also feel less invested in the problem. I don't carry the question with me anymore."*

Chapter 3: Creativity – From Polished Outputs to Original Insights

What This Capability Answers: When AI generates novel combinations at scale, professionals exercise creative reasoning by distinguishing between what is merely novel and what is genuinely valuable. Creativity makes you valuable and irreplaceable by practicing contextual evaluation that algorithms cannot replicate.

Practices:

- Implement the Creative Partnership Cycle across five phases: Diverge independently before consulting AI, Explore using AI to expand possibilities, Evaluate AI outputs through critical analysis, Embody ideas through physical prototyping and embodied exploration, and Integrate insights for sustainable implementation.
- Protect temporal separation by establishing AI-free creative moments. Schedule dedicated time for thinking without AI tools, allowing ideas to take shape through human imagination before AI challenge and refinement.
- Engage hands and bodies in physical making. Build prototypes, sketch by hand, manipulate materials directly. Embodied creation

builds creative confidence and reveals insights that purely digital exploration cannot access.

- Nurture your intrinsic motivation by reconnecting creative work to personal meaning beyond efficiency metrics. Ask regularly why the work matters to *you*, not just whether it can be completed faster with AI assistance.
- Practice invisible integration during creative presentation. Prepare extensively with AI support but deliver creative work with undivided human presence, ensuring audiences encounter authentic creative voice.

Illustrative Quote from Our Research: *"I realized I hadn't sketched anything truly weird in months. All my designs looked sophisticated and professional, but they also looked like they came from the same AI aesthetic rather than my own mind."*

Chapter 4: Critical Thinking – From Shallow Reasoning to Clear Judgment

What This Capability Answers: When AI analyzes faster and more comprehensively than humans, professionals determine what analysis means for *specific* situations, stakeholders, and purposes. Critical thinking makes you valuable and irreplaceable by practicing interpretive reasoning that algorithms cannot exercise.

Practices:

- Apply Toulmin's Argument model to examine what AI outputs suggest. Map claims, data, warrants, backing, qualifiers, and rebuttals to make the *Because* visible between evidence and conclusion before accepting algorithmic recommendations.
- Resist cognitive offloading by maintaining independent analytical assessment. Question AI outputs systematically rather than accepting confidence as competence, recognizing that polished presentation does not guarantee sound reasoning.
- Slow decisions when urgency threatens sound judgment. Insert deliberate pauses before high-stakes choices, creating space for the reflective reasoning that distinguishes wisdom from mere speed.
- Practice sceptical questioning that probes assumptions AI builds on. Ask what perspectives the analysis omits, whose interests it serves, what values it privileges. This is how you cultivate the dispositions of doubt that anchor critical thinking.
- Engage in structured dialogue and debate. Make reasoning visible to others through argument and counterargument, recognizing that critical thinking deepens through the friction of examining ideas publicly rather than accepting them privately.

Illustrative Quote from Our Research: *"More than ever, it's critical thinking. Not whether you can gather information, but whether you can judge what it means."*

Chapter 5: Communication – From Data Dashboards to Hybrid Authority

What This Capability Answers: When AI crafts eloquent messages instantly, professionals create authentic influence through embodied presence that no algorithm can replicate. Communication makes you valuable and irreplaceable by practicing meaning-making that requires the full spectrum of human interaction.

Practices:

- Master Aristotle's persuasive triad strategically. Use AI to enhance logos (logical argument) but provide ethos (credible character) and pathos (embodied emotion) through authentic human presence that builds trust beyond words.
- Establish the Preparation-Performance Boundary rigorously. Leverage AI extensively backstage for research and content development, then perform on stage with complete human presence without devices, no algorithmic consultation, undivided attention.
- Practice invisible integration as discipline. Keep AI support completely invisible to audiences during live communication, ensuring they encounter only your authority and connection rather than split attention between person and screen.
- Read the room continuously during communication. Modulate voice in response to audience energy, establish eye contact that builds trust, respond spontaneously to unstated concerns. This is how you hone your embodied eloquence (*eloquentia corporis*) that creates meaning beyond content.
- Internalize content through embodied preparation. Practice delivery physically until material becomes authentic expression rather than performed script, building the presence that transforms information into influence.

Illustrative Quote from Our Research: *"It took me out of the moment to interact with the AI tool. [When the facilitator] used AI visibly, it distracted the atmosphere and momentum."*

Chapter 6: Collaboration – From Human Teams to Bionic Collaboration

What This Capability Answers: When AI agents handle coordination with unprecedented efficiency, professionals design collective intelligence that algorithms cannot orchestrate. Collaboration makes you valuable and irreplaceable by creating the human dynamics that generate breakthrough thinking beyond mere task coordination.

Practices:

- Implement the Bionic Collaboration model: purposefully blend human intuition for meaning-making with AI computational strength for coordination. Let algorithms handle volume, speed, and consistency while you handle ambiguity, ethics, and meaning.
- Establish human-first protocols for important decisions. Begin with unassisted human framing before any AI or agent outputs appear, preserving agency in problem identification and definition, while still capturing algorithmic advantages for execution.
- Ritualize dissent windows in team processes. Create protected time for questioning agent recommendations and building shared understanding beyond statistical optimality, preventing premature AI-accelerated consensus that bypasses creative friction.
- Protect presence in collaborative spaces. Keep live meetings device-light, relocating AI to preparation and documentation phases. Preserve the unplanned conversations where trust builds, inefficient debates where creativity sparks, and messy disagreements where shared understanding emerges.
- Architect collaboration systems that preserve social-emotional exchange. Recognize that trust and psychological safety emerge through micro-interactions that algorithms abbreviate or eliminate. This is how you preserve the relational depth that enables teams to challenge assumptions and adapt under pressure.

Illustrative Quote from Our Research: *"When everything is automated, my unplanned conversations disappear."*

Chapter 7: Practical Wisdom – From Technical Mastery to Wise Action

What This Capability Answers: When algorithms optimize everything, professionals exercise practical wisdom that orients all capabilities toward purposes beyond efficiency. Practical wisdom makes you valuable and irreplaceable by practicing contextual judgment that cares about a greater good algorithms fundamentally cannot do.

Practices:

- Practice the Wisdom Compass systematically: *Perceive* stakes that algorithms cannot process (ask: what matters?), *Integrate* competing values that resist quantification (ask: what is right?), *Regulate* emotions to maintain clarity under uncertainty (ask: what resonates?), and *Act* with courage when context demands overriding algorithmic recommendations (ask: what works?)

- Implement the Deliberate Pause Protocol before AI-driven decisions. Ask three questions: What does this optimize? What does it sacrifice? Who bears the cost? Sixty seconds of reflection transforms acceptance into assessment.
- Draft contrarian scenarios that challenge AI forecasts. Before accepting algorithmic recommendations, generate alternative interpretations that question underlying assumptions, revealing blind spots that optimization cannot see.
- Stage moral dilemmas for judgment rehearsal. Practice navigating situations where values conflict and rules provide no clear guidance, building the capacity to act wisely despite uncertainty because the good requires it.
- Develop simple guiding principles as repositories of wisdom. Distil experience into portable maxims that orient action when procedures cannot and algorithms should not. This is how you honour the contextual particularity that resists universal optimization.

Illustrative Quote from Our Research: *"In our team, AI brings the options, but humans bring the meaning."*

Chapter 8: Your Human Magic – From Individual Capabilities to Irreplaceable Value

What Integration Means: Chapter 8 operationalizes the six capabilities through the Five Disciplines and the Human Magic Matrix, providing systematic approaches for sustained capability development. Integration is practice that transforms knowing into doing, intention into habit, knowledge into wisdom.

Practices:

- Practice the Five Disciplines that preserve capability while leveraging AI amplification: Frame questions independently before consulting AI (Curiosity), Protect temporal boundaries for AI-free creation (Creativity), Maintain analytical scepticism toward algorithmic outputs (Critical Thinking), Establish preparation-performance boundaries (Communication), and Architect human-first protocols for collaboration (Collaboration).
- Use the Human Magic Matrix as diagnostic tool. Map yourself quarterly across erosion-amplification axes for each capability, identifying where you risk cognitive offloading versus where you successfully leverage AI as amplifier of wisdom rather than replacement for judgment.

- Establish weekly capability audits. Spend fifteen minutes each Friday monitoring erosion patterns before they calcify into habits, asking: Where did I defer to AI this week when independent judgment was required? Where did I successfully amplify capability?
- Implement the 90-day development cycle. Complete self-assessments honestly, establish one new boundary practice per capability, monitor progress through visible metrics, and adjust based on observed erosion or amplification patterns.
- Cultivate professional citizenship over algorithmic citizenship. Make the daily choice to direct AI through irreducible human capacities rather than deferring to algorithmic authority. This is how you make choices that determine whether you remain irreplaceable or become redundant.

The Cumulative Principle

In Chapter 7, I talked about the use of principles to represent the fundamental concept behind an answer. If we were to identify the cumulative principle from the combined six capabilities, it would be this: *We can (re)claim our professional value creation by cultivating six human capabilities and exercising reasoning in ways that AI cannot replicate.* Specifically, we can:

1. **Frame the questions worth asking** through curiosity that tolerates productive uncertainty rather than rushing to algorithmic closure.
2. **Imagine possibilities beyond optimization** through creativity that distinguishes genuine value from mere novelty.
3. **Evaluate what analysis means** through critical thinking that interprets significance for specific contexts rather than accepting algorithmic confidence as competence.
4. **Convey meaning authentically** through embodied communication that creates trust through presence rather than transmitting information through screens.
5. **Orchestrate collective intelligence** through collaboration that preserves human dynamics essential for breakthrough thinking rather than merely coordinating tasks efficiently.
6. **Integrate all capabilities through practical wisdom** toward purposes that serve the common good: determining what deserves optimization, which values matter when they conflict, and when to override AI because meaning demands it.

We do not compete with algorithms but practice judgment in the way algorithms fundamentally cannot. Our reasoning is contextual rather than universal, values-integrated rather than metric-optimized, purpose-oriented rather than efficiency-maximized, and ethically grounded rather than merely computationally optimal. Where algorithms ask "what's most efficient?" we ask "what matters here?" Where algorithms optimize outcomes, we determine which outcomes are worth pursuing. Where algorithms recommend based on past patterns, we act with wisdom that honours a greater good.

This is the human magic: not supernatural ability but *systematic practice of capabilities that make professionals both valuable and irreplaceable precisely because they resist algorithmic replication.* The choice between erosion and amplification is the choice you and I make each morning when algorithms offer instant answers and when we must decide whether to pause, whether to question, whether to trust our hunch over machine confidence. Human Magic as professional citizenship means *directing* AI through these six human capabilities rather than deferring to algorithmic authority. It means making AI an amplifier of the reasoning and judgment only humans can exercise.

Appendix 2: How This Book Was Written

When I began writing a book about maintaining human capabilities in the age of AI, I faced an immediate question: How *should I write it?*

I could have written it entirely by hand, as if AI tools didn't exist. But that would have been dishonest. This book argues that the answer to AI is not avoidance but thoughtful engagement. I write about learning to use these tools in ways that amplify rather than erode our capabilities.

So I practiced what I teach.

My decision to engage thoughtfully with AI tools stems from decades of developing scholarly judgment through traditional research and writing methods. Since completing my doctoral dissertation in 1989, I have published more than a dozen books with major academic publishers including *Oxford University Press, Palgrave Macmillan*, and *Sage*, alongside over 30 peer-reviewed articles in journals such as *Strategic Management Journal, Long-Range Planning, Journal of Management Studies, Human Relations, Management Science, and Organization Studies*. This body of scholarship, spanning strategic management, knowledge management, and organizational studies, has accumulated over 20,000 citations in Google Scholar through entirely conventional research and writing processes. This foundation of proven academic rigor developed across three and a half decades without any AI assistance informs how I evaluate AI tools today, ensuring they amplify rather than substitute for the critical thinking, methodological precision, and original insights that scholarly publishing demands.

Throughout this project, I used AI tools systematically. Consensus and Perplexity Pro helped me search and evaluate academic literature, and I used Perplexity searches to rigorously check and Google Scholar to corroborate all sources for accuracy and validity. NotebookLM helped me organize my extensive research materials. Claude Sonnet 4.5–6, ChatGPT-5, and Mistral Le Chat served as sometimes competing writing coaches, refining prose and maintaining consistency across chapters. DALL-E helped me draft the visuals, which a human designer improved.

I also worked with a seasoned professional editor and writer with whom I have collaborated since 2011. He provided traditional editorial guidance throughout manuscript development, reviewing each chapter as it progressed and offering language refinement, argument tightening, inconsistency identification, and clarity improvements. Together, we completed three to six iterations of each chapter. These exchanges involved essential human editorial judgment that no AI tool can replicate. His expertise exemplifies the kind of human-to-human collaboration that remains central to scholarly writing.

At the very end of the journey, I proofread and fine-tuned everything before handing over manuscript to the publisher by end October 2025. After the copy editor at Taylor & Francis/Routledge checked for consistency of style, corrected errors, and clarified presentation, I reviewed the proofs again in January and February 2026.

The AI tools did not create the concept, models, or frameworks you'll encounter in these pages. They did not select the research or interpret its meaning. They did not make the arguments or draw the conclusions. Those came from three decades of research, teaching, and consulting on strategy, organizational learning, and human development, as well as 25 years of parallel hands-on leadership experience in several organizations.

What the AI tools did was amplify my ability to organize, articulate, and refine ideas that were already mine. They helped me work more efficiently through my research data from research projects designed and led by me, without compromising intellectual integrity. They helped me search through my notes, articles, and books from decades back, helping me bring to the forefront concepts, models, and tools that had been relegated to the aft. They allowed me to focus my cognitive energy on the creative and analytical work that only I could do.

This is exactly the approach I advocate in the book: Use AI to handle what it does well. None of us mere humans can match the incredible capacity and speed of deep neural networks-driven LLMs in searching, organizing, drafting, iterating. Like I argue in this book, we can and should focus on what only we can do. Let the tools amplify your reasoning, not replace it.

Wharton professor Ethan Mollick recently captured this dynamic precisely: the people who thrive with AI are those who know what good looks like and can explain it clearly enough for the AI to deliver it. Subject matter expertise, not prompting skill, determines whether AI amplifies or dilutes your work.[1]

Was this the right approach? I believe it was, though I've learned as much from the challenges as from the successes. It was also formally reviewed and approved by the publisher. There were moments when AI suggestions felt seductive but hollow and sometimes even out of touch with my reality. At times I had to resist the efficiency of a well-phrased suggestion in favour of the harder work of finding my own words. I experienced instances where I realized I was drifting toward the tool's patterns rather than my own thinking.

These struggles taught me that working well with AI requires constant vigilance and clear principles. You must know what you're willing to delegate and what you must do yourself. You must recognize when AI is amplifying your capability and when it's eroding it.

I share this not as a model to follow but as an honest account of how this book came into being. Every author must make their own choices about tools and methods. My hope is that by being transparent about mine, I honour both you as a reader and the argument I'm making in these pages.

The frameworks, insights, and practices you'll encounter here are the result of decades of work. The AI tools helped me give them shape and form. The responsibility for what you read, including its accuracy, its usefulness, its integrity, rests entirely with me.

If you find value in this book, it is because I learned to work with AI in a way that kept my human capabilities sharp and engaged.

That's the essence of *Human Magic*.

Note

1 Mollick (2026, January 27).

Reference

Mollick, E. (2026, January 27). Management as AI superpower: Thriving in a world of agentic AI. *One Useful Thing*. https://www.oneusefulthing.org/p/management-as-ai-superpower

Index

For Product Safety Concerns and Information please contact our EU representative GPSR@taylorandfrancis.com
Taylor & Francis Verlag GmbH, Kaufingerstraße 24, 80331 München, Germany

www.ingramcontent.com/pod-product-compliance
Ingram Content Group UK Ltd.
Pitfield, Milton Keynes, MK11 3LW, UK
UKHW020009200926
475702UK00015B/2555

* 9 7 8 1 0 4 1 2 1 6 7 6 6 *